The UN Declaration on the Rights of Indigenous Peoples

The UN Declaration on the Rights of Indigenous Peoples

A New Interpretative Approach

ANDREW ERUETI

OXFORD
UNIVERSITY PRESS

OXFORD
UNIVERSITY PRESS

Oxford University Press is a department of the University of Oxford. It furthers the University's objective of excellence in research, scholarship, and education by publishing worldwide. Oxford is a registered trade mark of Oxford University Press in the UK and certain other countries.

Published in the United States of America by Oxford University Press
198 Madison Avenue, New York, NY 10016, United States of America.

Library of Congress Cataloging-in-Publication Data
Names: Erueti, Andrew, author.
Title: The UN Declaration on the Rights of Indigenous Peoples : a new interpretative approach / Andrew Erueti.
Other titles: United Nations Declaration on the Rights of Indigenous Peoples
Description: New York : Oxford University Press, 2022. |
Includes bibliographical references and index.
Identifiers: LCCN 2021034883 (print) | LCCN 2021034884 (ebook) |
ISBN 9780190068301 (hardback) | ISBN 9780190068332 (digital-online) |
ISBN 9780190068325 (epub) | ISBN 9780190068318 (updf)
Subjects: LCSH: United Nations. General Assembly. Declaration on the Rights
of Indigenous Peoples. | Indigenous peoples (International law)
Classification: LCC KI30 2007. E78 2021 (print) | LCC KI30 2007 (ebook) | DDC 341.4/852—dc23
LC record available at https://lccn.loc.gov/2021034883
LC ebook record available at https://lccn.loc.gov/2021034884

DOI: 10.1093/oso/9780190068301.001.0001

1 3 5 7 9 8 6 4 2

Printed by Integrated Books International, United States of America

Contents

Acknowledgments

This book is based on my PhD thesis at the University of Toronto Faculty of Law, which provided terrific support from start to finish. I am particularly indebted to Professor Karen Knop who introduced me to Courtney Jung's work, *The Moral Force of Indigenous Politics*, and Karen Engle's book, *The Elusive Promise of Indigenous Development*. Engle's work in particular provided a key counterpoint to the argument made in this book. But it was Karen's generosity of time, intellectual rigor, and faith in the project that kept me going.

I want to thank my colleagues at Amnesty International for conversations on indigenous rights, but especially the Gender, Sexuality and Identity and Latin American team, and Craig Benjamin at Amnesty-Canada. I would also like to thank the communities I worked with over that time but in particular the indigenous activists and communities in the Chittagong Hill Tracts, Bangladesh. Not everyone will agree with the ideas in this book, but it was written in the spirit of seeking a solution to an enduring issue.

Looming large across this work is the scholarship of James Anaya. Practically anyone who has ever written about international indigenous rights is responding in some way to his seminal work, *Indigenous Peoples in International Law*. I am indebted to Professor Anaya for his scholarship, his friendship, and his tireless advocacy for indigenous peoples across the globe.

I want to acknowledge my colleagues at the law faculties of the University of Auckland, Waikato and Victoria, and the many indigenous rights scholars I have had the pleasure of meeting, including Brad Morse, Jérémie Gilbert, Gloria Valencia-Webber, Robert Clinton, Megan Davies, Brenda Gunn, Patrick Macklem, Doug Sanderson, Mattais Ahren, Les Malezer, Luis Rodríguez-Piñero, Kent McNeil, Alex Xanthaki, Benedict Kinsgbury, and Julian Burger.

Thanks too to the OUP editorial team for your support and attention to detail, and to Lane for his artwork.

To my whanau, Max and Mia, Mum, Dad, Andy and Kath, Trina, Caity, Claire and Hema, and Claire's family Barbara, Richard, Jack, Manfred, and Cristal—my love and gratitude. During the tough times I would often call on

Hema for strength. We miss you and this book is for you. And to my partner, Claire Charters. She radiates intellect, fun, and love. I am in constant amazement at how she manages to do it all—social, professional, and family life. Claire never doubted I would complete my thesis or this book. I often did. But it was Claire who always got me across the finish line. I feel blessed to be with you, Max and Mia.

Introduction

When the Declaration[1] was adopted by the UN General Assembly in 2007, it was quite rightly heralded as a breakthrough achievement for indigenous peoples first and foremost.[2] Although other international treaties, standards, and policies on indigenous rights exist, notably International Labour Organization Convention No. 169,[3] no other international instrument provides such robust protections for indigenous peoples or any minority group. Hundreds of activists toiled for three decades for a Declaration, negotiating the terms of twenty preambular paragraphs and forty-six "rights" in the UN offices of Geneva and later New York as the Declaration was brought before the UN General Assembly. Throughout this time, there was acceptance of the need for an exemplar at the international level to address indigenous peoples' specific, pressing needs.

The Declaration was also a significant achievement for the international human rights community at large. The Declaration is a product of the human rights system. It was created within the human rights arm of the United Nations and is largely an elaboration of human rights in core texts, including the International Covenant on Civil and Political Rights[4] and International Covenant on Economic, Social, and Cultural Rights[5] (International Human Rights Covenants). For example, while the Universal Declaration of Human

[1] *United Nations Declaration on the Rights of Indigenous Peoples*, G.A. Res. 61/295, UNGAOR, 61st Sess., Supp. No. 49, U.N. Doc. A/RES/61/295 (2007) [hereinafter The Declaration].

[2] For commentary on the politics of the negotiation of the Declaration, *see generally* Making the Declaration Work: The United Nations Declaration on the Rights of Indigenous Peoples (Claire Charters & Rodolfo Stavenhagen eds., 2009); Realizing the UN Declaration on the Rights of Indigenous Peoples: Triumph, Hope, and Action (Paul Joffe, Jackie Hartley, & Jennifer Preston eds., 2010); Alexandra Xanthaki, Indigenous Rights and United Nations Standards (2007); Reflections on the UN Declaration on the Rights of Indigenous Peoples: Studies in International Law (Steve Allen & Alexandra Xanthaki eds., 2011); The UN Declaration on the Rights of Indigenous Peoples: A Commentary (Jessie Hohman & Marc Weller eds., 2018).

[3] *Convention (No. 169) Concerning Indigenous and Tribal Peoples in Independent Countries*, June 27, 1989, 28 I.L.M. 1382 (entered into force Sept. 5, 1991).

[4] *International Covenant on Civil and Political Rights*, Dec. 16, 1966, 999 U.N.T.S. 171 (entered into force Mar. 23, 1976).

[5] *International Covenant on Economic, Social and Cultural Rights*, Dec. 16, 1966, 993 U.N.T.S. 3 (entered into force Jan. 3, 1976).

The UN Declaration on the Rights of Indigenous Peoples. Andrew Erueti, Oxford University Press. © Oxford University Press 2022. DOI: 10.1093/oso/9780190068301.003.0001

Rights (UDHR), upon which the covenants are based, states that all human beings are born free and equal, with a focus on individuals,[6] the Declaration extends this right to indigenous peoples as a collective: "Indigenous peoples and individuals are free and equal to all other peoples and individuals and have the right to be free from any kind of discrimination, in the exercise of their rights, in particular that based on their indigenous origin or identity."

At the same time, the Declaration has pushed the bounds of both our understanding of human rights and the way in which human rights are made. The Declaration stands against the classic human rights model in many ways. By seeking to uphold the human rights of collectives, the Declaration upends the principle that rights are vested in individuals. Unlike most human rights, which are prospective in nature—protecting rights now and into the future—the Declaration is in large part backward looking and reparative. It recognizes the effects of history and seeks to address its injustices through measures expressed as rights, such as the restoration of traditional lands and the observance of international treaties between indigenous peoples and settler governments.

In particular, the Declaration recognizes the collective right of indigenous peoples to self-determination. Article 3 of the Declaration states: "Indigenous peoples have the right to self-determination. By virtue of that right they freely determine their political status and freely pursue their economic, social and cultural development."[7] This restates the language in common article 1 of the International Human Rights Covenants, but with reference to *indigenous* peoples. Related to this are the rights to self-government and to give free, prior, and informed consent (FPIC) to any legislative measures that will affect indigenous peoples.

Self-determination is both a means to freedom and equality while also presenting the potential for great conflict and human rights violations. This is most starkly illustrated by the decolonization movement of the 20th century. Motivated by a quest for equality and enjoyment of all human rights, the leaders of colonized peoples in Asia, the Middle East, and Africa sought independence through the right to self-determination.[8] However, these independence movements often had the effect of uprooting people and

[6] *Universal Declaration of Human Rights*, G.A. Res. 217A (III), UNGAOR, 3d Sess., Supp. No. 13, U.N. Doc. A/810, at 71 (1948).

[7] The Declaration, *supra* note 1, art. 3.

[8] Roland Burke, Decolonization and the Evolution of International Human Rights (2010).

stoking ethnic tensions. The right to self-determination is contained in the International Human Rights Covenants, but it is commonly understood to apply to whole nation-states and not sub-national groupings like minorities and indigenous peoples.

Thus, the Declaration is not a typical human rights instrument. What accounts for these breakthrough rights is indigenous peoples' participation in their making. Typically, negotiations are governed by states with limited input from interest groups, and any subsequent disagreement about meaning requires reference back to states' negotiating positions.[9] However, what is remarkable about the Declaration negotiations is that indigenous peoples were able to participate in the Declaration negotiations alongside states. It would be going too far to say that they were accorded equal status. However, indigenous advocates were able to propose new text and counter any proposals made by states during the negotiations. Thus, *who* participated and *what* they said are important in terms of the resulting rights.[10]

This has significant implications not only for the specific rights ultimately embodied in the Declaration but for how they should be interpreted and applied at the international level and, more importantly, within domestic states. The diverse and extensive participation by indigenous peoples and numerous states in the Declaration negotiations and the particular arguments made and accepted is the subject of this book. It reveals a distinctive account of the Declaration's history and provides the basis for a fresh means of thinking about the Declaration's meaning and effects.

As we will see, there is much disagreement about the normative models underpinning the Declaration. In this book, I take up the question of the normative model(s) at work in the Declaration through the political history of the international indigenous movement as it intersected with the Declaration's drafting. The book's contribution is twofold. First, it offers a new account of this history—one that seeks to highlight the diversity and complexity of the Declaration negotiations, particularly the distinctive contributions made by Northern and Southern indigenous movements. Second, the book offers a new interpretative model that is supported by this political history together with legal justificatory argument. This mixed

[9] *Vienna Convention on the Law of Treaties*, May 23, 1969, 1155 U.N.T.S. 331, art. 32 (entered into force Jan. 27, 1980).

[10] Claire Charters, *The Legitimacy of the UN Declaration on the Rights of Indigenous Peoples*, *in* Making the Declaration Work: The United Nations Declaration on the Rights of Indigenous Peoples 280 (Claire Charters & Rodolfo Stavenhagen eds., 2009).

model of interpretation, as I call it, not only offers a path for a more fruitful global application of the Declaration, it also clarifies (1) the normative bases of international indigenous rights; and (2) in turn, the meaning of indigenous peoples for the purposes of international law.

Two Models of the Declaration

In the leading text, *Indigenous Peoples in International Law*, indigenous scholar James Anaya argues that indigenous rights in international law—specifically those set out in the Declaration—are an application of the universal human rights contained in core human right treaties, particularly the International Human Rights Covenants, to indigenous peoples.[11]

When the chair of the indigenous global caucus (the organizing body comprised of indigenous representatives), Les Malezer, addressed the UN General Assembly after it voted 144–4 to endorse the Declaration, he articulated this model, which I describe as a "human rights model" of international indigenous rights:[12]

> We emphasise once again that the Declaration on the Rights of Indigenous Peoples contains no new provisions of human rights. It affirms many rights already contained in international human rights treaties, but rights which have been denied to the Indigenous Peoples. As Indigenous Peoples we now see a guarantee that our rights to self-determination, to our lands and territories, to our cultural identities, to our own representation and to our values and beliefs will be respected at the international level . . . The Declaration carries a message for all States that have links and association with Indigenous Peoples. That message is not about secession, as some States may fear, but about co-operation and partnership to ensure that all individuals, regardless of race or beliefs, are truly equal and that all peoples are respected and allowed to develop.

This human rights model is now so prominent that it has effectively become the mantra of the international movement.[13] However, the human

[11] S. JAMES ANAYA, INDIGENOUS PEOPLES IN INTERNATIONAL LAW (2004).

[12] Les Malezer, Statement of Les Malezer for the Indigenous Global Caucus (statement delivered at the UN General Assembly, New York, Sept. 13, 2007).

[13] *See, e.g.*, the essays in Joffe, Hartley, & Preston, *supra* note 2; Charters & Stavenhagen, *supra* note 2.

rights model has difficulty accounting for all aspects of the Declaration. Ultimately, according to Anaya, the normative basis of his model is "freedom" and "inherent human equality."[14] The Declaration includes the right to self-determination;[15] self-government;[16] historical redress;[17] the right to FPIC;[18] and the right to the recognition, observance, and enforcement of treaties.[19] Throughout the book, I will refer to Article 3 and these related rights as constituting the Declaration's "self-determination framework." Although the right to self-determination is contained in common article 1 of the International Human Rights Covenants—and Article 27 of the International Covenant on Civil and Political Rights, on the rights of persons belonging to minorities, covers some of this ground for indigenous peoples—it is not obvious that the human rights model can support the self-determination framework.[20]

The calls for self-determination in common article 1 of the Covenants were initially grounded in a human rights argument. The right to self-government has often been based on human rights. However, it is more difficult to make the connection between human rights and the requirements of FPIC, observance of international treaties, and redress for historical wrongs. There are no close parallels in the human rights system. In short, the human rights model has to work hard to justify the self-determination framework. Furthermore, Malezer's assurance that—consistent with a human rights model—the Declaration's message is "not about secession" obscures quite fundamental disagreements within indigenous movements about whether the Declaration leaves open the possibility of independence, as recognized for the former colonies of Africa, Asia, and the Middle East. Indeed, the decolonization movement, as we will see, was the principal driving force behind the indigenous movement at its inception as led by indigenous peoples of North America.[21] This was a major concern for many states, especially those dealing with internal security and stability issues relating to minorities. These origins reveal an alternative justificatory model for indigenous

[14] Anaya, *supra* note 11, at Chapter 5.

[15] The Declaration, *supra* note 1, art. 3.

[16] *Id.*, art. 4.

[17] *Id.*, arts. 11(2) and 28.

[18] *Id.*, arts. 19 and 32(2).

[19] *Id.*, art. 37.

[20] *See* Helen Quane, *The UN Declaration on the Rights of Indigenous Peoples: New Directions for Self-Determination and Participatory Rights*, *in* Allen & Xanthaki, *supra* note 2 ("Notwithstanding assertions that the Declaration contains no new rights, it is anything but a codification of existing international law. Even a cursory glance at its provisions reveals significant innovations, particularly in the area of self-determination and participatory rights" at 259).

[21] *See* Chapter 1.

rights, what I describe as a "decolonization model" premised on the injustice of European colonization and settlement of indigenous peoples. However, Anaya sees decolonization as a largely completed project. Given the "contemporary absence of colonial structures in the classical form" and the desire of most indigenous peoples to maintain an enduring relationship with the state, ordinarily autonomy, not independence, is the appropriate remedy[22] (although his human rights model accepts the possibility of secession due to abuse of fundamental human rights).[23]

2 Turning to the Politics of the International Indigenous Movement

Until recently, scholars have not delved into the politics of the international indigenous movement and its implications for the interpretation of the Declaration. Political and legal theorists have inquired into the normative bases of indigenous rights[24] and questions of definition of indigenous peoples.[25] Social movement theorists and anthropologists have engaged with the rapid rise of indigenous peoples' movements in Latin America,[26] Asia,[27] and Africa.[28] However, the literature on the international indigenous movement

[22] Anaya, *supra* note 11 ("In most cases in the postcolonial world . . . secession would most likely be a cure worse than the disease from the standpoint of all concerned" at 86).

[23] *Id.* ("where there is a violation of self-determination and human rights, presumptions in favor of territorial integrity or political unity of existing states may be offset to the extent required by an appropriate remedy" at 67). However, it is not clear in international law that this creates an additional legal category to classic colonialism. *See Accordance with International Law of the Unilateral Declaration of Independence in Respect of Kosovo (Kosovo Opinion)*, Advisory Opinion (2010) I.C.J. Rep. 403, at 436. *See also Reference re Secession of Quebec* (1988) 2 S.C.R. 217, at para. 135.

[24] Jeremy Waldron, *Redressing Historic Injustice*, 52:1 UNIV. TOR. LAW. J. 135 (2002); Benedict Kingsbury, *Reconciling Five Competing Conceptual Structures of Indigenous Peoples' Claims in International and Comparative Law*, 34:1 N.Y. UNIV. J. INT. LAW POLIT. 189 (2001); PATRICK MACKLEM, THE SOVEREIGNTY OF HUMAN RIGHTS (1st ed. 2015); COURTNEY JUNG, THE MORAL FORCE OF INDIGENOUS POLITICS: CRITICAL LIBERALISM AND THE ZAPATISTAS (2008).

[25] Benedict Kingsbury, *'Indigenous Peoples' in International Law: A Constructivist Approach to the Asian Controversy*, 92:3 AM. J. INT. LAW 414 (1998).

[26] On Latin American indigenous movements, *see* ALISON BRYSK, FROM TRIBAL VILLAGE TO GLOBAL VILLAGE: INDIAN RIGHTS AND INTERNATIONAL RELATIONS IN LATIN AMERICA (2000); Jung, *supra* note 24; LUIS RODRÍGUEZ-PIÑERO, INDIGENOUS PEOPLES, POSTCOLONIALISM, AND INTERNATIONAL LAW: THE ILO REGIME (1919–1989) (2005); DEBORAH J. YASHAR, CONTESTING CITIZENSHIP IN LATIN AMERICA: THE RISE OF INDIGENOUS MOVEMENTS AND THE POSTLIBERAL CHALLENGE (2005); INDIGENOUS MOVEMENTS, SELF-REPRESENTATION, AND THE STATE IN LATIN AMERICA (Kay B. Warren & Jean E. Jackson eds., 1st ed. 2003).

[27] INDIGENOUS PEOPLES OF ASIA (R.H. Barnes, Andrew Gray, & Benedict Kingsbury eds., 1995); CHRISTIAN ERNI, THE CONCEPT OF INDIGENOUS PEOPLES IN ASIA: A RESOURCE BOOK (2008).

[28] Alan Barnard, *Kalahari Revisionism, Vienna and the Debate*, 14:01 SOC. ANTHROPOL. 1 (2006); Dorothy L. Hodgson, *Introduction: Comparative Perspectives on the Indigenous Rights Movement in Africa and the Americas*, 104:4 AM. ANTHROPOL. 1037 (2002); Dorothy L. Hodgson, *Precarious*

has tended to be limited to expositions written mostly by indigenous scholars and advocates, and their supporters, and directed at the domestic application of indigenous rights or comparative analyses.[29] It is surprisingly spare on critiques of the movement.[30]

However, since the Declaration was adopted in 2007, there have been several significant contributions on the politics of the international indigenous movement by non-indigenous scholars, notably Karen Engle's *The Elusive Promise of Indigenous Development*[31] and Courtney Jung's *The Moral Force of Indigenous Politics*.[32] Both argue that the movement has focused on the use of culture and related human rights to support claims to indigenous rights, to the neglect of more powerful agendas relating to structural economic and political redress.

There has also been quite strident criticism of the strategic use of culture by African indigenous peoples' movements and their supporters.[33]

These works sit within a larger body of scholarship critiquing the reification of culture by the identity-based movements that arose during the 1960s, including the Black Power, Second Wave Feminism, Gay and Lesbian, and Indigenous and Native American movements.[34] These groups had suffered marginalization and discrimination and as a result were disadvantaged structurally relative to dominant majority cultures. They saw their marginal

Alliances: The Cultural Politics and Structural Predicaments of the Indigenous Rights Movement in Tanzania, 104:4 AM. ANTHROPOL. 1086 (2002); DOROTHY L. HODGSON, BEING MAASAI, BECOMING INDIGENOUS: POSTCOLONIAL POLITICS IN A NEOLIBERAL WORLD (2011); Jim Igoe, *Becoming Indigenous Peoples: Difference, Inequality, and the Globalization of East African Identity Politics* 105:420 AFR. AFF. 399 (2006); Gabrielle Lynch, *Becoming Indigenous in the Pursuit of Justice: The African Commission on Human and Peoples' Rights and the Endorois*, 111:442 AFR. AFF. 24 (2012).

[29] *See, e.g.*, Joffe, Hartley, & Preston, *supra* note 2; Charters & Stavenhagen, *supra* note 2; Mauro Barelli, *The Role of Soft Law in the International Legal System: The Case of the United Nations Declaration on the Rights of Indigenous Peoples*, 58:4 INT. COMP. LAW. Q. 957 (2009). Brenda Gunn, *Overcoming Obstacles to Implementing the UN Declaration on the Rights of Indigenous Peoples in Canada*, 31 WINDSOR Y.B. ACCESS JUST. (2013) 147.

[30] For an exception to the rule, *see* Ahrén's description of the Declaration negotiations and the tensions between indigenous "hard-line" advocates and "pragmatists," Mattias Ahrén, *The UN Declaration on the Rights of Indigenous Peoples—How Was It Adopted and Why Is It Significant?*, *in* UNITED NATIONS DECLARATION ON THE RIGHTS OF INDIGENOUS PEOPLES (Henry Minde, Asbjorn Eide, & Mattias Ahrén eds., 2007).

[31] KAREN ENGLE, THE ELUSIVE PROMISE OF INDIGENOUS DEVELOPMENT: RIGHTS, CULTURE, STRATEGY (2010).

[32] Jung, *supra* note 24.

[33] *See* Justin Kenrick & Jerome Lewis, *Indigenous Peoples' Rights and the Politics of the Term 'Indigenous'*, 20:2 ANTHROPOL. TODAY 4 (2004); Barnard, *supra* note 29; John R. Bowen, *Should We Have a Universal Concept of 'Indigenous Peoples' Rights'?: Ethnicity and Essentialism in the Twenty-First Century*, 16:4 ANTHROPOL. TODAY 12 (2000).

[34] ANTHONY APPIAH, THE ETHICS OF IDENTITY (2005).

group status as connected to their inherent or essential character whether it was race, sexuality, gender, or ethnicity. Their search for justice was often made on the basis of this identity, and the movements often stressed their core cultural differences from other dominant cultures.[35]

A number of liberal theorists of "recognition" and "multiculturalism" supported these social movements. For example, Will Kymlicka emphasized the connection between culture and individual freedom.[36] According to Kymlicka, "liberals should be concerned about the fate of cultural structures, not because they have some moral status of their own, but because it is only through having a rich and secure cultural structure that people can become aware in a vivid way of the options available to them, and intelligently examine their value."[37] Mirroring the social movements themselves, multiculturalists often used a particular concept of culture to support their theories. For Kymlicka, a cultural group is complete and closed, has the capacity to govern, and members consider their culture is central to their way of life.[38] The idea of culture as distinctive, timeless, relativist, and antagonistic to progress has a long history in colonial policy, political theory, and anthropology.[39]

This idea of culture continues to influence contemporary thinking about social groups.[40] However, contemporary anthropology and political theory tend to have discarded it, preferring a "constructivist" understanding of culture as hybrid, contested, and constructed through historical processes, thus ever-changing.[41] As James Tully observes, cultures are not only "overlapping, interactive and internally negotiated but also densely interdependent in their formation and identity."[42]

In this vein, Nancy Fraser has been perhaps the most influential critic of the "politics of recognition" promoted by multiculturalism and identity-based movements.[43] According to Fraser, the politics of recognition encouraged

[35] Nancy Fraser, Adding Insult to Injury: Nancy Fraser Debates Her Critics (Kevin Olson ed., 2008).
[36] Will Kymlicka, Liberalism, Community, and Culture (1989).
[37] *Id.*
[38] *Id.*
[39] Sally Engle Merry, *Human Rights Law and the Demonization of Culture (and Anthropology Along the Way)*, 26:1 PoLAR Polit. Leg. Anthropol. Rev. 55 (2003).
[40] *Id.*
[41] *See, e.g.*, Nancy Fraser & Axel Honneth, Redistribution or Recognition?: A Political-Philosophical Exchange (2003); Nancy Fraser, *Rethinking Recognition*, 3 New Left Rev. 107 (2000); Merry, *supra* note 39; James Tully, Strange Multiplicity: Constitutionalism in an Age of Diversity (1995); Iris Marion Young, Inclusion and Democracy (2002).
[42] Tully, *supra* note 41, at 10.
[43] Fraser & Honneth, *supra* note 41.

essentialism and simplification of social groups and ran counter to a constructivist account of culture. This she called the "problem of reification."[44] However, Fraser's most significant contribution was the argument that the "politics of recognition" neglected the economic dimensions of an injustice resulting in the "problem of displacement."[45] It is one thing to recognize and respect one's gender or indigenous identity, and another to recognize that the social status of these identities in society may also result from economic injustice, or the "politics of distribution."[46] Fraser emphasized that matters of recognition and distribution are intertwined, and both need to be addressed to end an injustice.[47]

The problems of reification and displacement that Fraser identifies resonate with Engle's and Jung's critiques of indigenous peoples' politics. Engle seeks to dampen conventional readings of the Declaration as a "breakthrough" achievement for the international movement. She recognizes that in the early years of negotiations, indigenous advocates (predominately of the United States) advanced historically grounded "strong forms of self-determination," that is, asserting the "right of secession or independence as a nation state."[48] These advocates sought to shoehorn their domestic claims to Indian sovereignty into the Declaration negotiations and invoked the right of peoples to self-determination and decolonization.

However, Engle argues that several years into the Declaration negotiations, this line of argument was abandoned as advocates instead based their claims on human rights and, especially, the "human right to culture."[49] Under this human rights model, the focus is on maintenance of a way of life/tradition through land, heritage, and development.[50] Engle attributes this to a decision made by indigenous advocates to adapt to the realities of working within the UN human rights system. Many indigenous advocates saw strong claims to self-determination as a "futile attempt to affect international law too dramatically."[51] She cites James Anaya as one of the lead proponents of this shift in strategy.[52] She also notes that the human rights model was the

[44] Fraser, *supra* note 41, at 108.
[45] *Id.*
[46] *Id.* at 110–112.
[47] Fraser & Honneth, *supra* note 41, at 19, 25. Note Fraser's later recognition of a political dimension in Nancy Fraser, *Identity, Exclusion and Critique*, 6:3 EURO. J. POL. THEORY 305 (2007).
[48] Engle, *supra* note 30, at 3.
[49] *Id.*
[50] *Id.* at 6.
[51] *Id.* at 2.
[52] *Id.* at 98.

preferred approach of indigenous advocates of the former Spanish colonies of Latin America, where claims to political sovereignty were not realistic—given the presence of repressive regimes—or aligned with the aims of the Latin American movement.[53] When Latin American indigenous advocates did participate, their focus, as she shows, tended not to be political independence but cultural autonomy and basic human rights.

Conceiving indigenous rights as human and cultural rights, Engle argues, has not only raised the problem of reification, it has "largely displaced or deferred many of the economic and political issues that initially motivated much indigenous advocacy: issues of economic dependency, structural discrimination, and lack of indigenous autonomy."[54] The movement has, in short, drifted from its moorings in self-determination toward matters of culture, consultation, and land rights. Engle describes this as the "soft edge" of the claims of indigenous peoples, resulting in less of a threat to the state, and cites ILO Convention No. 169 as "both representative of and central to the move to protect indigenous rights under a human rights framework, particularly through the right to culture."[55]

This "soft approach," Engle argues, is evident also in the decisions of UN and Inter-American human rights treaty bodies. Advocates have largely couched their demands in terms of cultural rights as treaty bodies have proven increasingly receptive to these arguments. Here, Engle dwells especially on the Inter-American Court of Human Rights, which has upheld indigenous rights to consultation, land and resources, and FPIC.[56] All of this jurisprudence, as she rightly notes (and as I discuss in Chapter 4), is based on human rights and especially the right to culture.[57]

Like Engle, Courtney Jung seeks to free indigenous claims making from "the cultural straitjacket that has been imposed on it by a conception of

[53] *Id.* at 55–66.

[54] *Id.* at 3.

[55] *Id.* at 5. ILO Convention 169 has indeed become the prominent "go to" instrument for indigenous peoples in Latin America. The Convention contains basic rights for indigenous peoples. It affirms rights to traditional lands and the right to be consulted on activities that will affect them. *See Convention (No. 169) Concerning Indigenous and Tribal Peoples in Independent Countries, supra* note 3, at Preamble.

[56] Engle, *supra* note 31, Chapter 4.

[57] As I note in Chapter 4, the Inter-American Court has extended the human right to property to indigenous peoples' traditional lands. But instead of equality, the rights are said to be based on culture, which has led to the essentialization of indigenous rights. *See* Case of the Mayagna (Sumo) Awas Tingni Indigenous Community v. Nicaragua (2001), Inter-Am. Ct. H.R. (ser. C) No. 79.

legitimacy that relies on traditional practices and customs."[58] She does not delve as deeply as Engle into the use of the right to culture as a strategy in the international movement but instead focuses on the case of the Zapatista uprising in Chiapas, Mexico.[59] Applying a constructivist conception of culture, Jung argues that indigenous movements form around culture not because it expresses a people's deepest sense of itself, but because it is one of the core social markers used by the state to include or exclude them as fully fledged citizens.[60] Indigenous identity has been forged through state-sponsored policies that have used race, then class, and then ethnicity to categorize indigenous peoples.[61] Indigenous peoples have organized around these successive identities because access to power and resources has been regulated in these ways.

The Zapatista movement, Jung argues, emerged due to the decline of the power and connections provided through class-based *campesino* politics.[62] The Zapatistas increasingly came to assert their indigenous identity as they came to appreciate its potential politically to advance their aims of self-government and territory.[63] Peasants became indigenous peoples. But, in Jung's view, the strategy has ultimately boxed them in. Like Engle, she cites the limitations of claims based on indigenous culture, including failure to challenge structural injustices and the exclusion of groups by indigenous power brokers.[64]

Instead of grounding obligations to indigenous peoples in the cultural difference of groups, Jung advocates a "critical liberalism" that finds an alternative justificatory basis in the structural origins of marginalized social groups.[65] As Jung puts it, "the normative standing of these groups lies . . . in the political history that has forged them as groups not in the extent to which they are culturally distinct."[66] For indigenous peoples, the focus should therefore lie with historical and ongoing injustices. Cultural difference is relevant insofar as the state has helped to make it relevant to the nature and extent of the injustices.[67]

58 Jung, *supra* note 24, at 235.
59 *Id.*, Chapter 2.
60 *Id.* at 37.
61 *Id.* at 19.
62 *Id.* at 169–82.
63 *Id.*
64 *Id.* at 213–32.
65 *Id.* at 233.
66 *Id.* at 234.
67 *Id.* at 238.

3 An Alternative Political History of the Declaration

Engle's and Jung's compelling critiques have largely gone unanswered by indigenous advocates and scholars.[68] In this book, I seek to contribute to the welcome turn to indigenous politics in the international law literature by developing an alternative and unique political history of the Declaration. The historical narrative I offer contrasts with Engle's account of "strong forms of self-determination" being displaced by human rights and culture. As Engle and Jung demonstrate, cultural differences may have been significant to the Zapatista movement and Latin American and Northern indigenous movements generally. However, human rights and the human right to culture were not the only normative arguments that endured in the Declaration negotiations.

The narrative I develop in this book focuses on tensions between different regional indigenous movements that can broadly be separated along the lines of the "North" and "South." By the "North," I refer to the indigenous peoples of the former British Colonies of Canada, Australia, New Zealand, and the United States (often known as the "CANZUS" states). The "South" in this book refers to indigenous peoples in Latin America, Asia and Africa, and the Saami of the Nordic states (Sweden, Finland, Norway) principally, but it must be noted that there are now seven official UN indigenous regions.[69] In addition to the Pacific and North America, the UN recognizes Africa; Asia; Central and South America and the Caribbean; the Arctic; and Central and Eastern Europe, Russian Federation, Central Asia, and Transcaucasia. However, I focus in this book on the Asian and African movements given their lead role in extending the movement beyond its original focus on the Americas and Australasia to the South and their particular emphasis on

[68] Among the notable exceptions are Kirsty Gover, *Review Essay: The Elusive Promise of Indigenous Development: Rights, Culture, Strategy by Karen Engle*, 12:2 Melb. J. Int. Law 419 (2011); and Kirsty Gover, *Settler-State Political Theory, "CANZUS" and the UN Declaration on the Rights of Indigenous Peoples*, 26:2 Eur. J. Int. Law 345 (2015).

[69] Henry Minde, *The Destination and the Journey: Indigenous Peoples and the UN from the 1960s through 1985*, *in* United Nations Declaration on the Rights of Indigenous Peoples (Henry Minde, Asbjorn Eide, & Mattias Ahrén eds., 2007). While the Saami were early participants in the international movement and Northern-based, they share many historical similarities with "Southern" Asian and African indigenous peoples in that their peoples were gradually absorbed by adjacent colonizing powers rather than subjected to overseas colonization and settlement. They cannot, therefore, like the Asian and African movements, rely on the decolonization model. Other Southern indigenous peoples' movements could be included such as the "indigenous small numbered peoples" of the Russian Federation and the Tartar movement in Ukraine, *see, e.g.*, Alexandra Xanthaki, *Indigenous Rights in the Russian Federation: The Case of Numerically Small Peoples of the Russian North, Siberia, and Far East*, 26:1 Hum. Rights Q. 74 (2004).

human rights and culture to access the international movement. They effectively established the blueprint by which all other nascent indigenous movements would need to follow.

These Northern and Southern movements came to the international movement at different stages. As Engle notes, indigenous advocates of North America were the first to engage actively in the Declaration negotiations, followed shortly afterwards by advocates of Australia and New Zealand. Reacting against assimilationist policies, and drawing on their special historical relationship with the state, these activists sought restoration of the tribe's inherent prior sovereign rights and, given states' resistance to significant reforms, sought to shoehorn their aspirations into an international standard-setting process. The right to self-determination was critical to them.

When negotiations commenced, states sought a Declaration that would promote basic human rights of indigenous peoples[70] or minority rights;[71] in other words, standards that broadly reflected what most states had already committed to domestically in word if not in deed. Northern indigenous peoples also stressed the importance of basic human rights.[72] However, these indigenous advocates primarily advanced a "decolonization model." This model highlighted the parallels between Northern indigenous peoples' historical experience and that of colonized peoples of Asia, Africa, and the Middle East who had obtained their independence under UN supervision by virtue of the right to self-determination of peoples as developed from the chapters of the UN Charter on trust territories and non-self-governing territories (and earlier the provisions of the Covenant of the League of Nations on mandate territories).[73] Advocates sought to fit the decolonization model to the "historical sovereignty" arguments advanced against their states domestically, whereby indigenous peoples sought restoration of their prior,

[70] *See, e.g.*, New Zealand, "New Zealand Statement under Item 5" (1989) doCip Doc. 200284_1 (on file with author) (referring to UN Resolution 21/120 and the need to "ensure compatibility with existing human rights instruments" at 200284_2).

[71] *See, e.g.*, *Canada, Information received from Governments*, UNWGIP, 6th Sess., U.N. Doc. E/CN.4/Sub.2/AC.4/1988/2/Add.1 (1988) ("Canada is of the view that rights, referred to in the draft principles, should generally be oriented towards rights of individuals. In this regard we should emphasize Article 27 of the International Covenant of Civil and Political Rights where a right with a collective aspect has been stated in terms of individual rights" at 3).

[72] *See, e.g.*, "Statement of the Grand Council of the Crees (of Quebec)" (1988) doCip Doc. 210980_1 (on file with author) ("While we meet here, we are fighting for our survival as a people. Our collective rights are being denied in many lands, and even in the most wealthy countries of the world, our people are always the poorest of the poor" at 210980_1).

[73] Generally, *see* ANTONIO CASSESE, SELF-DETERMINATION OF PEOPLES: A LEGAL REAPPRAISAL (1998).

sovereign rights. Although overseas decolonization had led to independence for peoples as constituted by the colonially imposed borders, rather than for the previously sovereign peoples, the argument in the Declaration negotiations was that indigenous peoples were likewise colonized peoples entitled to the right to self-determination and independence; to deny them the right would be to discriminate against them.

In support of the decolonization model, Northern indigenous peoples pointed to treaty-making with European states, and a long-established practice of recognition of indigenous peoples as first peoples with a *sui generis* political-legal status.[74] This Northern experience of colonization and settlement was also relatively recent in that the most intensive period of settlement for these states was in the mid- to late-19th century.

The decolonization model, therefore, speaks to a nation-to-nation relationship between Northern indigenous peoples and CANZUS states, whereas a human rights model is directed at domestic issues of equality and political participation. The decolonization model indicated that self-determination in the Declaration offered indigenous peoples the option of independence should indigenous peoples and states fail to negotiate their terms of co-existence. It also indicated the need for international supervision of indigenous-state relations.

As noted above, Engle recognizes that this "strong form of self-determination," as she puts it, was advocated by Northern indigenous peoples. However, she argues that the decolonization model became less prominent due to a combination of (1) its shelving by indigenous advocates in the North and (2) a preference for human rights and culture in the Latin American indigenous movement.

In contrast, I argue that it is the globalization of the movement and, in particular, the participation of indigenous peoples of *Asia* and later *Africa* that saw a particular emphasis on human rights and culture in the Declaration negotiations. This threatened to undermine the decolonization model and unravel the self-determination framework. These movements placed particular emphasis on culture and human rights because this established common cause with indigenous peoples of the North. Although Northern indigenous peoples focused on the decolonization model, they also repeatedly referred to their marginalization, threatened cultural identity, and denial of basic

[74] For an illuminating account of this practice of indigenous-states relations in CANZUS states, *see* Kirsty Gover, Tribal Constitutionalism (2010).

rights. The Southern movement's emphasis on human rights was also an effort to defuse anxiety held by Southern states over minority security and stability issues. Asian and African states were particularly concerned about the right to self-determination in the Declaration. In response, Asian indigenous advocates held themselves out as "harmless" communities of remote, mountain, and hilltop areas seeking cultural survival in the face of unrelenting Western development and culture (not secession). Because Asian and African movements' participation in the Declaration negotiations is not featured in Engle's narrative, she misses a pivotal North–South tension.

There are two particular implications that follow from this alternative narrative of the Declaration's history. First, Engle overstates the emphasis on the human rights model by Northern indigenous advocates—indeed the Northern movement split between advocates of a human rights model and advocates of the decolonization model with the latter group persisting right up to the Declaration's UN General Assembly adoption (North–North tension). Second, by overlooking the impact of Asian and African indigenous peoples' participation in Declaration negotiations, Engle underestimates the pressure placed on Northern indigenous peoples to drop the decolonization model (broader South and North–South tension).

3.1 North–North Tension

In this book, contrary to Engle, I demonstrate that while many Northern advocates did come to shift their emphasis from the decolonization model toward a human rights model (witness the statement read by Malezer before the UN General Assembly), other Northern "hardline" advocates stayed the course. They did not want to compromise their core roots in radical sovereign tribal politics. Indeed, it is this persistence in advancing the decolonization model that accounts for the inclusion of the self-determination framework in the Declaration. By not according real weight to the connection between this model advanced by indigenous advocates of the North and the Declaration's self-determination framework, Engle limits the interpretive horizons of the Declaration. By this, I do not mean in the technical sense of understanding the travaux preparatoires as a subsidiary means of treaty interpretation,[75] but more broadly as predisposing the reader to assume that

[75] *Vienna Convention on the Law of Treaties*, *supra* note 9, art. 32. The Declaration is, of course, not a treaty.

the Declaration's wording cannot be read in an alternative way and/or that there is no longer a politics supporting this alternative reading. Contrary to Engle, the self-determination framework is thus directed at the restoration of tribal political power and tribal economic assets that would address issues of structural injustice.

3.2 A Broader South and North–South Tension

The participation of Asian and African indigenous peoples in the Declaration negotiations meant that there was significantly more emphasis on human rights and especially the human right to culture, and greater pressure to drop the decolonization model than Engle describes. Whereas Engle's account features the Latin American indigenous movement as the other factor explaining why the decolonization model was displaced, my research demonstrates the pivotal role played by Asian and African indigenous advocates. The decolonization model was neither practical nor persuasive in the context of Asia and Africa. Latin American indigenous peoples could at least claim the decolonization model—although I argue that the model is for the North only based, in particular, on treaty-making and the ongoing recognition broadly of the significance of indigenous peoples' prior occupation and sovereignty by successive settler governments. However, Asian and African indigenous peoples could not ground their claims in the same history of colonialism and thus could only benefit from alternatives to the decolonization model. Furthermore, Asian and African (and also Latin American) indigenous peoples were not as interested in historical injustices as they were with contemporary struggles—the need for their cultural survival and, in particular, access to basic human rights.

4 Reading the Declaration Anew

By recognizing the part played by the indigenous advocates of the South, particularly Asia and Africa, my account has the effect of sharpening the North–South politics of the trade-off involved in adopting the Declaration. However, the place of the North–North politics in my account suggests that we should also re-examine the final trade-off itself. Engle's rise-and-fall story of the indigenous advocacy behind the Declaration dovetails with a one-note interpretation of the Declaration as flowing from human rights and, especially, the human right to culture. Likewise, Anaya asks us to see the Declaration as a set of universal human rights elaborated to fit the indigenous context.

The few scholars who propose a more radical reading of the Declaration as grounded in rectificatory justice, notably Patrick Macklem, do so as a normative matter and not, as I do, through an account of its political history.[76] Moreover, Macklem offers a one-note interpretative model akin to the decolonization model—it is only about rectificatory justice for denial of sovereignty.

I take issue with both the one-note human rights reading and the one-note decolonization approach. The alternative political history outlined in this book shows that neither the impact of the Southern indigenous peoples' movement nor the Northern movement has been fully appreciated. The South contributed toward the human rights in the Declaration, while the North ensured the decolonization model was retained.

The picture of the Declaration that emerges in this book is normatively mixed. This mixed-model account sees the Declaration as containing two normative strands: one based on human rights and the other based on anti-colonialism.

The human rights model gives indigenous peoples of the South access to those rights that are grounded in human rights. These include the rights to practice and revitalize their cultural traditions and customs (Article 11); the right to manifest, practice, develop, and teach their spiritual and religious traditions, customs, and ceremonies (Article 12); and the right to determine and develop priorities and strategies for exercising their right to development (Article 23). This also includes the right to self-determination itself, although in the sense of promoting the right to effective participation in public life, inclusion of indigenous peoples in decisions affecting them, and local autonomy. Northern indigenous peoples also may rely on the human rights model.

However, the right to self-determination, self-government, historical redress, treaty rights, and FPIC—the self-determination framework—resulted from the decolonization model. Indigenous peoples are first peoples, prior to the current state, and entitled to recognition of their inherent sovereign status. For indigenous peoples of the CANZUS states, the self-determination

[76] Macklem, *supra* note 24.

framework is in the Declaration to address their specific circumstances. It also shows that Northern indigenous peoples' claims are not mired in claims to culture, as Engle argues, but rather directed at major economic and political reforms.

Others offer mixed models that view the Declaration as containing human rights and "aspirations"—the latter being the self-determination framework. However, these models seek to disconnect the self-determination framework from the decolonization model. The United States, Canada, and New Zealand argue that the aspirations are ultimately to be determined by states within their respective legal system and practices.[77] Benedict Kingsbury sees the aspirations as grounded in history and culture, not anti-colonialism.[78]

The important benefit of my mixed model is that it is not a zero-sum game between the North and South. This interpretation of the Declaration enables indigenous peoples of Africa and Asia (as well as Latin America) to access the rights in the Declaration that mean most to them and are grounded in their particular experience. It also helps address African and Asian states' opposition to their self-identification as indigenous peoples. This opposition was largely due to the self-determination framework in the Declaration, sparking fears of secession. It would also hopefully lead to less emphasis on culture. There would be less need to use culture to establish a common cause with the international movement and to defuse anxiety held by Southern states over minority security and stability issues. CANZUS states, of course, would oppose the inclusion of decolonization in the mixed model, but this is based on its concern about the power of the decolonization model rather than any question about its normative salience.

The question, however, is whether my mixed model is the better model of interpretation. Can the Declaration be given such a mixed-model interpretation so that it serves both Northern and Southern indigenous peoples at the same time? Is this argument within the bounds of current thinking in international law? I argue that the mixed model is for two reasons: (1) the "interpretive community" associated with the Declaration's negotiations and its implementation shared and continue to share a set of assumptions, expectations, and knowledge that support my mixed-model interpretation of the

[77] For example, according to the United States, self-determination in the Declaration is a "new and distinct international concept of self-determination specific to indigenous peoples." *See* United States State Department, *Announcement of U.S. Support for the United Nations Declaration on the Rights of Indigenous Peoples: Initiatives to Promote the Government-to-Government Relationship & Improve the Lives of Indigenous Peoples* (2010) at [3], <https://2009-2017.state.gov/s/srgia/154553.htm>.

[78] Kingsbury, *supra* note 25, at 244.

Declaration;[79] and (2) drawing on Thomas Franck's theory of international law and legitimacy, I argue that the self-determination model and human rights model as set out in the mixed model have a high degree of legitimacy because, among other things, it matches particular justifications with the people who made them, and the resulting norms. It thus should exert high compliance pull toward compliance by the CANZUS states and Southern states.

The contemporary challenge is to revive the normatively mixed account of the Declaration, which, I argue, is truest to its political history, maximizes the gains for all indigenous peoples, and is legally plausible. The human rights model is dominant in the South. Nevertheless, as I argue, there remains strong resistance to indigenous rights—especially in Asia and Africa—due to the Declaration's self-determination framework. In Latin America, there is a heavy emphasis on culture and not equality leading to the reification of indigenous rights. Ironically, even in the North, indigenous peoples rarely refer to the decolonization model. The challenge now for Northern indigenous advocates is to re-assert the self-determination framework in the Declaration and emphasize its basis in the decolonization model.

5 Outline of Chapters

Chapter 1 tracks the origins of the contemporary international indigenous movement in Northern indigenous rights advocacy and notes the use by these advocates of the decolonization model in the Declaration negotiations to support their self-determination claims.

Chapter 2 describes the emergence of an Asian indigenous movement supported by activist anthropologists from Western Europe and their focus on culture and human rights in the Declaration negotiations. Chapter 2 also describes the path toward the adoption of the Declaration by the UN General Assembly. These two chapters emphasizing indigenous voices in the Declaration negotiations draw on my personal experience working as an advocate and indigenous rights academic for the past twenty years for tribal communities in New Zealand and as an advocate in the UN, including as

[79] For comment on the notion of interpretive communities in international law, *see* Ian Johnstone, *The Power of Interpretive Communities*, *in* POWER IN GLOBAL GOVERNANCE (Michael Barnett & Raymond Duvall eds., 2004).

the first adviser on indigenous rights to Amnesty International's head office in London. At Amnesty, I worked with Asian and African advocates as well as many from the Americas and Australasia. The international perspective and discussions with indigenous rights leaders allowed me to test out many of the ideas in this book. The book's preparation was greatly aided by the documentation compiled by the Swiss-based NGO, doCip (the Center for Documentation, Research and Information), which has gathered documentation since the 1977 International Conference on "Discrimination against the Indigenous Populations in the Americas." In particular, I used the doCip CD Rom database of (i) reports drawn up by the members and special rapporteurs of the working groups negotiating the Declaration; and (ii) presentations and statements made by states, NGOs, intergovernmental bodies, and indigenous advocates during the Declaration negotiations. The database is particularly comprehensive because it contains written submissions that are not available in the UN documentation database, including many submissions made by indigenous advocates and NGOs. If you would prefer to read ahead of this descriptive account of the negotiations, to the case for a mixed model and how it differs from conventional normative accounts, I suggest reading from Chapter 3.

In Chapter 3, I make the case for a mixed-model interpretation of the Declaration based on the fact that throughout negotiations, two strands of argument were emphasized by two different types of social movements. The mixed model thus keeps faith with the Declaration's political history, particularly the diverse and extensive participation of indigenous peoples, while also clarifying the normative basis of indigenous rights and who indigenous people are for the purposes of international law.

In Chapter 4, I discuss the benefits of the mixed model to both the Northern and Southern indigenous movements. The model, I argue, can substantially benefit the Southern movements, particularly the Asian and African movements, by removing state concerns with the category of indigenous peoples and the self-determination framework. It would also emphasize the legal legitimacy that these rights have for Southern indigenous peoples and shift the focus of local movements from culture to equality. In the North, the challenge of my mixed-model approach is to avoid the decolonization model being absorbed by the human rights model through the practices of interpretation. By revealing the place of the decolonization model in the political history and thereby in the text of the Declaration, I seek to position indigenous advocates to re-assert the decolonization model so as to counteract the effects of both the one-note models and the mixed models exemplified by Benedict Kingsbury and Canada, the United States, and New Zealand. By way of illustration, I close by considering the implications of the mixed model in three case studies directed at aboriginal title claims in Canada, freshwater claims in New Zealand, and the application of the right to FPIC in the North and South.

The last chapter concludes by taking up the critique by several authors that the Declaration's universalized propositions on indigenous rights have limited utility in the domestic context, given the need for indigenous rights to engage with competing interests, economic issues, and extant constitutional structures. Certain on-the-ground practices, some even involving private industry, are noted as out ahead of international standards. In response, I argue that this critique overlooks the power of the mixed model to address fundamental gaps in the domestic indigenous rights architecture of both the North and South and thereby speak to these different contexts in ways that the conventional interpretation of the Declaration does not.

1

The Declaration and the Decolonization Model

1 Indigenous Movements in the North

From the late 1960s and early 1970s, indigenous social movements arose within the settler states of Canada, Australia, New Zealand, and the United States (CANZUS or Northern states). Inspired by the decolonization movement, indigenous activists worked alongside other social movements, including women's rights and Black Power movements, to mobilize for state reforms.[1]

Each national indigenous movement had its own distinctive flavor. However, there were also many commonalities given their shared origins as movements founded by "first peoples" colonized by European imperialists but particularly the British Crown. Early British colonial policy on indigenous peoples was aimed at engaging with local indigenous inhabitants through treaties and ad hoc local agreements. Between 1776 and 1871, the British Crown made hundreds of treaties with indigenous peoples in what was then known as British North America.[2] These treaties were not only about acquiring land, many were also about recognizing indigenous political authority. During this early phase of engagement, significant colonial judicial decisions and proclamations recognized an indigenous right to qualified sovereignty.[3] A rapidly growing settler population and demand for land led to a new phase of indigenous-settler relations. Colonial judicial

[1] *See generally* Paul G. McHugh, Aboriginal Societies and the Common Law: A History of Sovereignty, Status, and Self-Determination (2004) [hereinafter McHugh, "Aboriginal Societies"]; Paul G. McHugh, Aboriginal Title: The Modern Jurisprudence of Tribal Land Rights (2011) [hereinafter McHugh, "Aboriginal Title"].

[2] McHugh, "Aboriginal Societies," *supra* note 1.

[3] For example, the US Supreme Court in the trilogy of "Cherokee Cases" recognized Indian tribal rights to land and inherent sovereignty as "domestic, dependent nations." Johnson v. M'Intosh, 21 U.S. 543 (1823) [hereinafter *Johnson*]; Cherokee Nation v. Georgia, 30 U.S. 1 (1831) [hereinafter *Cherokee Nation*]; Worcester v. Georgia, 31 U.S. 515 (1832) [hereinafter *Worcester*]. *See royal proclamation 1873.*

The UN Declaration on the Rights of Indigenous Peoples. Andrew Erueti, Oxford University Press. © Oxford University Press 2022. DOI: 10.1093/oso/9780190068301.003.0002

decisions and policies turned against indigenous peoples.[4] International law doctrines of *terra nullius* and discovery were used to justify the taking and settlement of indigenous peoples' lands. Conflicts over land between settler governments and indigenous peoples resulted in the confiscation of tribal lands.[5] Those lands retained by indigenous peoples were often converted into individualized titles, undermining tribal sovereignty and collective control over their sale.[6] By the end of the 19th century, nearly the entire landmass of the CANZUS states passed out of indigenous ownership.[7] With the settler governments now well established, government policy in the early 20th century shifted again.[8] First, successive governments recognized the "tribe" or "Indian band" and applied special laws and codes to them, including the establishment of reserves,[9] the corporatization of tribes,[10] and regulation of tribal members and land rights.[11] Second, governments adopted a policy of gradual assimilation, encouraging tribal members to leave the land base and merge into the general citizenry.[12] The ultimate policy goal was to create a

[4] *See* Wi Parata v. the Bishop of Wellington (1877) 3 N.Z. Jur. 72 (NS). Only several decades after the Treaty of Waitangi, the judicial decision of *Wi Parata* ruled that Māori possessed no property in their traditional lands and that the Treaty was a "nullity."

[5] Almost one-quarter of New Zealand was acquired by the state through land confiscation from tribal "rebels" who resisted requests to sell their land to the Crown, *see* RAUPATU: THE CONFISCATION OF MĀORI LAND (Richard Boast & Richard S. Hill eds., 2009).

[6] ROBERT A. WILLIAMS JR., THE AMERICAN INDIAN IN WESTERN LEGAL THOUGHT: THE DISCOURSES OF CONQUEST (1990) (In the United States, the Dawes General Allotment Act of 1887 broke up tribal landholdings into individual plots that could become alienable); *see* RICHARD BOAST, MĀORI LAND LAW (2d ed. 2004) (In New Zealand, the Native Land Court converted Māori tribal title into an alienable freehold title).

[7] The Major Crimes Act, 18 U.S.C. § 1153 (1885) (which established paramount federal jurisdiction over certain crimes committed in Indian country, whether by an Indian or a non-Indian); *see also* the Public Law 280 of 1953, which extended state criminal and civil jurisdiction to Indian country in specified states; *see also* Russel L. Barsh, *The Red Man in the American Wonderland*, 11:3 HRTS 14 (1984). The jurisdiction recognized in the United States under the "Cherokee Cases" was whittled away by Congress under its so-called "plenary power."

[8] For Canada, *see* PATRICK MACKLEM, INDIGENOUS DIFFERENCE AND THE CONSTITUTION OF CANADA (2001); for New Zealand, *see* ANDREW SHARP, JUSTICE AND THE MĀORI: MĀORI CLAIMS IN NEW ZEALAND POLITICAL ARGUMENT IN THE 1980S (1990); for Australia, *see* RICHARD BROOME, ABORIGINAL AUSTRALIANS: A HISTORY SINCE 1788 (2010); BAIN ATTWOOD & FIONA MAGOWAN, TELLING STORIES: INDIGENOUS HISTORY AND MEMORY IN AUSTRALIA AND NEW ZEALAND (2001). For comparative approaches, *see* Bradford Morse, *Common Roots but Modern Divergences: Aboriginal Policies in Canada and the United States*, 10 STTLR 115 (1997); Ralph W. Johnson, *Fragile Gains: Two Centuries of Canadian and United States Policy Toward Indians*, 66 WASH L. REV. 643 (1991). PAUL HAVEMANN, INDIGENOUS PEOPLES' RIGHTS IN AUSTRALIA, CANADA, & NEW ZEALAND (1999). For analysis that focuses on the CANZUS states, *see* KIRSTY GOVER, TRIBAL CONSTITUTIONALISM (2010); McHugh, "Aboriginal Societies," *supra* note 1.

[9] McHugh, "Aboriginal Societies," *supra* note 1, at 276–84.

[10] *Id.* at 224–43.

[11] *Id.* at 245–62, 264–74.

[12] McHugh, "Aboriginal Title," *supra* note 1 ("[t]he implicit presumption, sometimes made explicit, was that tribes would become an urban proletariat. It was generally believed that their movement to

race of North American Indians or Māori or Aboriginal people and put an end to the tribe as a historical-political institution.

It was this drive to assimilate indigenous peoples, coinciding with the rise in the 1960s and 1970s of identity-based movements and the UN decolonization movement, that inspired indigenous activism across the CANZUS states.[13] What were these activists seeking and why? Their ambitions were different from most other social movements of the North. Their agenda was political power for indigenous peoples based on their prior sovereign status—in particular, the restoration of indigenous historical-political institutions and traditional lands and resources. This "historical sovereignty" argument challenged the legitimacy of the contemporary state.[14] While many radical activists spoke of indigenous independence and sovereignty, most called for political autonomy within the modern state. What was ultimately required was a comprehensive inquiry by the CANZUS states into the injustices of the past and a process of historical rectification for tribes—including the restoration of tribal political autonomy.[15]

In a new phase of indigenous-state relations, government policies came to increasingly recognize group-differentiated rights through exemptions and the granting of specific rights. The reforms were based on the notion of indigenous peoples as first peoples with a special relationship with the state. President Nixon's 1977 "Self-Determination Policy" looked to a "new era in which the Indian future is determined by Indian Acts and Indian decisions."[16] Tribes would have greater control over the planning and

the cities would dissolve their customary polities and that those old forms would be superseded by new patterns of ethnic association and cultural identity" at 34).

[13] For comment on the emergent indigenous movement in Australia, *see* Gary Foley, Andrew Schaap, & Edwina Howell, The Aboriginal Tent Embassy: Sovereignty, Black Power, Land Rights and the State 123 (2013); for factors leading to the rise of indigenous movements in New Zealand, *see* Sharp, *supra* note 8; for the rise of the Red Power movement, *see* Roxanne D. Ortiz, Indians of the Americas: Human Rights and Self-Determination 1984) [hereinafter Ortiz, "Indians of the Americas"]; *see also* Russell Means, Where White Men Fear to Tread: The Autobiography of Russell Means (1995); for Canada, *see* George Manuel, The Fourth World: An Indian Reality (1974).

[14] For a description of this "historical sovereignty" argument, *see* James Anaya, *Divergent Discourses about International Law, Indigenous Peoples, and Rights over Lands and Natural Resources: Toward a Realist Trend*, 16 Colo. J. Intl. Envtl L. & Pol'y. 237, 241 (2005).

[15] Ward Churchill, *Charades, Anyone? The Indian Claims Commission in Context*, 24:1 Am. Indian Cult. Res. J. 43 (2000). The United States had sought to comprehensively resolve the grievances of Indian tribes in 1946 with the Indian Claims Commission. However, the only remedy provided under the relevant statute was monetary compensation upon a finding of extinguishment or taking of rights, leaving many fundamental issues unresolved.

[16] Richard M. Nixon, *Special Message on Indian Affairs*, *in* Public Papers of the Presidents of the United States: Richard Nixon. Containing the Public Messages, Speeches and Statements of the President, 1970 564 (1970).

administration of federal Indian programs.[17] The Alaska Native Claims Settlement Act (ANCSA) 1971 sought to resolve the long-standing issues surrounding aboriginal land claims in Alaska.[18] In Australia, statutory land agreements resulted in the return of large tracts of land to Aboriginal peoples. The Aboriginal Land Rights (Northern Territory) Act 1976 (ALRA) resulted in approximately half of the Northern Territory—the state with the largest aboriginal population—being held by Aboriginal peoples under a collective form of freehold title.[19] The Waitangi Tribunal was granted power in 1985 to inquire into the historical violations of the Treaty of Waitangi in New Zealand, ushering in a new era of historical inquiry and redress through modern treaty settlements.[20] In Canada, the British Columbia Treaty Commission was established to address aboriginal land claims in British Columbia.[21] These reforms were also accompanied by a series of judicial decisions in an emergent era of public interest litigation recognizing native interests in fisheries, minerals, and other resources.[22]

However, Indian activists, particularly the more radical elements, were frustrated at their relatively weak bargaining power as small minorities. An enduring problem throughout the history of indigenous-settler state relations was the one-sided manner in which reforms were determined, and this continued to plague policymaking in the new era of indigenous rights recognition. Furthermore, indigenous rights in the CANZUS states tended to fall within the realm of the executive branch of government, which left indigenous peoples at the mercy of prevalent political attitudes.[23] The courts, on occasion, would intervene and prompt government action by, for example,

[17] *See* Russel L. Barsh, *Aboriginal Rights, Human Rights, and International Law*, 2 Aust. Aboriginal Studies 2 (1984).

[18] Alaska Native Claims Settlement Act, 43 U.S.C. § 1601–24 (1971).

[19] Marcia Langton, Settling with Indigenous People: Modern Treaty and Agreement-Making (2006).

[20] Treaty of Waitangi Act, 1975 (NZ), 1975/114. On the early work of the Tribunal, *see* Sharp, *supra* note 8, at Chapter 4.

[21] McHugh, "Aboriginal Societies," *supra* note 1.

[22] In the United States, in the early 1970s, there was judicial recognition of treaty rights to fish in Washington State, *see* United States v. Washington, 384 F. Supp. 312 (1974) (which ruled that treaties signed in 1854 and 1855 reserved the right to fish); *see also* Santa Clara Pueblo v. Martinez, 49 U.S. 436 (1978) (the Supreme Court upheld the right of recognized tribes to determine their membership base in accordance with their inherent sovereignty); Mabo v. Queensland (No. 2), [1992] 175 C.L.R. 1. (rejecting principle of *terra nullius*); Te Weehi v. Regional Fisheries Officer, [1986] 1 N.Z.L.R. 680 (recognizing a Māori customary right to fisheries); Calder v. Attorney-General of British Columbia, [1973] S.C.R. 313 (recognizing aboriginal title in Canada).

[23] Gover, *supra* note 8; *see also* Mark Hickford, Lords of the Land: Indigenous Property Rights and the Jurisprudence of Empire (2011).

recognizing aboriginal rights to land and resources. However, the courts tended to defer to the executive.[24]

The reformist decisions and policies were no doubt influenced by the historic sovereignty arguments of indigenous movements. But at the same time, they seemed to be the tweaking of old policies. As was the case for many other social movements of the time, reform was neither fast enough nor radically transformational. What advocates sought—and continued to be denied to them—was the restoration of indigenous historical-political institutions and traditional lands and resources.

Indigenous peoples did not trust domestic governments to address their calls for major reform. What offered greater hope was international law—the notion of appealing to a supra-national authority that applied objective standards directed to indigenous peoples' core concerns. As the Grand Council of the Crees would remark during the Declaration negotiations:[25]

> History has shown us that domestic law is not a reliable standard for protection of human rights. It is a fundamental principle of the United Nations that we set higher ideals. We attempt to transcend national and municipal law, and bind ourselves to a higher ideal in order to overcome the misguided interests, greed, and political motivations that can result in abhorrent domestic legislation.

In the late 1970s, there were already signs that the UN would be inquiring into the rights of indigenous peoples due to the lobby efforts of indigenous advocates.[26] To have a set of international standards—especially if they were set high—would be a significant advancement for the cause of indigenous

[24] In New Zealand, *see* Te Runanga o Wharekauri Rekohu Inc v. Attorney-General, [1993] 2 N.Z.L.R. 301 ("[p]arliament is free to enact legislation on the lines envisaged in the Deed or otherwise. Whether or not it would be wise to do so and whether there is a sufficient 'mandate' for any such legislation are political questions for political judgment. The Court is not concerned with such questions" at 309); *see also* New Zealand Māori Council v. Attorney-General [2013] 3 N.Z.L.R. 31 (the Supreme Court declined to stop privatization of a hydro-project on the basis that Māori could access redress from the government).

[25] *See* "Statement of the Grand Council of the Crees (of Quebec)" (Aug. 1, 1988) doCip Doc. 210980_2 (on file with author) at 2.

[26] *See*, especially, International Indian Treaty Council, *International NGO Conference on Discrimination Against Indigenous Populations-1977-In the Americas*, 1:7 Treaty Council News (1977) [hereinafter "Report on Geneva NGO Conference"]. *See also* José R. Martínez Cobo, *Study of the Problem of Discrimination Against Indigenous Populations, Final Report (First Part)*, UNESCOR, 43rd Sess., U.N. Doc. E/CN.4/Sub.2/1986/7 & Adds. 1–4 (1986) [hereinafter "Final Report"].

peoples' movements. The aim, then, was to shoehorn domestic historic sovereignty-based claims into this international project.

2 The Rise of the International Indigenous Rights Movement

2.1 Indigenous Movements of the North

The first indigenous organizations to participate in international politics in the UN emerged from North America as extensions of domestic Indian sovereignty movements. The two leading organizations were the International Indian Treaty Council (Treaty Council) and the World Council of Indigenous Peoples (WCIP). The Treaty Council was formed in June 1974, at the first International Indian Treaty Conference, by the American Indian Movement (AIM) and traditional leaders of the Sioux Nation.[27] The Sioux Nation maintains many separate tribal governments scattered across several reservations and communities in North and South Dakota, Nebraska, Minnesota, and Montana in the United States. The landmass of the four largest reservations—Cheyenne River, Standing Rock, Rosebud, and Pine Ridge—would match the size of a small nation-state.[28] Many of the AIM activists were from Pine Ridge or other Sioux reservations. AIM was originally formed by young urban-based activists in Minnesota to fight mistreatment by police and to improve prospects for jobs, education, and housing.[29] However, it formed alliances with the Sioux Nation during the 1973 occupation of the town of Wounded Knee on the Pine Ridge Sioux reservation in South Dakota.[30] The AIM was invited to join a "traditionalist" faction of the Pine Ridge reservation, the Pine Ridge Sioux Oglala Civil Rights Organization, who not only were protesting against non-compliance with treaty obligations but also corruption and nepotism in the Pine Ridge tribal government.[31] Wounded Knee was chosen due to its symbolic significance

[27] Ortiz, *supra* note 13.

[28] Roxanne D. Ortiz, Human Rights, the United States, and American Indians 78 (1978) [hereinafter Ortiz, "Human Rights"].

[29] *Id.* AIM was founded in 1968 as a Red Power defense organization, analogous to and allied with the Chicano (Mexican) Brown Berets and the Black Panthers (*Id.*). *See* American Indian Movement of Des-Moines, *By-Laws of the American Indian Movement of Des Moines*, online: History Matters <http://historymatters.gmu.edu/d/6897>.

[30] Ortiz, "Indians of the Americas," *supra* note 13.

[31] Ortiz, "Human Rights," *supra* note 28.

as the site of the 1890 Wounded Knee Massacre of Indians by US cavalry soldiers.[32] The protest, which resulted in the death of a US marshal and two tribal activists during shootouts, drew substantial media attention and put the AIM in the national spotlight. The AIM's alliance with the traditional leaders of the Sioux and other nations made good sense. While the original object of the AIM was to combat urban racism, it became increasingly clear that the greater cause was tribal sovereignty.[33] As an urban-based organization, it lacked legitimacy without some connection with the tribal base. Tribal sovereignty meant much more than the jurisdiction exercised by the federally recognized Indian governments—which were seen as corrupt agents of the state.[34]

From the outset, the Treaty Council was particularly interested in the anticolonial movement and the UN decolonization process. The Treaty Council's first director, Jimmie Durham, a member of the Cherokee nation, had lived in Geneva during the late 1960s and been inspired by the decolonization movement.[35] In Geneva, Durham befriended a number of African liberation leaders seeking independence for their nations. Durham and other founders of the Treaty Council were particularly encouraged by the decolonization of small island states in the Caribbean and South Pacific. As Dunbar-Ortiz notes, "few of [them] were larger in size or more populated than a number of Indian territories in the United States."[36] This suggested that nations like the Sioux might achieve their stated aim of independent nation status, and if the Sioux obtained this, other nations might follow.[37]

The other major organization was the WCIP, established in 1975 at the International Conference of Indigenous Peoples in British Columbia.[38] Compared to the Treaty Council, the World Council had closer ties with officially recognized tribal governments. It was affiliated with the National Indian

[32] *Id.*; Means, *supra* note 13.

[33] Ortiz, "Human Rights," *supra* note 28.

[34] Ortiz, "Indians of the Americas," *supra* note 13.

[35] Dan Berger, The Hidden 1970s: Histories of Radicalism (2010).

[36] Ortiz, "Human Rights," *supra* note 28, at 34.

[37] Ortiz, "Indians of the Americas," *supra* note 13 (As its first measure, the Treaty Council established "the Declaration of Continuing Independence" that outlined the responsibilities of the Treaty Council including "a mandate to open offices in New York and elsewhere in order to facilitate access to international political forces"; and noted that Indian people allied themselves with the "colonized Puerto Rican people in their struggle for independence from the same United States" at 33).

[38] Henry Minde, *The Destination and the Journey: Indigenous Peoples and the UN from the 1960s through 1985*, *in* United Nations Declaration on the Rights of Indigenous Peoples 17–18 (Henry Minde, Asbjørn Eide, & Mattias Ahrén eds., 2007); Douglas Sanders, The Formation of the World Council of Indigenous Peoples 20 (1977).

Brotherhood (NIB) of Canada—a collective of Indian band governments—through its founding chair, and former head of the NIB, George Manuel,[39] and it obtained financial support from states including Canada, Norway, and Denmark.[40] Also, unlike the Treaty Council, which was directed at the United States, Canada, and to a lesser extent, Latin America, the World Council membership was more diverse, including indigenous peoples of CANZUS, Latin America, Saami of the Nordic states, and Inuit of Greenland.[41] At this very early stage, the World Council envisaged a global indigenous movement, whereas the Treaty Council was largely focused on North America. As a result, there were some tensions between the Treaty Council and the World Council.[42] At the time, there were questions about whether Saami were indigenous peoples given they had not been subjected to overseas colonization and settlement.[43]

The event that marked the beginning of indigenous peoples' direct engagement in the international system was the 1977 International NGO Conference on Indigenous Peoples of the Americas, held at the UN in Geneva.[44] The conference was organized by the Treaty Council and attended by over a hundred activists from North America and Latin America. The delegates met over several days at the UN's Palais des Nations and discussed an agenda for obtaining international law recognition of their sovereign status. The delegates produced an international instrument setting out their rights-based agenda, entitled the "Draft Declaration of Principles for the Defense of the Indigenous Nations and Peoples of the Western Hemisphere."[45]

While the Declaration did not expressly refer to self-determination, its focus was nationhood and independence. Article 4 of the Declaration noted: "Indigenous nations or groups shall be accorded such degree of independence as they may desire in accordance with international law." Article 7 referred to "Jurisdiction," noting "no state shall assert or claim to exercise any right of jurisdiction over any indigenous nation or group unless pursuant to a valid treaty or other agreement freely made with the lawful representatives

[39] Minde, *supra* note 38 at 17.

[40] Sanders, *supra* note 38 at 20.

[41] *Id.* at 15.

[42] *Id.* at 21.

[43] *Id.* at 20.

[44] For an account of this conference, *see* "Report on Geneva NGO Conference," *supra* note 26. *See also* Cobo, "Final Report," *supra* note 26, at paras. 81–113.

[45] *Draft Declaration of Principles for the Defense of the Indigenous Nations and Peoples of the Western Hemisphere*, UNESCOR, U.N. Doc. E/CN.4/Sub.2/L.684, at Annex IV (1978).

of the indigenous nation or group concerned."[46] Treaties between indigenous peoples and states were to "be recognized and applied in the same manner and according to the same international laws and principles as the treaties and agreements entered into by their states."[47] In relation to claims to territory, the Declaration noted: "No state shall claim or retain, by right of discovery or otherwise, the territories of an indigenous nation or group, except such lands as may have been lawfully acquired by valid treaty or other cessation freely made."[48]

As a precursor of the forthcoming tensions between Northern and Southern indigenous movements, Articles 1 and 2 referred to two different types of nations. Article 1 was clearly directed at the indigenous peoples of North America. Indigenous people were to be recognized as: "nations and proper subjects of international law, provided the people concerned desire to be recognized as a nation and meet the fundamental requirement of nationhood, namely: (a) having a permanent population; (b) having a defined territory; (c) having a government; (d) having the ability to enter into relations with other states."[49] Article 2 was directed at indigenous peoples of Latin America. It referred to "Indigenous groups not meeting the requirements of nationhood"—these would also be "subjects of international law and are entitled to the protection of this Declaration, provided they are identifiable groups having bonds of language, heritage, tradition, or other common identity."[50] This contrast between the aims of the North American advocates and those of Latin America can be seen in a video documentary on the Conference prepared by indigenous advocates and supporters entitled "An Indian Summer in Geneva."[51] The documentary shows the arrival of Indian advocates of North America and those from Latin America with a focus on Brazilian activists of Mato Grosso dol Sul. Jimmie Durham is interviewed and speaks of his aspirations for "making our sovereignty as Indian nations primarily with each other, as we started out before we were colonised. Of making a real organisation of Indian nations, like the [Organisation of American States] that would work together economically."[52] Other

[46] *Id.*, art. 7.
[47] *Id.*, art. 5.
[48] *Id.*, art. 8.
[49] *Id.*, art. 1.
[50] *Id.*, art. 2.
[51] Kisos Films, *Indigenous Summer in Geneva*, YouTube (Feb. 28, 2011), <https://www.youtube.com/watch?v=_gQrilz25tI>.
[52] *Id.* at 00h:32m:45s.

interviews with Latin American indigenous advocates adopt a very different stance. They speak about land rights and basic rights to health care and education. Their focus is on human rights and the human right to culture.

In closing, the Conference established a "program of action" to be carried out by indigenous organizations—the most significant being the establishment of a working group in the UN to focus on the elaboration of an instrument on indigenous peoples' rights. Clearly, the aim was to have the UN draft an international instrument along the lines of the Draft Declaration of Principles for the Defense of the Indigenous Nations and Peoples of the Western Hemisphere.

3 The Working Group on Indigenous Populations

The advocacy efforts of the Treaty Council and other indigenous NGOs coincided with efforts within the UN human rights system to address the status of indigenous peoples. Since the late 1960s, the UN Human Rights Division and Sub-Commission on Prevention of Discrimination and Protection of Minorities (Sub-Commission on Human Rights) began to inquire into the status of indigenous peoples. These efforts expanded as part of the UN Decade for Action to Combat Racism and Racial Discrimination (1973 to 1983). Chilean diplomat Hernan Santa Cruz wrote a report on the economic, social, and cultural discrimination of minorities, which contained two chapters on the situation of indigenous peoples.[53] However, the Commission on Human Rights had to be persuaded that indigenous peoples should be treated as a distinct category of study from minorities.[54] Finally, in 1971, acting on a recommendation of the Sub-Commission on Human Rights, through the Commission on Human Rights, a study on indigenous peoples was approved by the Economic and Social Council (ECOSOC).[55] Later, Jose R. Martinez

[53] HERNAN S. CRUZ, STUDY ON RACIAL DISCRIMINATION IN THE POLITICAL, ECONOMIC, SOCIAL AND CULTURAL SPHERES, U.N. Doc. E/CN.4/Sub.2/307 (1970), at para. 1094 (recommending that a new report be made only on indigenous peoples).

[54] *See* Augusto Willemsen Diaz, *How Indigenous Peoples' Rights Reached the UN*, *in* MAKING THE DECLARATION WORK: THE UNITED NATIONS DECLARATION ON THE RIGHTS OF INDIGENOUS PEOPLES (Claire Charters & Rodolfo Stavenhagen eds., 2009) (noting his personal lobby efforts for a separate UN study on indigenous peoples).

[55] ECOSOC Resolution 1589 (L), U.N. ESCOR, 50th Sess., Supp. No. 1 at 16, U.N. Doc. E/5044 (May 21, 1971) (authorizing the Sub-Commission to conduct a general and complete study into the problem of discrimination against indigenous populations and to suggest the necessary national and international measures by which to eliminate this).

Cobo was appointed to carry out the study, which came to be known as the "Cobo Report."[56] Originally, this was a racial discrimination project directed at the basic human rights of indigenous peoples. But as the study advanced, Cobo noted that existing human rights standards "are not fully applied" to indigenous peoples and, moreover, are "not wholly adequate" to the task.[57] For Cobo, "[s]elf-determination, in its many forms, must be recognized as the basic pre-condition for the enjoyment by indigenous peoples of their fundamental rights and the determination of their own future."[58] Thus, self-determination would provide a path to human rights. Cobo did not discount the possibility of self-determination granting independence—it had both its "internal and external expressions," though the right would ordinarily be "expressed in various forms of autonomy within the State."[59]

Within the UN, several Nordic states led a proposal for a Working Group on indigenous peoples.[60] Eventually, a proposal was put to the UN Commission on Human Rights by the Sub-Commission on Human Rights to establish a working group directed at the current status of indigenous peoples and the elaboration of standards of protection. This was approved by the ECOSOC, in 1982.[61]

In terms of working procedure, the working group was comprised of five members of the Sub-Commission on Human Rights elected annually from its ranks of independent experts, one from each regional grouping. These experts would have the task of preparing each new draft of the Declaration. The first Chair was a Norwegian human rights expert, Asbjørn Eide, chosen due to his country's role in establishing the working group. However, Eide was replaced in 1985 by Erica-Irene Daes who went on to lead the negotiations for the balance of the working group's ten-year tenure. The working group would meet annually for up to five working days at the Palais des Nations in Geneva before the annual sessions of the Sub-Commission on Human Rights in August—although this was later extended to ten working days.

At the first working group meeting, almost all indigenous advocates were of the North. Thirteen Northern indigenous organizations and only one Latin American indigenous organization attended the meeting. There were

[56] Cobo, "Final Report," *supra* note 26.

[57] *Id.* at paras. 624, 625.

[58] *Id.* at para. 580.

[59] *Id.* at para. 581.

[60] Asbjørn Eide, *UN Action on the Rights of Indigenous Populations*, *in* The Rights of Indigenous Peoples in International Law: Selected Essays on Self-Determination 31 (1987).

[61] ECOSOC Res. 1982/34.

no indigenous organizations representing Asian or African indigenous peoples.[62] Northern indigenous peoples—as they had done in the 1977 Geneva NGO Conference—immediately linked their struggle to the international anti-colonial agenda. As with the 1977 Conference, indigenous advocates represented the more radical element in domestic indigenous politics. The organizations tended to be specialist international NGOs—established for the specific task of appealing to international standards and bodies. It was easier for them to adopt a stronger stance against states because they were not dependent on government subsidies in the way many officially recognized tribes were. The Treaty Council and the WCIP were prominent, and there were new groups. The Saami Council represented the Saami of Norway, Sweden, Finland, and Russia. Several bodies were effectively the vehicles of individuals. This included the Indian Law Resource Center run by a Potawatomi lawyer, Tim Coulter,[63] with links to the New York Akwasasne Mohawk community;[64] the Indigenous World Association founded by Roxanne Dunbar-Ortiz—who was a founding member of the Treaty Council;[65] and the National Aboriginal and Islander Legal Services Secretariat (NAILSS) run by Paul Coe, a longtime aboriginal activist and lawyer.[66] The Four Directions Council originally represented four Canadian Nations but was increasingly represented by Russel Barsh, a non-indigenous lawyer and academic.[67] The Latin American organizations tended to be (mostly) urban-based organizations often called "Indianista organizations," including the Indian Council of South America or "Consejo India de Sudamerica" (CISA).[68] CISA was originally a branch of the WCIP though it would eventually operate independently.[69] But like many others from Latin America, CISA had tenuous connections with specific tribal communities and advanced a Quechua Indianist ideology—a return to the basic institutions and values of Incan

[62] *See* Working Group on Indigenous Populations, *Report on the First Session,* UNESCOR, 35th Sess., U.N. Doc. E/CN.4/Sub.2/1982/33, at 3 (1982) [hereinafter First Working Group meeting].

[63] Joëlle Rostkowski, Conversations with Remarkable Native Americans 85 (2012).

[64] Todd Leahy & Raymond Wilson, The A to Z of Native American Movements 79 (2009).

[65] Douglas Sanders, *The Legacy of Deskaheh: Indigenous Peoples as International Actors, in* The Human Rights of Indigenous Peoples 78–79 (Cynthia Price Cohen ed., 1998).

[66] *Id.* at 179. NAILSS was the first Australian indigenous organization to obtain NGO consultative status with ECOSOC. *See* Sarah Pritchard, *Declaration on the Rights of Indigenous Peoples: Drafting Nears Completion in the UN Working Group,* 60:2 Aboriginal Law Bulletin 9, 10 (1993).

[67] Sanders, *supra* note 38, at 78.

[68] *Id.*

[69] *Id.*

society, and not the more day-to-day struggles faced by rural community-based Quechua and Aymara Indians.[70]

A unique feature of the working group was its open process of participation. According to standard rules, representatives of governments, specialized agencies, and regional international organizations were entitled to participate as observers. Representatives of NGOs that had been given consultative status by the ECOSOC were also entitled to participate as observers. These included long-established NGOs such as Amnesty International, Survival International, and the Anti-Slavery Society. But in 1982, at the first meeting, there were only five indigenous organizations with ECOSOC consultative status.[71] This threatened to exclude large numbers of indigenous peoples as the process for applying for consultative status was cumbersome. However, due to prompting by UN officials and the Sub-Commission on Human Rights, a special registration procedure was established for any indigenous advocate attending the working group.[72] Given the working group's mandate, it was essential that indigenous advocates be permitted to participate.[73] Moreover, Northern indigenous peoples indicated that as nations they could not be relegated to mere observer status but should be given equal rights to participate in the negotiations alongside states.[74]

3.1 Which Conceptual Model—Human Rights or Decolonization?

(a) Human Rights

The Working Group on Indigenous Populations was originally a human rights project. It was located in the human rights division of the UN as a subsidiary body beneath the Sub-Commission on Human Rights. The Sub-Commission itself was a subsidiary body of the UN Commission on Human

70 Nilo Cayuquo, Zoltán Grossman, & Jo Tucker, *Interview with Nilo Cayuquo*, 9:2 LAT. AM. PERSPECT. 100 (1982).

71 First Working Group meeting, *supra* note 62, at 6.

72 *See* Augusto W. Diaz, *supra* note 54, at 26–27.

73 Douglas Sanders, *The UN Working Group on Indigenous Populations*, 11:3 HUM. RIGHTS Q. 406, 408 (1989).

74 *See* "International Indian Treaty Council" (Aug. 9–13, 1982) doCip Doc. 200252_1 (on file with author). ("We believe that the elaboration of standards should include the direct participation of indigenous peoples in the discussions and drawing up of instruments, and should take into account the right of indigenous peoples to self-determination" at 200252_2). *See also* KAREN KNOP, DIVERSITY AND SELF-DETERMINATION IN INTERNATIONAL LAW Chapter 5 (2002) (noting how the working group adopted an open process of negotiations treating indigenous peoples on the same basis as states).

Rights. The working group's task was to (1) review developments concerning the promotion and protection of the *human rights* and fundamental freedoms of indigenous populations; and (2) give special attention to the evolution of standards concerning the rights of indigenous populations.[75]

The prominent states participating in the Declaration negotiations included the CANZUS, Latin American, Nordic, and Asian states. The CANZUS states would have great influence, given their economic and political clout but also their recognized experience of settler-government-indigenous relations and the presence of significant numbers of indigenous peoples in their countries. During the annual meetings of the working group, each member of the CANZUS group normally made several oral and written interventions.

Unsurprisingly, the human rights model was the preferred approach of CANZUS and other states.[76] It found support in the resolution that established the working group as well as the UN General Assembly's 1986 resolution on standard setting in the field of international human rights. General Assembly resolution 41/120 read in part:[77]

> Recalling the extensive network of international standards in the field of human rights . . .
>
> *Emphasizing* the primacy of the Universal Declaration of Human Rights, the International Covenant on Civil and Political Rights and the International Covenant on Economic, Social, and Cultural Rights in this network,
>
> *Recognizing* the value of continuing efforts to identify specific areas where further international action is required to develop the existing international legal framework in the field of human rights . . .
>
> 2. *Urges* Member States and United Nations bodies engaged in developing new international human rights standards to give due consideration in this work to the established international legal framework . . .

[75] *Study of the Problem of Discrimination against Indigenous Populations*, E.S.C. Res. 1982/34, UNESCOR, U.N. Doc. E/RES/1982/34 (1982) [emphasis added].

[76] *See, e.g.*, New Zealand, "New Zealand Statement under Item 5" (1989) doCip Doc. 200284_1 (on file with author) (Referring to UN Resolution 21/120 and the need to "ensure compatibility with existing human rights instruments" at 2). *See also* Working Group on Indigenous Populations, *Information Received from Governments: Canada*, UNESCOR, 6th Sess., U.N. Doc. E/CN.4/Sub.2/AC.4/1988/2/Add.1 (1988) ("Canada is of the view that rights, referred to in the draft principles, should generally be oriented towards rights of individuals. In this regard we should emphasize Article 27 of the International Covenant on Civil and Political Rights where a right with a collective aspect has been stated in terms of individual rights" at 3) ["Information from Canada"].

[77] *Setting International Standards in the Field of Human rights*, G.A. Res. 41/120, UNGAOR, 97th Plen. Mtg., U.N. Doc. A/RES/41/20 (1986).

4. Invites Member States and United Nations bodies to bear in mind the following guidelines in developing international instruments in the field of human rights; such instruments should, inter alia:
   (a) Be consistent with the existing body of international human rights law . . .
   (e) Attract broad international support;

According to CANZUS states, the precarious state of indigenous peoples indicated that the priority should be the basic human rights set out in the International Human Rights Covenants and the Universal Declaration of Human Rights of 1948 (UDHR).[78] According to this view, all that is needed is the conscientious application of human rights standards to the problems suffered by members of indigenous groups. But the UDHR's emphasis on universal individual rights—irrespective of the person's cultural, religious, or political allegiances—meant that it failed to address those matters that were of most importance to Northern indigenous activists; that is, restoration of political sovereignty and territory.[79] The UDHR also had a checkered history, as imperial nations had unsuccessfully sought to exclude its application to peoples in colonies through a "colonial exemption clause." This proposal provided added impetus to the decolonization movement.[80]

More fundamentally, for indigenous activists, human rights were closely attached to the construction of, and implied fidelity to, the modern liberal democratic state. As Samuel Moyn notes, rights established the boundaries of citizenship as a means of solidifying the power of the nation-state.[81] The classic liberal equality model, which provided the core foundation for the drafting of the UDHR in the post-war years, was not about protection of the citizen against the state, but the promotion of the state itself.[82] Indigenous activists, on the other hand, questioned the existence and legitimacy of the state. The state had no right to govern indigenous peoples and their territories without their consent.[83]

[78] *Universal Declaration of Human Rights*, G.A. Res. 217A (III), UNGAOR, 3d Sess., Supp. No. 13, U.N. Doc. A/810, at 71 (1948).

[79] Also, a particular quirk of human rights instruments was, and remains, their ahistorical nature. *See* Richard A. Falk, Human Rights Horizons: The Pursuit of Justice in a Globalizing World 290 (2000).

[80] Roland Burke, Decolonization and the Evolution of International Human Rights (, 2010).

[81] Samuel Moyn, The Last Utopia: Human Rights in History Chapter 1 (2010).

[82] *Id.*

[83] For liberal accounts of how the absence of legitimacy and consent require rectificatory justice for indigenous peoples, *see* Margaret Moore, *The Right of Indigenous Peoples to Collective Self-Determination, in* Secession and Self-Determination (Stephen Macedo & Allen E. Buchanan eds., 2003); Allen E. Buchanan, Justice, Legitimacy, and Self-Determination: Moral Foundations for International Law (2007).

Human rights were important to Northern indigenous advocates. Some spoke of the need for existing human rights to be better implemented, strengthened, or supplemented to provide greater protection for indigenous peoples.[84] Northern indigenous peoples frequently noted that while they lived in an affluent liberal democracy, they experienced deeply entrenched poverty.[85] They also expressed concern about the violation of indigenous peoples' fundamental human rights in Latin America.[86] However, the prominent view was that human rights were deficient. As noted by the Inuit Circumpolar Conference:[87]

> In regard to the objectives and scope of the Draft Principles [of the draft Declaration], it is not sufficient to simply confirm that existing international standards apply to indigenous peoples. Nor is it adequate to adapt such standards to meet particular indigenous requirements. What is necessary is to ensure that the Draft Principles will also create new standards.

An alternative model, related to human rights, was a minority rights model, that is, an elaboration of the right of minorities in Article 27 of the ICCPR:[88]

> In those States in which ethnic, religious or linguistic minorities exist, persons belonging to such minorities shall not be denied the right, in

[84] *See* "Statement of the Chiefs of Alberta" (1982) doCip Doc. 200286_1 (on file with author) (requesting that "in the event that indigenous peoples continue to be not recognized by the UN as a peoples with their own homelands . . . the Working Group . . . consider putting forward amendments to [the International Covenants] in order that indigenous peoples rights are specifically protected within those existing Covenants" at 200286_5).

[85] *See* "Statement of the Grand Council of the Crees (of Quebec)" (1988) doCip Doc. 210980_1 (on file with author) ("[w]hile we meet here, we are fighting for our very survival as a people. Our collective rights are being denied in many lands, and even in the most wealthy countries of the world, our people are always the poorest of the poor" at 210980_1).

[86] At the first working group meeting, the Indian Legal Resource Centre insisted that it give "priority attention to the grave human rights problems now facing Indians of Central and South America." *See* ILRC, "Summary of Oral Statement Presented by the ILRC" (Aug. 11, 1982) doCip Doc. 200284_1 (on file with author) (The genocide in Guatemala demonstrated to the ILRC "the need to study (1) why present governing human rights standards . . . have failed to protect the rights of Indians, and (2) whether there are means whereby existing standards might be strengthened or supplemented to provide protection for the most fundamental human rights which are now being denied Indians" 200284_1).

[87] *See* Inuit Circumpolar Conference, *Information Received from NGOs*, UNESCOR, U.N. Doc. E/CN.4/Sub.2/AC.4/1988/5, at 6 (1988).

[88] *International Covenant on Civil and Political Rights*, Dec. 19, 1966, 999 U.N.T.S. 171, art. 27 (entered into force Mar. 23, 1976) [hereinafter *ICCPR*].

> community with the other members of their group, to enjoy their own culture, to profess and practise their own religion, or to use their own language.

The recognition of the rights of minorities within a state has always been controversial because of their ability to undermine state stability. While human rights struggled to emerge during the post-war years, despite the adoption of the UDHR, minority rights barely rated a mention. When the United Nations was established, the UN Charter contained no reference to minority rights,[89] nor did the UDHR.[90] The Genocide Convention,[91] adopted in 1948, contained no reference to "cultural genocide" or "ethnocide."[92] The European Convention on Human Rights (1950)[93] does not speak of minority rights, nor do the American Declaration of the Rights and Duties of Man (1948)[94] and the American Convention on Human Rights (1969).[95] It was not until several decades after the UDHR that the UN elaborated minority rights protections in the form of Article 27 of the ICCPR. Even then, Article 27 is framed as the rights of individuals belonging to minorities, as opposed to collective rights. Article 27 has been successfully invoked in a series of cases brought before the UN Human Rights Committee to protect indigenous cultural practices.[96] However, Article 27 has clear limitations as a framework for articulating indigenous claims. As Will Kymlicka notes:[97]

> To oversimplify, Article 27 can be invoked to contest discrete laws or policies adopted by states, but it does not contest the structure of the state itself. It sets limits on how states govern their indigenous peoples, but it does not

[89] *Charter of the United Nations*, June 26, 1945, Can. T.S. 1945 No. 7 (entered into force Oct. 24, 1945).

[90] *Universal Declaration of Human Rights*, *supra* note 78.

[91] *Convention on the Prevention and Punishment of the Crime of Genocide*, Dec. 9, 1948, 78 U.N.T.S. 277 (entered into force Jan. 12, 1951).

[92] *Id.*

[93] *Convention for the Protection of Human Rights and Fundamental Freedoms*, Nov. 4, 1950, 213 U.N.T.S. 221 (entered into force Sept. 3, 1953).

[94] OAS, Conference of American States, *American Declaration on the Rights and Duties of Man*, OEA/Ser.L/V/II. 82/Doc. 6/Rev. 1 (1948).

[95] *American Convention on Human Rights*, Nov. 22, 1969, 1144 U.N.T.S. 123 (entered into force July 18, 1978).

[96] *See, e.g.*, Bernard Ominayak v. Canada (Communication No. R. 167/1984), UNGAOR, 45th Sess., Supp. No. 40, U.N. Doc. A/45/40 Vol. II (1990); Ivan Kitok v. Sweden (Communication No. R. 197/1985), UNGAOR, 43rd Sess., Supp. No. 40, U.N. Doc. A/43/40 (1988); Ivan Kitok v. Sweden (Communication No. 197/1985), UNGAOR, 43rd Sess., Supp. No. 40, U.N. Doc. A/43/40 (1988).

[97] Will Kymlicka, *Beyond the Indigenous/Minority Dichotomy*, *in* REFLECTIONS ON THE UN DECLARATION ON THE RIGHTS OF INDIGENOUS PEOPLES 189 (Steve Allen & Alexandra Xanthaki eds., 2011). Also, note that the UN Human Rights Committee has rejected complaints alleging violation of the Article 1 right of self-determination in the ICCPR on the ground that this is a collective

> put in question the right of states to govern indigenous peoples and their territories. Yet it is precisely the structure of the state that is the central issue for many indigenous peoples. They do not simply want the state to govern them differently; rather, they want to govern themselves.

Much the same could be said for any other regional or international formulation of minority rights. The UN Declaration on the Rights of Minorities, for example, contains a set of human rights as applied to minorities but does not endorse collective rights or any rights like those in the self-determination framework.[98]

(b) The Decolonization Model

For several decades following the Second World War, the dominant international movement for the freedom of peoples was the anti-colonial movement directed by the UN.[99] The purposes of the UN Charter included a reference to developing "friendly relations among nations based on respect for the principle of equal rights and self-determination of peoples," which seemed to offer the promise of independence for colonies.[100] However, this formulation of self-determination was ambiguous and the development of a right to self-determination from the Charter proved, instead, to emerge from the chapters on self-government for trust territories and non-self-governing territories.[101]

The founding states of the UN, most of them imperial powers, were ambivalent about self-determination and its connection with decolonization. Mark Mazower notes:[102]

right and only complaints relating to individual rights can be considered by the Committee. *See* Apirana Mahuika et al v. New Zealand (Communication No. 547/1993), UNGAOR, 56th Sess., Supp. No. 40, U.N. Doc. A/56/40 (2000). Nevertheless the Human Rights Committee has recognized that Article 27 may be interpreted in light of the Article 1 right of self-determination (*Id.* at paras. 1, 9.2).

[98] UN General Assembly, *Declaration on the Rights of Persons Belonging to National or Ethnic, Religious and Linguistic Minorities*, Feb. 3, 1992, A/RES/47/135.

[99] Moyn, *supra* note 81; Jan Eckel & Samuel Moyn, The Breakthrough: Human Rights in the 1970s (2013); Mark Mazower, No Enchanted Palace: The End of Empire and the Ideological Origins of the United Nations (2009).

[100] *Charter of the United Nations*, *supra* note 89 (Lists as one of the UN purposes: "To develop friendly relations among nations based on respect for the principle of equal rights and self-determination of peoples, and to take other appropriate measures to strengthen universal peace" at art. 1(2)).

[101] *Id.* at Chapters XI (governing non-self-governing territories), XII, and XIII (establishing the trustee system).

[102] Mazower, *supra* note 99, at 8.

> One can view the Charter and especially its preamble, along with the UDHR and the Genocide Convention, as testifying to the foundational imperatives of the new world order established in the fight against Nazism. Or one can read them as promissory notes that the UN founders never intended to cash.

Like the League of Nations, the UN was a club of Western states concerned about shoring up and maintaining their power.[103] However, this changed due to a battle of ideas about the protection of minorities and agitation from former colonial nations who were early entries to the UN system. India's Prime Minister, Jawaharlal Nehru, led his country's protests at the South African government's treatment of its Indian population and found a receptive audience despite the UN's formal prohibition on intervening in internal matters.[104] This triggered a major shift in direction for the UN from its initial project of protecting imperialism to the active promotion of decolonization. Relying in particular on the principle of self-determination set out in the UN Charter, the decolonization movement succeeded in making the UN an instrument for the emancipation of colonial peoples throughout the world. Self-determination, then, moved from a principle of international law to a widely accepted legal right. This movement and the process of decolonization radically shifted international politics.[105] While at its inception in 1945 the UN was comprised of fifty-one states, mostly representative of the Americas and Western Europe, with minimal representation from Asia and Africa, by 1970 there were over seventy new member states. These additions were almost all newly decolonized nations of Asia and Africa. In 1960 alone, seventeen African states joined the UN.[106]

The decolonization movement was so powerful that the reference to self-determination in the International Human Rights Covenants was largely due to this shift in representation in the UN. When the UN organs debated the Covenants in the 1950s, the post-colonial states insisted that the Covenants

[103] *Id.*

[104] *Id.*, Chapter 4.

[105] David A. Kay, *The Politics of Decolonization: The New Nations and the United Nations Political Process*, 21:4 INT. ORGAN. 786 (1967); THOMAS D. MUSGRAVE, SELF-DETERMINATION AND NATIONAL MINORITIES 67–68 (2000).

[106] The countries were Cameroon, Central African Republic, Chad, Congo (Brazzaville), Congo (Leopoldville), Cyprus, Dahomey, Gabon, Ivory Coast, Malagasy Republic, Mali, Niger, Nigeria, Senegal, Somalia, Togo, and Upper Volta.

contain the right of peoples to self-determination as the threshold right.[107] In this, they found support from the Soviet Union and Communist bloc countries.[108] Lenin had long advocated for the self-determination of colonized peoples as did subsequent Soviet political leaders.[109]

For the post-colonial states, the right to self-determination was about the liberation of "peoples under foreign domination."[110] Self-determination was thus linked to anti-colonialism. This was the right upon which all other rights depended. Western states were opposed to any provision on self-determination in the International Human Rights Covenants, with the UK, France, and Belgium taking the lead given their concern about retaining control over their colonies and resources.[111] Western states advanced a number of technical arguments to support their opposition, including that self-determination was a political principle, not a justiciable right, or that it was too nebulous and vague to be included in an international treaty.[112] When it became clear that the right to self-determination would be included in the text—and as a result constitute a legal right—Western states sought to define the right in terms of their own political tradition of popular sovereignty and representative government.[113] Indeed, this interpretation of self-determination can be traced back to the statements of President Woodrow Wilson endorsing self-determination in "human rights terms" as supporting "democratic self-government" and "internal self-determination."[114]

When the International Human Rights Covenants came before the UN General Assembly, most Western states voted against them, and the

[107] ANTONIO CASSESE, SELF-DETERMINATION OF PEOPLES: A LEGAL REAPPRAISAL (1998) ("[t]he socialist countries—soon joined, at least at the political level, by an increasing number of freshly independent Third World countries—were the most active advocates of anti-colonial self-determination. They adopted and developed Lenin's thesis that self-determination should first and foremost be a postulate of anti-colonialism" at 44).

[108] *Id.* at 47–52 (noting how in 1950 the Soviet Union proposed a provision regarding self-determination in the International Covenants—"the primary concern was the right of self-determination of colonial peoples" at 48).

[109] *Id.* at 14–19 (although as Cassese notes "the Soviet leader championed self-determination more to further his ideological and political objectives than to safeguard peoples" at 18).

[110] Moyn, *supra* note 81.

[111] Cassese, *supra* note 107, at 49–50 ("By and large, it can be contended that Western countries opposed the provision on self-determination either on account of their colonial interests, or out of fear that the paragraph relating to the free disposition of natural resources imperiled foreign investments and enterprises in developing countries" at 50). *See also* Musgrave, *supra* note 105, at 67–68.

[112] Cassese, *supra* note 107, at 50–51. As we will see, these reasons are advanced by CANZUS states to oppose the inclusion of self-determination in the Declaration. *See, e.g., Information Received from Governments, United States*, UNESCOR, U.N. Doc. E/CN.4/WG.15/2/Add.1, at 7 (1995) (noting "uncertainty about the meaning of self-determination in international law").

[113] Musgrave, *supra* note 105, at 68.

[114] Cassese, *supra* note 107, at 19–23.

post-colonial states, the Soviet Union, and the Communist bloc states voted overwhelmingly in favor of them.[115] Common Article 1 of the covenants thus provides:[116]

> All peoples have the right of self-determination. By virtue of that right they freely determine their political status and freely pursue their economic, social and cultural development.

In addition to Article 1, the freshly minted states together with the Soviet Union and the Communist bloc states sought a series of resolutions in the UN General Assembly that linked self-determination to decolonization.[117] The most significant statement was Resolution 1514 (XV) of Dec. 14, 1960, entitled the "Declaration on the Granting of Independence to Colonial Countries and Peoples" (1960 Declaration on the Granting of Independence), which declared self-determination to be a "right" for "all peoples"[118] and stressed "the necessity of bringing to a speedy and unconditional end colonialism in all its forms and manifestations."[119] The Declaration also contained a reference to territorial integrity in Article 6:[120]

> Any attempt aimed at the partial or total disruption of the national unity and the territorial integrity of a country is incompatible with the purposes and principles of the Charter of the United Nations.

Territorial integrity was not referred to in the International Human Rights Covenants. However, it has always been an integral aspect of international law and is set out in Article 2(4) of the UN Charter.[121] And it became increasingly significant during decolonization. Newly decolonized states sought a reference to territorial integrity to ensure that their independence would be safe

[115] Musgrave, *supra* note 105, at 68.

[116] *International Covenant on Economic, Social and Cultural Rights*, Dec. 16, 1966, 993 U.N.T.S. 3 (entered into force Jan. 3, 1976); *ICCPR*, *supra* note 88.

[117] Musgrave, *supra* note 105, at 69–77.

[118] *Declaration on the Granting of Independence to Colonial Countries and Peoples*, G.A. Res. 1514, UNGAOR, 15th Sess., Supp. No. 15, U.N. Doc. A/4684 (1960), art. 2 [hereinafter *Declaration on the Granting of Independence*].

[119] *Id.* at para. 6.

[120] *Id.*, art. 6. To reaffirm the point, Article 7 provided: "All States shall observe faithfully and strictly the provisions of the Charter of the United Nations, the Universal Declaration of Human Rights and the present Declaration on the basis of equality, non-interference in the internal affairs of all States, and respect for the sovereign rights of all peoples and their territorial integrity."

[121] *Charter of the United Nations*, *supra* note 89, art. 2(4).

from internal secessionist claims and unwanted foreign interference in their domestic affairs. Eighty-nine states voted in favor of the 1960 Declaration on the Granting of Independence; there were nine abstentions. Those abstaining were the United States and mostly European colonial powers, including the United Kingdom, Belgium, Portugal, Spain, and France.[122]

However, Western states did support Resolution 2625 (XXV) of Oct. 24, 1970, entitled "Declaration on Principles of International Law Concerning Friendly Relations and Cooperation among States in Accordance with the Charter of the United Nations" (1970 Declaration on Friendly Relations).[123] Adopted by consensus, it contained a clear compromise between the self-determination aims of the Communist bloc countries and post-colonial states and the aims of the West. The Declaration endorsed self-determination and, like the 1960 Declaration on the Granting of Independence, noted the need to bring "a speedy end to colonialism."[124]

However, this resolution did not limit the right to self-determination to colonized peoples. Paragraph 1 provided that "by virtue of the principle of equal rights and self-determination of peoples . . . all peoples have the right to freely determine their political status."[125] Moreover, paragraph 7 linked self-determination to representative government and subjected territorial integrity to the maintenance of representative government and respect for human rights:[126]

> Nothing in the foregoing paragraphs shall be construed as authorizing or encouraging any action which would dismember or impair, totally or in part, the territorial integrity or political unity of sovereign and independent States conducting themselves in compliance with the principle of equal rights and self-determination of peoples as described above and thus possessed of a government representing the whole people belonging to the territory without distinction as to race, creed or colour.

This extension of self-determination beyond decolonization to include representative government was prompted by Western states' concern about

[122] Cassese, *supra* note 107, at 71.

[123] *Declaration on Principles of International Law Concerning Friendly Relations and Cooperation among States in Accordance with the Charter of the United Nations*, G.A. Res. 2526, UNGAOR, 25th Sess., Supp. No. 28, U.N. Doc. A/Res/25/2625 (1970).

[124] *Id.*

[125] *Id.*, para. 1 [emphasis added].

[126] *Id.*, para. 7. *See also* Cassese, *supra* note 107, at 109 (noting Western states had originally sought language in the Declaration that would explicitly equate self-determination with representative democracy).

human rights violations within the Soviet and post-colonial states. However, it also met with a long-term agenda to promote democracy and representative government. Subsequently, scholars have argued that paragraph 7 should be read as granting a right to independence in cases of gross abuses of human rights.[127] However, it is not clear in international law that this notion of remedial secession constitutes an additional legal category to classic colonialism.[128]

Decolonization was a significant movement, but it was denied to indigenous peoples. The 1960 Declaration indicated that decolonization applied to any colony geographically separate from the country administering it. Thus, there had to be salt water between the colonizing country and the colony or, at least, a geographically discrete set of boundaries.[129] This "salt water thesis," endorsed by the United States and Latin American states, excluded indigenous peoples of the Americas and Australasia from decolonization. At the time, Belgium—which was required to surrender its colonies in Africa and Asia under the decolonization program—advanced the argument that decolonization should include "indigenous peoples" within independent nations.[130] But this "Belgian thesis" was defeated. It therefore seemed indigenous peoples would not be able to call upon the right to self-determination and decolonization because of the salt water thesis.

3.2 The Declaration Negotiations and the Decolonization Model

A key feature of decolonization that would prove significant later in the context of the international indigenous movement was the tension between decolonization and human rights. There are contested views about the

[127] Cassese, *supra* note 107, at 118–20. *See also* JAMES CRAWFORD, THE CREATION OF STATES IN INTERNATIONAL LAW, 126–27 (2d ed. 2006); Robert McCorquodale, *Self-Determination: A Human Rights Approach*, 43:4 ICLQ 857, 857–85 (1994); Musgrave, *supra* note 105, at 188–99, 258; Buchanan, *supra* note 83.

[128] *Accordance with International Law of the Unilateral Declaration of Independence in respect of Kosovo (Kosovo Opinion)*, Advisory Opinion, [2010] I.C.J. Rep. 403 at 436. *See also Reference re Secession of Quebec*, (1988) 2 S.C.R. 217 (noting: (1) it is "unclear" whether such a remedial legal category is an "established law standard"; and (2) even if it did exist, "the current Quebec context cannot be said to approach such a threshold" at para. 135).

[129] *See* G.A. Res. 1514 (XV), *supra* note 118; and *1970 Friendly Relations Declaration*, *supra* note 104.

[130] GOVERNMENT OF BELGIUM, THE BELGIAN THESIS: THE SACRED MISSION OF CIVILIZATION, TO WHICH PEOPLES SHOULD THE BENEFIT BE EXTENDED? (1953).

attitudes of post-war anti-colonialists toward human rights. Samuel Moyn argues that these leaders were suspicious of the human rights program given its links to citizenship and state sovereignty.[131] Thus, human rights could detract from the main prize of self-determination and independence. Instead of emphasizing human rights, the decolonization movement appropriated and applied human rights to the ends of decolonization.[132] The notions of equality, non-discrimination, and liberty were used to support decolonization. Roland Burke, on the other hand, argues that at least in the 1950s and early 1960s, "although national independence was the highest priority, conventional human rights was almost always the central justification for recognition of a right to self-determination."[133] This was prompted in part by the efforts of colonizing powers to deny human rights to peoples in the colonies, exemplified by the special colonial exemption clause in the draft International Human Rights Covenants.[134] For these leaders, self-determination was said to offer up a path to the full enjoyment of human rights. Some saw the human rights and self-determination models as interdependent. Attitudes hardened once colonies acquired independence, though, given concerns about Western intervention and the use of human rights to justify questions about the new states treatment of their peoples, including minorities.

For the indigenous peoples' movement, leading figures such as Jose R. Martinez Cobo and some indigenous advocates spoke of self-determination as a path to human rights,[135] and many indigenous advocates saw human rights and self-determination as connected—even more so once the human rights model began to take hold. However, for the pioneers at the 1977 conference and UN working group meetings, independence was the priority, and human rights had potential to undermine the path to independence. Moreover, human rights were rarely part of the domestic movement's discourse especially during this initial phase. The right to self-determination

[131] Moyn, *supra* note 81, at 85.

[132] *See* Kay, *supra* note 105 (for the newly decolonized states, "the traditional concern of the United Nations with human rights has been but another vehicle for advancing their attack on colonialism and associated forms of racial discrimination" at 802).

[133] Roland Burke, Decolonization and the Evolution of International Human Rights 39 (2010).

[134] *Id.*

[135] *See, e.g.*, Four Directions Council, "Statement Concerning Racism in the Application of the Principles of Self-determination and Legal Equality of States" (1983) doCip Doc. 200479_1 (on file with author) ("the equal rights of all peoples to self-determination is fundamental to the universal realization of human rights generally" at 200479_1).

was seen in the context of prior sovereignty, and international treaty-making with settler governments. Of course, for many indigenous leaders, secession was not the aim; most sought greater political independence within the state, but it was important nonetheless to have the choice of full independence.

Human rights, therefore, largely supported the goal of independence in this sense, particularly non-discrimination and the right to equality. Indigenous advocates argued that the right to self-determination was a right for all "peoples," including indigenous peoples. This non-discrimination argument was important in the context of the salt water thesis. As noted above, this sought to limit self-determination and decolonization to *overseas* colonized peoples. However, indigenous advocates stressed that all peoples—including indigenous peoples and not just those in salt water states—should be entitled to self-determination and decolonization. As noted by the Four Directions Council:[136]

> Looking around the world today, we observe a curious phenomenon. Peoples of every race, with one exception, have been achieving self-determination and decolonization under the auspices of the UN. There are independent States today of every colour, save one. Is this a temporary oversight, or the result of institutionalized discrimination?

During the initial working group meetings, the WCIP,[137] the Four Directions Council,[138] the Indian Law Resource Center,[139] and the Treaty Council[140] provided the working group with their own indigenous rights declarations. Apart from *references* to the International Human Rights Covenants and the

[136] Four Directions Council, "Statement Concerning Racism in the Application of the Principles of Self-determination and Legal Equality of States" (1983) doCip Doc. 200479_2 (on file with author). *See also* "Submission to the Working Group by the Coalition of First Nations and Treaty Council Delivered by Sharon Venne" (1984) doCip Doc. 200518_A (on file with author) (urging the Working Group on Indigenous Populations to consider a recommendation to the Sub-Commission that: "The standards and obligations enunciated in the UN Charter on non-self-governing and trust territories, chapter 11, Article 73 must apply to self-determining Indigenous peoples" at 200518_I).

[137] *Information Received from NGOs: WCIP International Covenant on the Rights of Indigenous Peoples,* UNESCOR, U.N. Doc. E/CN.4/Sub.2/1983/5 (1983) (noting "all peoples have the right to self-determination. By virtue of that right Indigenous peoples may freely determine their political status and pursue their economic, social and cultural development" at 13).

[138] Four Directions Council, *Statement on Legal Standards,* UNESCOR, U.N. Doc. E/CN.4/Sub.2/AC.4/1983/CRP.1 Annex (1983) "Draft Resolution Declaring the Universality of all Human Rights."

[139] Indian Law Resource Center, "Principles for Guiding the Deliberations of the Working Group on Indigenous Populations" (1982) doCip Doc. 200253_1 (on file with author).

[140] *See* International Indian Treaty Council, *Information Received from NGOs, International Indian Treaty Council, Draft Principles for Guiding Deliberations of the Working Group,* UNESCOR, U.N. Doc. E/CN.4/1983/5/Add.2 (1982) [hereinafter "Treaty Council Model Declaration"].

UDHR, and specifically the right to equality and right of peoples to self-determination, the declarations themselves did not mirror human rights in the conventional sense. Rather, they were all directed at rights connected with obtaining political autonomy and control over their territories. Self-government, cultural integrity, religion, land rights, and natural resources were key rights in the model declarations, with each referring to the need for indigenous peoples' jurisdiction over these matters.

For example, the Treaty Council's declaration provided:[141]

> Article 1. Indigenous populations are subject to an economic and/or political and/or social domination which is alien and colonial or neo-colonial in nature.
>
> Article 2. Indigenous populations are composed of nations and peoples which are collective entities entitled to and requiring self-determination. The Working Group should, therefore, develop a definition of the ultimate goals of self-determination, appropriate to indigenous populations, and procedures for achieving those goals.
>
> Article 3. Indigenous nations and peoples who so desire should be granted the full rights and obligations of external self-determination.
>
> Article 4. Indigenous nations and peoples who wish to limit themselves to the exercise of internal self-determination only should be granted the freedom to do so. The rights of internal self-determination should include, but not be limited to, the right to:
>
> (a) control their own economies;
>
> (b) freely pursue their economic, social and cultural development in conformity with their tradition, custom and social mores;
>
> (c) engage in foreign relations and trade if they so desire
>
> (d) restore, practice and educate their children to their cultures, languages, traditions and way of life;
>
> (e) and the right to the ownership of land as the territorial base for the existence of indigenous populations as such.

Throughout the balance of the declaration, the Treaty Council refers not to human rights but to "Treaties,"[142] "National and Cultural Integrity,"[143]

[141] *Id.*
[142] *Id.*, Part IV.
[143] *Id.*, Part VI.

"Religious and Spiritual Freedom,"[144] "Child Welfare,"[145] "Land and Environment,"[146] and "Indigenous Membership"[147] and all in the context of indigenous peoples' control over these themes. The declaration did not assume that sovereignty would be exercised subject to human rights—any attempt to impose laws on indigenous peoples required their prior consent.[148] The language in the declarations correlates more with activists' domestic priorities and goals than with human rights.

Advocates in the working group referred to historical treaties to support their claims to self-determination and decolonization. However, in this international setting, the argument had particular bite. According to the Four Directions Council:[149]

> Treaty relations are evidence of international recognition of statehood, and recognition, once given, cannot ordinarily be withdrawn. Yet we find in the reports of international arbitration and human rights proceedings an assumption that treaties made with peoples of the Indian race are not treaties at all, and have no international legal consequences. The United Nations cannot afford to admit that a document calling itself a "treaty" and signed by the representatives of two nations is without effect, merely because one of the nations signing it is of the wrong race.

While many of the treaties were manifestly unfair toward indigenous peoples, within the UN working group, it was the concept of an international treaty between two independent nations that was all important.[150] In the case of Australian aboriginal advocates, where no historical treaty was made, a different tack was adopted. The absence of a treaty was used to signify that they had never ceded sovereignty or consented "to incorporate themselves with Euro-Australians."[151]

[144] *Id.*, Part VII.
[145] *Id.*, Part VIII.
[146] *Id.*, Part X.
[147] *Id.*, Part XI.
[148] *Id.*, art. 7.
[149] *See* Four Directions Council, *supra* note 136, doCip Doc. 200479_2.
[150] Indigenous advocates of the United States were also able to point to the Cherokee Supreme Court cases recognizing inherent aboriginal sovereignty, *see Johnson, supra* note 3; *Cherokee Nation, supra* note 3; *Worcester, supra* note 3.
[151] Russel Barsh, *Aboriginal Rights, Human Rights and International Law*, 2:4 AUST. ABORIGINAL STUDIES. (1984) 4.

However, the major difficulty with indigenous advocates' use of the anti-colonialism model was the increasing prominence of the principle of territorial integrity. As noted above, territorial integrity is directed at protecting the sovereignty of existing states. The 1960 Declaration on the Granting of Independence, while directed at decolonization for colonial peoples, contained a reference to territorial integrity, but this was aimed at affirming the territorial integrity of the newly independent states.

During the Declaration negotiations, states concerned about indigenous advocates' calls for self-determination would repeatedly stress that the right had to be read as including the exercise of forms of autonomy, or effective participation within the bounds of the modern state. To make this perfectly clear, some states sought an express reference to territorial integrity in the Declaration to protect their national unity.[152] A reference to territorial integrity would ensure that self-determination signified something other than independence. Instead, it would indicate the right to a form of "internal self-determination." As the Declaration advanced through the working group process, more and more states sought an express reference to territorial integrity. Several states also had concerns about collective rights[153] and references to historical redress.[154] States objected to the use of the word indigenous "peoples" in the Declaration given the UN Charter and common Article 1 of the International Human Rights Covenants spoke of self-determination as a right of "peoples." States preferred references to "populations," "minorities," or "people" in the singular. Hence, the working group was called the Working Group on Indigenous *Populations*.[155]

[152] *See, e.g.*, "Canada" (1991) doCip Doc. 200166_1 (on file with author) ("Any reference to a right to self-determination, explicit or implicit, must be put in the context of not implying any right to threaten the boundaries or political integrity of existing states, as is done in the context of the UN Declaration on Principles of International law on Friendly Relations and Cooperation among States in Accordance with the Charter of the UN" at 200166_1). *See also* "New Zealand" (1991) doCip Doc. 200176_1 (on file with author) (noting its "insistence that the Declaration contain a proviso regarding the use of the term 'peoples' has not found its way into the text . . ." at 200176_4).

[153] *See, e.g.*, "Canada" (1991) doCip Doc. 200165_1 (on file with author) ("As classical human rights instruments typically are formulated in terms of individual rights, we believe that the general emphasis in this Declaration should be on individual rights" at 200165_3).

[154] *See, e.g.*, "Canada" (1992) doCip Doc. 960245_A (on file with author): ("the wording of 'lands, territories and resources' in the past tense is very broad. Its use in the document may imply possession over all lands traditionally occupied by indigenous people at all previous stages of their history . . ." at 960245_K).

[155] *See* "Statement of the Treaty Council" (1984) doCip Doc. 200514_1 (on file with author) (calling for "the word 'Peoples' to be substituted for the word 'Populations' in the title of the Working Group on Indigenous Populations").

Northern indigenous advocates, on the other hand, rejected any reference to territorial integrity. Again, the principle of equality for all peoples was stressed. Common Article 1 of the International Human Rights Covenants was not conditioned by any reference to territorial integrity. Therefore, any attempt to counterbalance self-determination in the Declaration with the right of states to territorial integrity would be discriminatory to indigenous peoples. It was argued that the distinction could only be due to indigenous peoples' cultural difference.

3.3 The Right to Independence Had to Be an Option

This emphasis on self-determination and decolonization by the Treaty Council and other Northern indigenous organizations and advocates did not mean that the substantive goal had to be independence. Most indigenous advocates sought self-determination in a relational sense—that is, self-determination exercised within the modern state through self-government and other expressions of autonomy.[156]

Domestically, this was the position taken by most indigenous advocates. As we have seen, while some called for complete sovereign rule over their countries, most were seeking political autonomy and control over their territories. At the international level, this is clear from the Declaration of Defense issued at the 1977 Geneva NGO Conference, and the "declarations" presented by the Treaty Council, and other Northern indigenous organizations. For example, the Treaty Council's declaration presented to the working group, notes in Article 3: "Indigenous nations and peoples *who so desire* should be granted the full rights and obligations of external self-determination."[157]

However, the right to independence had to be an option. Autonomy within the state may be preferable to independence, but this did not rule out secession as a possibility. Just as colonized peoples had a choice between full independence and other forms of autonomy, so should indigenous peoples. CANZUS states knew that there was no ever-present threat of secession by

[156] *See, e.g.*, the declarations produced by the Treaty Council and others, *supra* notes 137–40.

[157] Treaty Council Declaration, *supra* note 140 (referring to indigenous peoples' right to "such degree of independence as they may choose," and states are forbidden to "assert or claim" any political jurisdiction over indigenous communities except under a "valid treaty or agreement freely made with the lawful representatives [of the people]").

indigenous peoples.[158] Indigenous peoples wanted a backup plan to ensure that states would recognize their political and territorial rights.

Both CANZUS states and indigenous advocates knew that self-determination without qualification provided indigenous peoples with tremendous leverage in negotiating their status within the state. This indicated that self-determination in the Declaration was connected to self-determination as set out in common Article 1 of the International Human Rights Covenants and, in turn, the decolonization project. It made self-determination a supranational issue. It also indicated that disputes between indigenous peoples and states need to be resolved at the international level through an independent international mechanism.

Treaties provided the means to realize these goals.[159] Historical treaties could provide evidence of indigenous peoples' prior sovereignty, but contemporary treaties between indigenous peoples and the state, as two sovereigns, could set out the terms of their co-existence. At the 1991 working group session, Mick Dodson, speaking for the Australian Northern Land Council, simply insisted that the Australian government negotiate a contemporary treaty with Aboriginal peoples.[160] This potential for treaty-making was noted in the early declarations prepared by indigenous advocates. The declaration prepared at the 1977 Geneva NGO Conference noted:[161]

> No state shall assert or claim to exercise any right of jurisdiction over any indigenous nation or group or the territory of such indigenous nation or group unless pursuant to a valid treaty or other agreement freely made with the lawful representatives of the indigenous nation or group concerned. All actions on the part of any state which derogate from the indigenous

[158] Roderic Pitty & Shannara Smith, *The Indigenous Challenge to Westphalian Sovereignty*, 46:1 AUST. J. POLIT. SCI. 121 (2011).

[159] *See* Four Directions Council, "Strengthening the Working Groups Standard Setting Role" (1988) doCip Doc. 210975_1 (on file with author) ("[t]he study of past treaties will lead to an understanding of the role that future treaties and agreements could play in adjusting the political relations between indigenous peoples and states—and thus could form an important element of the implementation strategy for any declaration of indigenous rights" at 210975_3). *See also* "Statement of the Grand Council of the Crees (of Quebec)" (1988) doCip Doc. 210980_1 (on file with author) ("[t]reaties are important in our consideration here both because they have been a source of abuse and have led to tragedy, but also because they provide recognition of indigenous self-determination, and may offer a practical mechanism to protect indigenous rights in the future" at 210980_3).

[160] "Statement by Mick Dodson, Director, Northern Land Council" (1991) doCip Doc. 200189_8 (on file with author).

[161] For description of the many conferences and meetings convened by activists and supporters, including the International NGO Conference on Discrimination against Indigenous Populations in 1977, *see* Cobo, "Final Report," *supra* at note 26, at Chapter 4.

nations' or groups' right to exercise self-determination shall be the proper concern of existing international bodies.

Indeed, in order to direct attention toward treaties and their potential for setting out the terms of co-existence between indigenous nations and states, indigenous advocates called for a special UN study on treaties between states and indigenous peoples.[162]

It should be stressed that this decolonization model was not the only game in town for indigenous advocates. US-based indigenous scholar, James Anaya, took the classic human rights model and sought to renovate it. Anaya argued that the indigenous rights proposed by indigenous peoples—including the right to self-determination—be viewed as human rights adapted to the specific situation of indigenous peoples.[163] Anaya stressed self-determination's fundamental connection with "freedom" and "inherent human equality."[164] According to Anaya, denial of the human right to self-determination to colonized peoples called for the *sui generis* remedy of decolonization.[165] Denial of the right to indigenous peoples called for another *sui generis* remedy represented by the human rights in the Declaration and ILO Conventions on Indigenous and Tribal Peoples, with independence arising in a remedial sense for extreme violation of indigenous peoples' human rights (for example, as set out in the 1970 Friendly Relations Declaration).[166] In this new approach, Anaya was part of a new school of thought about self-determination and human rights. During the early 1990s, leading international law scholars, Hurst Hannum,[167] Robert McCorquodale,[168] and Thomas Franck[169] were all writing about self-determination in a human rights sense in terms of promoting representative government and democratic governance.

[162] *See* "Statement of the Treaty Council" (1981) doCip Doc. 200516_1 (on file with author) (calling for "the Working Group on Indigenous Populations to advise the Sub-Commission to carefully study the Indian Treaties, the lack of observance of these Treaties and its influence on the human rights situation of indigenous peoples in the United States and Canada, and the viability of these treaties today . . ." at 200516_2).

[163] S. James Anaya, Indigenous Peoples in International Law (1996).

[164] *Id.* at 75–76.

[165] *Id.* at 80–85.

[166] *Id.* at 84–85.

[167] Hurst Hannum, *Rethinking Self-Determination*, 34:1 VA J. Int. Law 1 (1993).

[168] Robert Mccorquodale, *Self-Determination: A Human Rights Approach*, 43:04 Int. Comp. Law Q. 857, 857–85 (1994).

[169] Thomas M. Franck, *The Emerging Right to Democratic Governance*, 86:1 Am. J. Intl. Law 46 (1992).

This human rights reading of self-determination had much support in international law, including the insertion of self-determination in the International Human Rights Covenants—although, as we have seen, common Article 1 was also connected to decolonization and independence. The 1970 Friendly Relations Declaration accepted that self-determination meant decolonization, but paragraph 7 made it clear that it also meant representative government.

The shift from a decolonization model was a politically astute move. Anaya's human rights model would address states' concerns with self-determination's connection with decolonization. As a human right, self-determination would be exercised within states—it is not directed at secession.[170] Thus, there was no need for an express reference to territorial integrity in the Declaration, or even if there was a reference, it would not be inconsistent with the right to self-determination so conceived as a human right. In addition, cast as a human rights instrument—or the elaboration of widely ratified human rights—the rights in the Declaration have binding qualities, despite its technical status as a non-binding instrument. They are not *special* rights but part of the set of human rights guaranteed to all peoples and denied to indigenous peoples. Indeed, several states accepted this notion toward the end of the working group sessions. However, by viewing the Declaration as based on human rights, Anaya's account indicated that remedies would ordinarily be provided for, and located within, the modern state. The human rights model applies to, and in fundamental ways depends on, the existing configurations of state power. The decolonization model challenges the very existence of the modern state. It extended indigenous peoples' claims to the international plane as a nation-to-nation concern, and that offered the promise of real change. The dominant model, then, in the working group was the decolonization model, and it led to the inclusion of the self-determination framework in the Declaration. Anaya's human rights model would, however, gain increasing traction as the Declaration advanced toward the UN General Assembly for adoption.

4 ILO Convention 169 and the Self-Determination Model

Several years into the Declaration negotiations, a similar standard-setting process for indigenous peoples commenced several miles down the road

170 Anaya, *supra* note 163, at 86.

from the UN offices in Geneva. The ILO decided to revise ILO Convention 107, negotiated in the 1950s for indigenous peoples and tribal peoples. The ILO Convention 107 contained a set of social and economic rights, but its overall objective was to modernize subsistence-based indigenous and tribal peoples so as to integrate them into the modern economy.[171] Its theme was thoroughly outdated although the ILO thought a revision could allow for the incorporation of a new vision of cultural autonomy for indigenous peoples.[172]

For Northern indigenous advocates, the stakes were high because the revision had potential to recognize their vision of self-determination in an international convention.[173] The revision would also potentially set important precedents for the Declaration negotiations in terms of both procedures of participation and substantive norms.

The first pressing issue was indigenous advocates' participation in the drafting process.[174] Following ILO standard procedures, the drafting of ILO Convention 169 involved state delegations that comprised government representatives, employers' organizations, and trade unions representing workers. Some efforts were made to incorporate indigenous advocates into employer's and worker's delegations.[175] However, as Rodríguez-Piñero notes, these processes "proved insufficient to placate the feeling of frustration and exclusion of many indigenous organisations present at the [Convention negotiations]."[176] Even so, it is unclear whether their participation would have made much of a difference. As noted by Rodríguez-Piñero, "the need to involve the indigenous movement in the revision process weighed

[171] Luis Rodríguez-Piñero, Indigenous Peoples, Postcolonialism, and International Law: The ILO Regime (1919–1989) (2005) (for discussion on drafting of ILO Convention No. 107).

[172] *See* Lee Swepston, *New Step in the International Law on Indigenous and Tribal Peoples: ILO Convention No. 169 of 1989*, 15 Okla. City U. L. Rev. 677, 690 (1990) [hereinafter Swepston, "New Step in the International Law"]. Russel Lawrence Barsh, *Revision of ILO Convention No. 107*, 81:3 Am. J. Intl. Law 756 (1987); Lee Swepston, *Indigenous and Tribal Populations: A Return to Centre Stage*, 126 Int. Labour Rev. 447 (1987).

[173] Indigenous advocates of the North included the Four Directions Council, Indigenous World Association, International Organization of Resource Development, the World Council of Indigenous Peoples, and the Treaty Council. Apart from the North, there was the Indian Council of South America (CISA), the Inuit Circumpolar Conference, and the Nordic Saami Council. There were also the international human rights NGOs IWGIA and Survival International. There were no indigenous organizations from Asia or Africa.

[174] Rodríguez-Piñero, *supra* note 171, at 300–19 (discussing indigenous peoples' participation in the drafting process).

[175] *Id.* at 312–19. *See also* Swepston, "New Step in the International Law," *supra* note 172, at 686–87 (for an account of the drafting process and indigenous peoples' participation by the then lead ILO Officer).

[176] Rodríguez-Piñero, *supra* note 171, at 317.

considerably less than the Office's drive to advance its own decision and priorities concerning the revision of Convention 107."[177]

As with ILO Convention 107, the ILO's mandate was fundamentally utilitarian, i.e., the protection of basic rights, not more ambitious political rights.[178] There are no measures in ILO Convention 169 directed at self-determination, historical redress, or treaties, or forms of self-government.[179] The Convention does refer to indigenous "peoples" and not indigenous "populations." However, the ILO adopted a savings clause: "The use of the term 'peoples' in this Convention shall not be construed as having any implications as regards the rights which may attach to the term under international law."[180] The Convention guarantees rights to employment,[181] social security and health,[182] and education.[183] It also requires governments to recognize land rights,[184] customs,[185] and natural resources within their territories.[186] There is a right of indigenous peoples to be consulted and to give their consent to projects on their lands.

The ILO noted the ambitions of indigenous advocates "seeking to bring about radical changes in the nature of their relationship with the governments of the states in which they reside."[187] However, for the ILO, that enterprise was better suited to the UN working group.[188] The ILO was more concerned with "other indigenous and tribal groups and organizations . . . whose primary concerns are local autonomy and self-fulfillment."[189] This not only included "peasant communities and tribal groups" of Latin America but also groups in "Africa and Continental Asia," who were at an "embryonic stage"

[177] *Id.* at 319.

[178] Rodríguez-Piñero, *supra* note 171, at 293. As Knop notes, this stance was predetermined by the utilitarian approach of the ILO Convention 107, and the fact that this was a "partial revision" of that Convention, not an entirely new instrument, *supra* note 74.

[179] *Id.* at 690–91 (discussing disagreement in the drafting process on whether indigenous peoples should consent to measures that may affect them). ILO Convention concerning Indigenous and Tribal Peoples in Independent Countries, 1989 (ILO 169), 72 ILO Official Bulletin 59; 28 ILM 1382 (entered into force on Sept. 5, 1991).

[180] *Id.*, art. 1(3).

[181] *Id.*, art. 20

[182] *Id.*, arts. 24–25.

[183] *Id.*, arts. 26–31.

[184] *Id.*, art. 14(1).

[185] *Id.*, art. 9.

[186] *Id.*, art. 15.

[187] *See* International Labour Office, *Partial Revision of the Indigenous and Tribal Populations Convention, 1957 (No 107),* Report VI(1), International Labour Office, 75th session, Geneva (1988) at 15 [hereinafter *ILO Report VI(1)*].

[188] Swepston, "New Step in the International Law," *supra* note 172, at 692–95.

[189] *Id.*

or yet to be formed altogether.[190] An additional factor for the ILO was that it wanted the convention to be widely ratified by states, and according to the ILO officer, Lee Swepston, "any reference to self-determination would simply guarantee that the Convention would not be ratified."[191]

The convention was a disappointment for Northern indigenous advocates and most opposed its ratification. Sharon Venne described the negotiations as "paternalistic and racially discriminatory" and the ILO as "the most inappropriate forum to determine the rights of Indigenous Peoples."[192] When an ILO official took the floor in the UN working group to introduce the new Convention, indigenous advocates walked out in protest.[193] At the same time, Anaya notes "much of the criticism was couched in highly legalistic terms and worst case scenario readings of the convention without much regard to overall context."[194]

Indigenous advocates of Latin America and the Nordic states showed their support. The Saami Council lobbied for the Nordic states to ratify the convention, and Norway did so promptly in 1990.[195] Almost all Latin American states ratified the convention. There was recognition too, by several indigenous advocates of the North that there could be value in the ILO Convention 169 for movements in the South.[196]

190 *Id.* at 16.

191 *See* Lee Swepston, *Reply to Howard Berman by Lee Swepston*, (1989) 42 IRICJ 44, 45, cited in Rodríguez-Piñero, *supra* note 171, at 294.

192 Sharon Venne, *The New Language of Assimilation: A Brief Analysis of ILO Convention 169*, 2 WITHOUT PREJUDICE 53 (1990). According to Sharon Venne, a Canadian aboriginal lawyer, the ILO Convention 169 provided "an invitation to further assimilation."

193 *See* "Indigenous Peoples Resolution on ILO Convention 169" (1989) doCip Doc. 211021_1 (on file with author) (calling on states not to ratify the convention and noting lack of indigenous peoples' participation).

194 *See* Anaya, *supra* note 163, at 48.

195 "Statement by Nordic Sami Council" (1989) doCip Doc. 211072_1 (on file with the author) ("We share the opinion expressed by some other indigenous NGOs that the adoption of this convention has to be considered as a step forward in the general efforts of developing more positive and adequate universal standards on the rights of indigenous peoples and our member organizations are most likely to recommend the Nordic government to ratify the ILO Convention 169 as soon as possible" at 211072_1).

196 *See* "Statement of Chief Littlechild for the International Indigenous Organisations of Indigenous Peoples Resource Development" (1989) doCip Doc. 211022_1 (on file with author) ("I do not think we are in a position today to tell states that they should or should not ratify this convention. I was co-chairman of the indigenous peoples Working Group on the revision of ILO Convention 107 in Canada. We worked long and hard on the text of the revision; and I attended the ILO conference. I was personally insulted and demeaned by the process at the ILO conference . . . Nevertheless there are some good and important provisions in the revised convention that some indigenous peoples may find useful. Some of our brothers and sisters live in such terrible circumstances that even some means for improvement, and some means of redress, however inadequate, are worth having" at 211022_2).

The ILO Convention 169 should be recognized as an important contribution to international indigenous rights. Its overall framework was about strengthening indigenous institutions and land rights. There are important measures aimed at addressing deep-rooted economic inequality through improving working conditions, social welfare, health, and education. However, it fell well short of the aspirations of Northern indigenous peoples and set an unwelcome precedent for the Declaration negotiations in the UN.

5 The Declaration with a Self-Determination Framework

The initial resolution establishing the working group had referred to "the evolution of standards concerning indigenous populations" but did not specify the type of instrument. Candidates were a mere "body of principles," a declaration, or a convention. Quickly, it became apparent that it made sense to aim for a Declaration. Like the UDHR, a declaration adopted by the UN General Assembly is technically a resolution and not legally binding on member states. However, a declaration posed less of a threat to states. As the first working group Chair, Asbjørn Eide, noted:[197]

> [a Declaration] will be more easily negotiated, exactly because it will not carry binding obligations. If a convention is to be adopted it must be assumed that states, in the negotiating process, will be cautious in order not to bind themselves to more than a minimum. A Declaration which might be more advanced in its contents might still influence policies and legislation at the national level.

Indigenous advocates also appeared to support the idea of a declaration as a first step before negotiating a convention.[198] At the 1985 session, the working group agreed to "aim at producing in due course, and as a first formal step, a

[197] Asbjørn Eide, *supra* note 60, at 31.

[198] *See* Working Group on the Rights of Indigenous Populations, *Report of the Working Group on Its Fourth Session*, UNESCOR, 38th Sess., U.N. Doc. E/CN.4/Sub.2/1985/22 (1985) ("There was more or less general agreement from all sides that the standards to be drafted by the Working Group should in the first instance form a declaration, eventually to be adopted by the General Assembly of the United Nations. The possibility of a convention was also mentioned, but there seemed to be general agreement, also on this point, that this kind of instrument would emerge further down the road, possibly with inspiration from the declaration" at para. 85).

draft Declaration on indigenous rights, which may be proclaimed by the UN General Assembly."[199]

Early Declaration drafts presented by the working group in 1985 and 1986 contained basic human rights and affirmations of culture. For example, seven principles were considered at the fourth session in 1985:[200]

1. the right to the full and effective enjoyment of the fundamental rights and freedoms universally recognized in existing international instruments, particularly in the Charter of the United Nations and the International Bill of Human Rights.
2. the right to be free and equal to all other human beings in dignity and rights and to be free from discrimination of any kind.
3. the collective right to exist and to be protected against genocide, as well as the individual right to life, physical integrity, liberty, and security of person.
4. the right to manifest, teach, practice, and observe their own religious traditions and ceremonies, and to maintain, protect, and have access to sites for these purposes.
5. the right to all forms of education, including the right to have access to education in their own languages and to establish their own educational institutions.
6. the right to preserve their cultural identity and traditions, and to pursue their own cultural development.
7. the right to promote inter cultural information and education, recognizing the dignity and diversity of their culture.

States were obviously advancing the human rights model with an emphasis on basic human rights and cultural rights. However, the maintenance of the decolonization model by advocates of the North increasingly gained traction in the working group. As Karen Knop notes, over the eight years that the Declaration was prepared, it "developed from an inoffensive standard setting exercise to a bold frontrunner of the rights of indigenous peoples."[201]

As negotiations advanced, the working group began to incorporate references to the self-determination framework in the Declaration. By 1989,

199 *Id.*
200 *Id.* at Annex II.
201 Knop, *supra* note 74, at 263.

in addition to references to equality and minority rights, the Declaration referred to land rights, treaty rights, political participation, and autonomy.[202] There were measures on historical redress: paragraph 12 recognized a right of indigenous peoples to "collective and individual ownership of . . . lands or resources which they have traditionally *occupied* or used";[203] that is, occupied in the present and past tense, which implied a right to recover lands that were confiscated or settled upon by outsiders in the past without indigenous consent. In addition, paragraph 15 referred to "the right to reclaim land and surface resources or, where this is not possible, to seek just and fair compensation for the same when the property has been taken away from them without their consent, in particular, if such deprival has been based on theories such as those related to *terra nullius*, waste land or idle lands."[204]

There was a provision on the need to honor treaties in paragraph 27—although it noted the "right to *claim* that States honour treaties and other agreements concluded with indigenous peoples." Paragraph 23 noted the "collective right to autonomy in matters relating to their own internal and local affairs" over matters such as education, culture, housing, land and resources, and the environment.[205] Paragraph 24 referred to the right to "decide upon the structures of their autonomous institutions, to select the membership of such institutions, and to determine the membership of the indigenous people concerned for these purposes."

At this point, all references to collective rights were enclosed in square brackets (meaning there was no consensus on their inclusion in the Declaration), but all references to indigenous *peoples* were in the plural form. However, the only reference to self-determination was a preambular paragraph noting that nothing in the Declaration may be used to deny the right of self-determination to any people "which otherwise satisfies the criteria generally established by human rights instruments and international law. . . ."[206] This possibly indicated the right to self-determination in those cases of gross

[202] *See* Working Group on the Rights of Indigenous Populations, *Report of the Working Group on Its Seventh Session*, UNESCOR, U.N. Doc. E/CN.4/Sub.2/1989/36, at Annex II (1989) (First revised text of the draft Universal Declaration on the Right of Indigenous Peoples, as presented by the Chairman/Rapporteur Ms. Erica-Irene Daes); for a prior version, *see* Working Group on the Rights of Indigenous Populations, *Report of the Working Group on Its Fifth Session*, UNESCOR, U.N. Doc. E/CN.4/Sub.2/1987/22, at Annex II (1987).

[203] *Id.* at 33 (Operative para. 12).

[204] *Id.* at 33 (Operative para. 15).

[205] *Id.* at 33 (Operative para. 23).

[206] *Id.* at 31 (10th preambular paragraph).

human rights abuses as recognized by the 1970 Declaration on Friendly Relations.

At the working group's ninth session in 1991, a more developed version was completed.[207] The preamble of the Declaration noted that the International Human Rights Covenants "affirm the fundamental importance of the right to self-determination."[208] However, it did not connect this right with indigenous peoples. The first paragraph referred to the right of indigenous peoples to self-determination "in accordance with international law" which left self-determination's meaning unclear. However, a new paragraph 13 appeared to qualify self-determination—it provided nothing in the Declaration was to be interpreted as implying any right to engage in any activity contrary to the UN Charter or to the 1970 Declaration on Friendly Relations.[209] The reference to the Declaration on Friendly Relations could be seen as an attempt to indirectly incorporate a reference to the territorial integrity of states. At the same time, it could be read as allowing secession as a last resort if a group is subjected to gross violation of human rights.

In relation to historical redress, the Declaration continued to refer to the right to own land traditionally occupied in the past tense (paragraph 15) and now contained a new reference to the right to "restitution" (paragraph 16)—not the mere right to reclaim land or surface resources—or if this was not possible, compensation for lands and territories confiscated, occupied, used, or damaged without their informed consent.[210] There continued to be a reference to autonomy in internal and local affairs (paragraph 23)[211] and the right to claim that states honor treaties (paragraph 27)—although this now noted that indigenous peoples had the right to "submit any disputes that may arise in this matter to competent national or international bodies."[212]

Instead of consultation, there were now references to informed consent. Paragraph 22 noted "the right of indigenous peoples to be involved . . . in devising any laws or administrative measures that may affect them directly, and to obtain their free and informed consent through implementing such measures."[213] Military activities and the storage and disposal of hazardous

[207] Working Group on the Rights of Indigenous Populations, *Report of the Working Group on Its Ninth Session,* UNESCOR, U.N. Doc. E/CN.4/Sub.2/1991/40/Rev.1, at Annex II (1991).
[208] *Id.* at 31 (13th preambular paragraph).
[209] *Id.* at 34 (Operative para. 13).
[210] *Id.* at 34 (Operative paras. 15 and 16).
[211] *Id.* at 36 (Operative para. 23).
[212] *Id.* at 36 (Operative para. 27).
[213] *Id.* at 36 (Operative para. 22).

substances could not occur on indigenous peoples' land and territories without their agreement.[214]

In 1992, paragraph 1 on self-determination was extended. Instead of ending with a reference to the right of indigenous peoples to self-determination, "in accordance with international law," it went on to say "by virtue of which they may freely determine their political status and institutions and freely pursue their economic, social and cultural development. An integral part of this is the right to autonomy and self-government."[215] The former paragraph 13 prohibiting an interpretation of the Declaration implying any right to engage in any activity contrary to the UN Charter or the 1970 Declaration of Friendly Relations was now moved up to paragraph 4, closer to the paragraph 1 reference to self-determination.[216] Paragraph 25 referred to "the right to autonomy in matters relating to their own internal and local affairs. . . ."[217] The Declaration continued to refer to the right to lands "traditionally occupied" and the right to the restitution of lands taken.[218] Paragraph 31 continued to refer to "the right to claim that states honour treaties" and a right to submit disputes to national and international bodies.[219]

While most states were consistently opposed to any reference to self-determination in the Declaration, during the 1991 and 1992 working group sessions, Australia and Canada accepted a reference to self-determination in the Declaration provided it was clear that it did not relate to decolonization. Australia at the 1991[220] and 1992 sessions of the working group observed:[221]

> Realization of the right to self-determination is not limited in time to the process of decolonization nor is it accomplished by a single act or exercise. Rather it entails the continuing right of all peoples and individuals within

[214] *Id.* at 34 (Operative para. 17).

[215] Working Group on the Rights of Indigenous Populations, *Report of the Working Group on Its Tenth Session,* UNESCOR, U.N. Doc. E/CN.4/Sub.2/1992/33 at Annex I, at 46 (1992) (Operative para. 1).

[216] *Id.* (Operative para. 4).

[217] *Id.* at 50 (Operative para. 25).

[218] *Id.* at 48 (Operative paras. 16 and 17).

[219] *Id.* at 51 (Operative para. 31).

[220] Australia, "Speaking Notes on Self-Determination" (1991) doCip Doc. 200175_1 (on file with author) ("Events in all parts of the world show . . . that the concept of self-determination must be considered broadly, that is, not only as the attainment of national independence. Peoples are seeking to assert their identities, to preserve their languages, cultures, and traditions and to achieve greater self-management and autonomy, free from undue interference from central governments" at 200175_2) [emphasis in original].

[221] "Statement by Colin Milner on Behalf of Australian Delegation" (July 24, 1992) doCip Doc. 960255_3 and 960255_4 (on file with author).

> each state to participate fully in the political process by which they are governed. Clearly enhancing popular participation in this decision-making is an important factor in realizing the right to self-determination. It is evident that, even in some countries which are formally fully democratic, structural, attitudinal and procedural barriers exist which inhibit the full democratic effective participation of particular groups.

Australia was detaching self-determination from its historical connection with decolonization. Not wishing to be too prescriptive about the precise form self-determination should take, Australia noted that for its own country, "a system which guarantees full and genuine participation and fundamental human rights as well as recognizing the special position of indigenous peoples could provide an adequate and real realization of self-determination."[222] To assuage the concerns of states with self-determination, Australia suggested that the Declaration contain a reference to territorial integrity similar to that set out in the 1970 Friendly Relations Declaration.[223] By this reading, self-determination was a means of advancing such human rights as effective participation in public life and other basic democratic rights. This approach chimed with the human rights model being advanced by James Anaya, although Anaya envisaged self-determination as also encompassing self-government and other forms of autonomy.

Similarly, the Canadian approach was to disconnect self-determination from decolonization and produce a new concept of self-determination as internal self-determination.[224]

> Canada supports the principle of self-determination for indigenous people, within the framework of existing nation-states, where there is an inter-relationship between indigenous and non-indigenous jurisdiction that gives indigenous people greater levels of autonomy over their own affairs but that also recognizes the jurisdiction of the state.

For Canada, this internal self-determination was to be negotiated between indigenous peoples and state governments.[225]

222 *Id.* at Doc. 960255_3.
223 *Id.* at Doc. 960255_6.
224 *See* "Canada's Suggestions on Draft Operative Paragraphs" (1992) doCip Doc. 960245_A (on file with author).
225 *Id.*

Otherwise, states continued to call for the elaboration of existing basic human rights and minority rights to the situation of indigenous peoples. The United States was opposed to any reference to self-determination since it "might be construed as guaranteeing the right to full independence as a separate state to all indigenous groups."[226] The United States could, however, accept the right of indigenous peoples to "autonomy," provided there was recognition of the state's right in some cases to limit indigenous peoples' autonomy:[227]

> . . . the environmental law adopted at a national level may restrict the ability of persons belonging to indigenous groups to take certain decisions. The ability of indigenous groups to decide on the duties indigenous people owe to their group is likewise limited, properly, by the rights accorded individuals under national law.

By 1993, the year of the final working group meeting, the Declaration was comprised of a preamble with nineteen preambular paragraphs and forty-five articles and contained the self-determination framework.[228] The Declaration contained a reference to self-determination in almost identical terms to the rights as expressed in common Article 1 of the International Human Rights Covenants. Article 3 of the Declaration provided:[229]

> Indigenous peoples have the right of self-determination. By virtue of that right they freely determine their political status and freely pursue their economic, social and cultural development.

Prior versions had stated that nothing in the Declaration should permit any activity contrary to the UN Charter and the 1970 Declaration on Friendly Relations. But due to prompting from indigenous advocates, the reference to the Declaration on Friendly Relations was removed. Article 45 only prohibited any activity "contrary to the Charter of the United Nations."[230] There was no express reference to territorial integrity.

[226] "United States" (1992) doCip Doc. 960247_3 (on file with author).
[227] "United States" (1992) doCip Doc. 960247_7 (on file with author).
[228] *See* Working Group on the Rights of Indigenous People, *Report of the Working Group on Its Eleventh Session*, UNESCOR, U.N. Doc. E/CN.4/Sub.2/1993/29 at Annex 1 (1993) (Draft Declaration as agreed upon by the members of the Working Group on the Declaration at Its Eleventh Session).
[229] *Id.* at 48 (art. 3).
[230] *Id.* at 56 (art. 45).

Article 31 referred to the right of indigenous peoples to "autonomy or self-government":[231]

> Indigenous peoples, as a specific form of exercising their right to self-determination, have the right to autonomy or self-government in matters relating to their internal and local affairs, including culture, religion, education, information, media, health, housing, employment, social welfare, economic activities, land and resource management, environment and entry by non-members, as well as ways and means for financing these autonomous functions.

Indigenous peoples were concerned that this right was stated to be "a specific form of exercising their right to self-determination." This could indicate that self-determination ought to be limited to internal self-determination (or self-government) only, thus excluding any form of external self-determination. However, this article was positioned at the end of the Declaration so as not to indicate that self-government was the only means by which self-determination could be exercised.

With respect to land rights, the Declaration guaranteed the right to "own, develop, control and use the lands and territories, and other resources," which they have "traditionally owned or otherwise occupied or used."[232] Also, land was not necessarily limited to surface rights and included the total environment of the lands, air, waters, coastal seas, sea-ice, flora and fauna, and other resources, which they have traditionally owned or otherwise occupied or used. The Declaration also recognized "the right to the restitution of the lands, territories and resources which they have traditionally owned or otherwise occupied or used, and which have been confiscated, occupied, used or damaged without their free and informed consent."[233]

In terms of consultation with indigenous peoples, the Declaration contained requirements to obtain free and informed consent in the context of "any project affecting their lands, territories and other resources";[234] "legislative or administrative measures" affecting indigenous peoples;[235] or proposals to relocate them;[236] or proposals to conduct military activities on

[231] *Id.* at 54 (art. 31).
[232] *Id.* at 52 (art. 26).
[233] *Id.* at 53 (art. 27).
[234] *Id.* at 53 (art. 30).
[235] *Id.* at 51 (art. 20).
[236] *Id.* at 49 (art. 10).

their traditional lands.[237] In relation to treaties, indigenous peoples had the right to the "recognition, observance and enforcement of treaties, agreements and other constructive arrangements" and "conflicts and disputes which cannot otherwise be settled" were to be "submitted to competent international bodies."[238]

The linchpin and significant breakthrough was Article 3. What did it mean? There is no doubt that the right to self-determination was a response to the decolonization arguments of indigenous peoples of the North. The repeated assertion of the decolonization model in the working group led to the self-determination framework in the Declaration.

After completion of the working group sessions and acceptance of the Declaration by the Sub-Commission on Human Rights, the working group Chair, Erica-Irene Daes, published an interpretation of the Declaration that endorsed the decolonization model.[239] She notes:[240]

> With few exceptions, indigenous peoples were never a part of State-building. . . . They did not have an opportunity to participate in designing the modern constitutions of the States in which they live, or to share, in any meaningful way, in national decision-making.

As a result, they were "not now, full partners in the political process and lack others' ability to use democratic means to defend their fundamental rights and freedoms." How should the international community respond to this?[241] According to Daes:

[T]he existing State has the duty to accommodate the aspirations of indigenous peoples through constitutional reforms designed to share power democratically. It also means that indigenous peoples have the duty to try to reach an agreement, in good faith, on sharing power within the existing State, and to exercise their right to self-determination by this means and other peaceful ways, to the extent possible.

Daes continued:[242]

[237] *Id.* at 49 (art. 11).
[238] *Id.* at 54 (art. 36).
[239] Erica-Irene Daes, *Explanatory Note Concerning the Draft Declaration on the Rights of Indigenous Peoples*, UNESCOR, 45th Sess., U.N. Doc. E/CN.4/Sub.2/1993/26/Add.1 (1993).
[240] *Id.* at para. 24.
[241] *Id.* at para. 25.
[242] *Id.* at para. 26.

> Furthermore, the right of self-determination of indigenous peoples should ordinarily be interpreted as their right to negotiate freely their status and representation in the State in which they live. This might best be described as a kind of "belated State-building," through which indigenous peoples are able to join with all the other peoples that make up the State on mutually-agreed and just terms, after many years of isolation and exclusion. This does not mean that assimilation of indigenous individuals as citizens like all others, but the recognition and incorporation of distinct peoples in the fabric of the State, on agreed terms.

The emphasis by Daes is on domestic reform negotiated peacefully and on fair terms. She seems to contemplate—as indigenous peoples did in the working group—the creation of contemporary treaties negotiated under the supervision of international institutions. However, the right to negotiate implied that indigenous peoples could also *choose to remain outside the state* should there be no mutual agreement on just terms.[243] This approach is consistent with the decolonization model.

However, Erica-Irene Daes also endorsed another construction of self-determination as a right to "share power democratically,"[244] endorsing a right to decolonization and independence in cases of gross human rights abuses as recognized by the Friendly Relations Declaration 1970:[245]

> Once an independent State has been established and recognized, its constituent peoples must try to express their aspirations through the national political system, and not through the creation of new States. This requirement continues unless the national political system becomes so exclusive and non-democratic that it no longer can be said to be "representing the whole people." At that point, and if all international and diplomatic measures fail to protect the peoples concerned from the State, they may perhaps be justified in creating a new State for their safety and security.
>
> . . .
>
> The concept of "self-determination" has accordingly taken on a new meaning in the post-colonial era. Ordinarily, it is the right of the citizens of an existing, independent State to share power democratically. However, a

[243] *See* Knop, *supra* note 74, at 272–73 (noting this mixed approach toward reading self-determination in the Declaration).

[244] Daes, *supra* note 239, at para. 23.

[245] Daes, *supra* note 239, at para. 21 and 23.

> State may sometimes abuse this right of its citizens so grievously and irreparably that the situation is tantamount to classic colonialism and may have the same legal consequences."

Thus, Erica-Irene Daes was applying a mixed interpretative approach to self-determination. It included the possibility of secession based on historical denial of self-determination. However, she also endorsed a human rights model recognizing a right to secession as a remedy for the abuse of fundamental human rights.

6 Conclusion

The Declaration on the Rights of Indigenous Peoples represented a major breakthrough in two fundamental respects. First, while initially there was a very strong institutional bias toward human rights—given the working group's mandate and setting—this was effectively subverted by Northern indigenous peoples. Human rights were important to the movement but principally as a means of advancing broader claims to self-determination and independence. The parallels between the historical experience of colonial peoples and indigenous peoples of the North were consistently made throughout the working group negotiations. In the end, the self-determination framework was inserted into the Declaration.

Second, the decolonization model resulted in a novel approach to UN standard setting. While normally standard setting is controlled by states that will seek input from NGOs and other interested groups, the working group shifted from this approach to treat indigenous peoples substantially as equals with states.[246] The working group panel of experts thus mediated the concerns of both states and indigenous peoples as it prepared each iteration of the Declaration. The working group approach was no doubt influenced by the historical-based decolonization model. The adaptation of the process not only allowed Northern indigenous peoples to continually assert the decolonization model, it also had a feedback effect boosting the normative claims to the self-determination framework. If indigenous peoples were participating alongside states, like states, then they ought to be entitled to the right to self-determination just like other states/peoples. This open process and resulting

[246] Knop, *supra* note 74, at 248–55.

standards set a precedent that would prove to be enormously difficult for states to disassemble.

Yet, at the same time, a human rights model was emerging—as can be seen from the commentary by Erica-Irene Daes on the Declaration. As we will see in the next chapter, the emphasis on human rights and, especially, the human right to culture was significantly enhanced due to the increased participation of Asian indigenous advocates (followed by the African indigenous movement) in the Declaration negotiations. This threatened to undo the achievements made in the first working group.

2

The Human Rights Model

1 The Second Working Group

As demonstrated in Chapter 1, indigenous advocates from the Northern or CANZUS states were prominent in the working group negotiating the Declaration from 1982 through 1993. These advocates advanced a historic-based decolonization model for the Declaration, according to which indigenous peoples were first peoples with the same sovereign rights as other peoples. Drawing parallels with colonized peoples in Asia, the Middle East, and Africa, these advocates sought recognition of their right to self-determination, including the possibility of independence. They were successful in having the self-determination framework included in the Declaration.

However, the Declaration did not advance from the working group toward the UN General Assembly as hoped for. Instead, the working group's parent body, the UN Sub-Commission on the Prevention of Discrimination and Protection of Minorities (Sub-Commission on Human Rights), approved the Declaration in 2004.[1] The Sub-Commission text as it came to be known was then forwarded to the UN Commission on Human Rights. This commission comprising representatives of UN member states did not send the Declaration on to its parent body, the ECOSOC or the UN General Assembly, for endorsement but instead decided to establish a second working group to "elaborate the Declaration."[2]

Asian state representatives on the Commission noted the lack of a definition of indigenous peoples in the Declaration. Bangladesh and India were particularly critical of the UN Centre of Human Rights and its promotion of indigenous peoples in Asia.[3] Nicaragua noted "care should be taken to ensure

[1] *Report of the Sub-Commission on Prevention of Discrimination and Protection of Minorities on Its 46th Session*, UN Commission on Human Rights, 46th Sess., U.N. Doc. E/CN.4/SUB.2/1994/56 (1994).

[2] *Establishment of a Working Group of the Commission on Human Rights to Elaborate a Draft Declaration in Accordance with Paragraph 5 of General Assembly Resolution 49/214*, ESC Res 1995/32, UNESCOR, 52nd Sess., Supp. No. 2, U.N. Doc. E/CN.4/1996/177 (1995).

[3] *Id.* at 10 and 12.

The UN Declaration on the Rights of Indigenous Peoples. Andrew Erueti, Oxford University Press. © Oxford University Press 2022. DOI: 10.1093/oso/9780190068301.003.0003

that the final version was acceptable to the international community, and that its provisions did not undermine the sovereignty and territorial integrity of States."[4]

This second working group was different in character to the first. It was higher in status and instead of being led by a panel of independent human rights experts, had five state representatives of the UN Commission on Human Rights as panelists. Many indigenous advocates saw this as a measure to dilute the many gains made in the first working group—specifically the self-determination framework. The view held by many states was that the first working group had been a largely indigenous-led process and what was needed now was a compromise between the positions of indigenous peoples and what was acceptable to the international community.[5]

Northern indigenous advocates were strongly opposed to the establishment of the second working group.[6] A real concern was the presence of indigenous peoples of Asia and then Africa. In this working group, Southern indigenous peoples were even more prominent than in the first. Northern indigenous advocates had to contend with not only Southern states and their opposition to the self-determination framework but also Asian and African indigenous advocates advancing the human rights model. Whether the right to self-determination was limited was not of great importance to Asian and African indigenous advocates. Their concern was access to basic human rights.[7] There was little Northern indigenous advocates could do to stop the Declaration advancing to another working group, so their task was to ensure that the integrity of the self-determination framework was maintained.

The Working Group on the Draft Declaration, as it was called, held its first session in November 1995. The goal was to finish this work within the next decade. That same year, the UN General Assembly proclaimed 1996–2005 the International Decade of the World's Indigenous People with adoption of the Declaration by the UN General Assembly being a major goal of the decade.[8]

[4] *Id.* at 9.

[5] *Id.* at 11.

[6] *See* Moana Jackson, *The Face Behind the Law: The UN and the Rights of Indigenous Peoples*, 8:2 Yearbook of New Zealand Jurisprudence—Te Purenga 28 (2005).

[7] *See, e.g.*, Suhas Chakma, *The Working Group on the Draft Declaration: As Alive as Fossil*, 101 Asian Centre for Human Rights Rev. (2005) >.

[8] *Programme of Activities of the International Decade of the World's Indigenous People*, UNGAOR, 57th Sess., U.N. Doc. A/58/505 (2003).

In this chapter, I trace the negotiations in the second working group from 1993 to its adoption by the UN General Assembly in 2007, including the divisions not only between the Northern and Southern movements but within the Northern movement as the human rights model became the Declaration's principal interpretative model. However, first, I describe how Southern indigenous movements became such a prominent figure in the international movement.

2 Asian and African Indigenous Peoples in the Declaration Negotiations

2.1 Asian Indigenous Peoples in the Second Working Group

From the late 1960s, during the earliest stages of the international indigenous movement, NGOs made up of "activist anthropologists" played a key role in raising awareness of the plight of indigenous peoples. In the Americas, virtually every state had some law or decree regulating the sale and use of tribal lands and special administrative agencies to deal with the "Indians." However, most states vacillated between policies of benign neglect and assimilation. Originally, the NGOs' focus was on the most vulnerable and culturally distinctive indigenous peoples of Latin America. Anti-Slavery, consistent with its mandate, drew attention to indigenous peoples being kept in conditions tantamount to slavery as serfs to landlords.[9] In addition, Latin American states were opening up areas to settlement and development, leading to the encroachment on indigenous lands of ranchers, miners, loggers, military personnel, and missionaries.[10] From the late 1970s, there were increasing reports of torture and extrajudicial killings of indigenous peoples in Peru,[11] El Salvador,[12] and Guatemala.[13]

[9] *See, e.g.*, Judith Ennew, Debt Bondage: A Survey (1981).

[10] *See* Jacques Lizot, The Yanomami in the Face of Ethnocide (1976) (noting the encroachment by gold miners on territory of the Yanonami of the Brazilian Amazonia).

[11] From 1980, Peru was embroiled in a civil conflict that would run for two decades. *See* Steve J. Stern, Shining and Other Paths: War and Society in Peru, 1980–1995 (1998).

[12] El Salvador's civil war commenced in the 1980s and led to the death of more than 70,000 people, many of them being rural *campesino* and indigenous peoples. *See* Robin M. DeLugan, Reimagining National Belonging: Post-Civil War El Salvador in a Global Context (2012).

[13] *See generally* Edward Fischer, *Beyond Victimisation: Maya Movements in Post-War Guatemala*, *in* The Struggle for Indian Rights in Latin America (Nancy G. Postero ed., 2004); *See also* Kay B. Warren, Indigenous Movements and Their Critics: Pan-Maya Activism in Guatemala (1998).

The anthropology NGOs sought to shine a light on these issues by distributing newsletters and publications in newspapers.[14] Three European organizations—International Working Group of Indigenous Affairs (IWGIA), Survival International, and Anti-Slavery—were at the vanguard of this new movement. All of these organizations shared their founders' background in anthropology. They were scholars with an academic interest in indigenous peoples, but became activist-anthropologists given their concerns surrounding the plight of indigenous peoples. As Wright notes, "with their critique of the 'colonial situation,' anthropologists began to look critically at the legacy and goals of the profession, 'awakening' to their ethical responsibilities, and directing their interests to the concerns of native peoples."[15] Anthropology was perceived as giving succor to the colonial ideologies that supported the settlement and colonization of indigenous peoples.[16]

Many of the communities that the anthropology NGOs wrote about had been their subjects in fieldwork. They were mostly remote and culturally distinctive communities in Central and South America. The view was that these peoples lacked political know-how and sophistication to protect themselves, with little contact with the outside world. Survival International did not undertake work on the struggle of the Kurds, Basque, Ukrainians, or First Nations of the United States who were said to be "relatively more sophisticated politically and have their own informed and articulate spokepeoples,"[17] neither did IWGIA or Anti-Slavery.

Throughout the 1970s, these NGOs were busy collecting and disseminating information and reports on Latin American indigenous peoples.[18] Increasingly, these organizations also campaigned on the situation of indigenous peoples in Asia, in light of the clear similarities between their situation and that of "Amazonian Indians" in Latin America. Indigenous peoples of Asia, like those of the Americas, were culturally distinct and remote communities struggling with the onslaught of modern life. This joining up of distinctive vulnerable tribal communities across two continents heralded the beginnings of an international indigenous peoples' movement. As we saw in

[14] Jens Dahl, IWGIA: A History (2009).

[15] Robin Wright, *Anthropological Presuppositions of Indigenous Advocacy*, 17 ANNUAL. REV. Anthropol. 267 (1988) 365, at 367 (according to Wright the Declaration of Barbados became "the manifesto of anthropology's alliance with the liberation struggles of native people"); *see The Declaration of Barbados: For the Liberation of Indians*, 14:3 Curr. Anthropol. 267 (1973).

[16] Wright, *supra* note 15.

[17] *Id.* at 70.

[18] Dahl, *supra* note 14.

Chapter 1, the US indigenous leaders were seeking to establish a process in the UN to develop standards of protection for indigenous peoples. The internationalization of tribal issues by these anthropologists would provide a platform for Asian indigenous peoples to access that UN process.

The most important action in terms of incorporating Asian indigenous peoples into the international movement was the move from the late 1970s by IWGIA, Survival International, and Anti-Slavery to channel their reports on Asian and Latin American indigenous peoples into international human rights monitoring bodies. The International Labour Organization (ILO) was the initial site of interest—until the UN working group was formed—because of ILO Convention 107. Drafted by the ILO, this was the first international treaty directed at indigenous and tribal peoples' rights.[19] Although not, strictly speaking, a human rights treaty, it was part of a body of standards developed over the 20th century to address the living and working conditions of indigenous peoples in the global South. Originally, indigenous peoples in this context meant the peoples of European colonies, but the ILO Convention 107 was directed at a subset of this group—culturally distinctive tribal communities or minorities of the South. However, ILO Convention 107 was focused on the protection of the basic rights of the tribe through their absorption into the nation's citizenry.[20] The convention, therefore, promoted basic rights to social security,[21] health,[22] vocational training,[23] and education.[24] There was recognition of the need to respect indigenous values, institutions, language, and, significantly, the protection of indigenous peoples' traditional lands.[25] But the recognition of these rights could not undermine the project of integration. The protections were temporary measures, as indigenous and tribal peoples gradually became "more acculturated and productive members of society."[26] Land rights, for example, were to be protected but with the expectation that indigenous peoples would leave the land and participate in the social and economic life of society. If their traditional way

[19] *Convention (No. 107) Concerning the Protection and Integration of Indigenous and Other Tribal and Semi-Tribal Populations in Independent Countries*, June 26, 1957, 328 U.N.T.S. 247 (entered into force June 2, 1959) [hereinafter *Convention (No. 107)*].

[20] *See* Luis Rodríguez-Piñero, Indigenous Peoples, Postcolonialism, and International Law: The ILO Regime (1919–1989) (2005) (discussing the drafting of ILO Convention No. 107).

[21] *Convention (No. 107), supra* note 19, art. 19.

[22] *Id.* art. 20.

[23] *Id.* arts. 16–18.

[24] *Id.* arts. 21–25.

[25] *Id.* arts. 11–14.

[26] Rodríguez-Piñero, *supra* note 20, at 124.

of life obstructed economic development, it had to be "gradually eliminated" or "at least adapted to the economic and social needs of the communities concerned."[27]

However, the anthropology NGOs advanced an interpretive spin consistent with the emerging era of indigenous rights promotion and protection.[28] After an initial phase of relative indifference toward implementation of the convention, Rodríguez-Piñero refers to a second phase from 1975 to 1989, whereby the "interaction between the international NGO movement and the [ILO] organization's supervisory system gradually fostered an interpretation of Convention No 107 as an instrument for the defence of indigenous rights, opening the most active phase thus far of the international protection of the rights of Indigenous Peoples by the ILO."[29] Efforts were made by the ILO to engage directly with the states being monitored, including the conduct of research visits to conflict zones under its "direct contact procedure."[30]

Through submissions made to the ILO by IWGIA, Survival International, and Anti-Slavery, the situation of both indigenous peoples of the settler states and tribal peoples of South Asia was highlighted.[31] Bangladesh had attracted the attention of international media and human rights NGOs due to the Chittagong Hill Tracts conflict following the government's policy of encouraging Bengali settlement of the Hill Tracts as a means to control and supplant local Jumma tribal authorities and land rights.[32] The transmigration policy brought to mind the settlement policies of the American Amazon in Brazil, Ecuador, and Peru. The conflict between the Jumma, the army, and Bengali settlers resonated with similar experiences of indigenous peoples in Guatemala, Chile, Peru, and El Salvador. The Sardar Sarovar dam

[27] ILO, *Living and Working Conditions of Indigenous Populations in Independent Countries*, Report VIII(1) International Labour Conference, 39th Session, Geneva (1956) at 69. *See also* Rodríguez-Piñero, *supra* note 20, at 124.

[28] Rodríguez-Piñero, *supra* note 20, at 251.

[29] *Id.*; *see, e.g.*, *Observations of the ILO Committee of Experts on the Application of Conventions and Recommendations (CEACR) in Relation to India and the Sardar Hydro Project*, UNILOOR, 1988, Report III (Part 4A), 75th Session (noting that recent occupation of government-owned lands did not mean that tribal peoples had no land rights) [hereinafter ILO CEACR India].

[30] Douglas Sanders, *The UN Working Group on Indigenous Populations*, 11:3 Hum. Rights Q. 406 (1989) (noting the ILO conducted two "direct contact missions" to Bangladesh in 1985 and 1987 at 424).

[31] Rodríguez-Piñero, *supra* note 20, at 249–52 (commenting on IWGIA and Survival International's engagement with the ILO supervisory mechanism to bring attention to tribal peoples in Brazil, India, and Bangladesh).

[32] Amena Mohsin, The Chittagong Hill Tracts, Bangladesh: On the Difficult Road to Peace (2003).

project in India[33] and the World Bank-funded Chico River Dam project in the Cordilleras of the Philippines,[34] both of which had displaced significant numbers of indigenous peoples, chimed with similar developments in Latin America.

Outside of the ILO, the UN working group negotiations on the Declaration was the most significant forum. To be accepted with credibility in this forum would offer Asian indigenous peoples several opportunities. First, while not a complaint mechanism, it was engaged in gathering empirical evidence to support its standard setting work, and this would direct more international attention toward their cause. Second, minority rights in the Asian states—as well as ILO Convention 107—were notoriously weak while the Declaration appeared to be on the path toward creating robust standards in relation to the protection of culture, traditional lands, and autonomy. As Kymlicka notes, "If they come to the international community under the heading of national minority, they get nothing other than generic Article 27 [minority] rights; if they come instead as 'Indigenous Peoples', they have the promise of rights to land, control over natural resources, political self-government, language rights and legal pluralism."[35]

Once the first UN working group was established, the anthropology NGOs attended its sessions and again spoke in the same breath of the struggle of indigenous peoples in Asia and the Americas.[36] Initially, there were only a few submissions on Asian indigenous peoples made by Anti-Slavery and other NGOs. However, within a few years, indigenous advocates from Southeast Asia began to arrive and make their own statements so that toward the end of

[33] This was part of the Narmada dam project initially supported by the World Bank that resulted in large-scale displacement of tribal peoples, *see* AMITA BAVISKAR, IN THE BELLY OF THE RIVER: TRIBAL CONFLICTS OVER DEVELOPMENT IN THE NARMADA VALLEY (2004).

[34] Survival International, Survival International News (1983) (announcing the cancellation of the Chico River Dam project).

[35] WILL KYMLICKA, MULTICULTURAL ODYSSEYS: NAVIGATING THE NEW INTERNATIONAL POLITICS OF DIVERSITY (2007).

[36] *Information Received from NGOs (Anti-Slavery Society) in Relation to the Hmong of Thailand, West Papua, Guatemala, CHT, Bangladesh*, UNESCOR, U.N. Doc. E/CN.4/Sub.2/AC.4/1983/5/Add.1 (1983); "Report by Anti-Slavery Society" (1989) doCip Doc. 211057_1 (on file with author) (commenting on Chittagong Hill Tracts); "Report by Anti-Slavery Society" (1989) doCip Doc. 211060_1 (on file with author) (commenting on Burma); *Report of the Secretary-General, Information Communicated by Non-Governmental Organizations, Survival International*, UNESCOR, U.N. Doc. E/CN.4/Sub.2/AC.4/1984/4, at 5 (1984) (commenting on land rights of "indigenous minority groups" in the Philippines, "tribal minority peoples" in Bangladesh, "Indians" of the Americas, "indigenous peoples" of Guatemala, and "Melanesian peoples" of West Papua) [hereinafter *Information from Survival International*].

the first working group there were a prominent number of Asian indigenous advocates.

2.2 Opposition to Asian Indigenous Peoples

Within the UN working group, the participation of Asian indigenous advocates was vigorously opposed by Asian states, especially China, Indonesia, India, and Bangladesh. These states asserted that the working group had no business looking into the situation of minorities in their states, arguing that "indigenous peoples" related to the specific historic experience of colonization and settlement of first peoples by Europeans in the Americas and Australasia. The following statement made by China in the working group in 1995 typifies the argument:[37]

> The Chinese Government believes that the question of Indigenous Peoples is the product of European countries' recent pursuit of colonial policies in other parts of the world. Because of these policies, many Indigenous Peoples were dispossessed of their ancestral homes and lands, brutally oppressed, exploited and murdered, and in some cases even deliberately exterminated. To this day, many Indigenous Peoples still suffer from discrimination and diminished status . . . As in the majority of Asian countries, the various nationalities in China have all lived for aeons on Chinese territory. Although there is no Indigenous Peoples' question in China, the Chinese Government and people have every sympathy with Indigenous Peoples' historical woes and historical plight. China believes it absolutely essential to draft an international instrument to protect their rights and interests . . . The special historical misfortunes of Indigenous Peoples set them apart from minority nationalities and ethnic groups in the ordinary sense. For this reason, the draft declaration must clearly define what Indigenous Peoples are, in order to guarantee that the special rights it establishes are accurately targeted at genuine communities of indigenous people and are not distorted, arbitrarily extended or muddled.

[37] *Consideration of a Draft of a United Nations Declaration on the Rights of Indigenous Peoples: Information Received from Governments (China)*, UN Commission on Human Rights, 52nd Sess., Supp. No. 2, U.N. Doc. E/CN.4/1995/WG.15/2 (1995) at 7.

According to China, "indigenous peoples" related to the West's colonization project in the settler states of the Americas and Australasia. Asia does not have indigenous peoples but "minorities"—a different category altogether. Asian states attending the working group negotiations, therefore, sought a definition of indigenous peoples that made clear that they were to be found in the settler states and asserted that it was ultimately for states to determine who constituted an indigenous people. India highlighted the need to focus on Latin America where "in the last few decades indigenous peoples in some countries have been subjected to ethnocide and decimation on such a large scale that their very survival is at stake."[38] The implication was that the claims of Asian indigenous peoples were a distraction from the more pressing issue of fundamental human rights abuses in Latin America. China, Bangladesh, India, and Indonesia were consistent and strong opponents of indigenous rights applying to their states throughout the Declaration negotiations.

These states were concerned about the domestic consequences of indigenous rights given the presence of local minority movements seeking greater autonomy or independence. Above all, Asian states were concerned about the claims of Northern indigenous advocates to self-determination. For them, the stakes were much higher compared to the CANZUS states;[39] there has never been a serious threat to the territorial integrity of these states. Although Northern indigenous peoples sought self-determination, almost all of them envisaged an enduring relationship within the state. Additionally, indigenous rights threatened to undermine state-sponsored development projects, and the private investment considered essential to the economic growth and independence of these states.

The activities of the working group invited unwanted international scrutiny of domestic policy on minorities. Indonesia, for example, was repeatedly criticized in international fora for its annexation of the Moluccas and West Papua;[40] Burma for its oppressive treatment of the Chin and Karen and other "hill-tribes" on its eastern border with Thailand;[41] and Bangladesh for its

[38] *Statement by the Indian Delegation*, UNESCOR, U.N. Doc. E/CN.4/Sub.2/AC.4/1984/2/Add.2, at 9 (1984).

[39] Roderic Petty & Shannara Smith, *The Indigenous Challenge to Westphalian Sovereignty*, 46:1 AUST. J. POLIT. SCI. 121, 136 (2011) (noting that the African concern about territorial integrity and local secession claims was different to the CANZUS states where the "rhetoric of opposition to self-determination focused on excluding external scrutiny of what government regard as domestic policy making."). However, CANZUS concerns were not merely about intervention but, as I argue in Chapter 1, the normative power with obvious legal and political consequences that came with a reference to self-determination without a reference to territorial integrity.

[40] CHRIS LUNDRY, SEPARATISM AND STATE COHESION IN EASTERN INDONESIA (2009).

[41] MARTIN SMITH, BURMA: INSURGENCY AND THE POLITICS OF ETHNICITY (1999).

transmigration policy of settling Bangladesh settlers on Jumma homelands in the Chittagong Hill Tracts.[42] China was concerned about its annexation of Nepal and claims to Taiwan. As most of these nations had emerged from a long period of Western imperial rule, they were sensitive to foreign intervention and the imposition of "Western-derived" human rights standards.[43] Thus, Asian states frequently referred to *their* history of Western oppression and described their whole nation-states as comprising indigenous peoples.[44] We are all indigenous peoples, we have all suffered from Western rule, and we identify with those still subject to "Western imperial rule."[45]

The issue was compounded by suspicions that indigenous rights were being used to undermine post-colonial states—some of which were allied with the Soviet Union. As Will Kymlicka notes:[46]

> There is a widespread perception that international organisations are internationalising minority rights precisely in order to destabilise certain countries. In particular, it is widely believed in many post-colonial states that the international sponsorship of minority rights is simply a conspiracy by the West, and particularly the US, to weaken and divide post colonial states.

Kymlicka also notes how post-colonial states resented the intrusion of foreign powers in local affairs, given that imperial rulers collaborated with small minorities and granted them power and privilege in order to maintain control over the rest of the population.[47] In addition, tensions resulted from the creation of kin-state minority groups due to the arbitrary delineation of country borders, whereby a minority may have ethnic links and higher loyalty to the population of a neighboring kin-state thereby creating security concerns.[48]

[42] *Information from Survival International*, *supra* note 36, at 5 (commenting on land rights of "tribal peoples" in Bangladesh).

[43] *Compare* ROLAND BURKE, DECOLONIZATION AND THE EVOLUTION OF INTERNATIONAL HUMAN RIGHTS Chapter 2 (2010) (noting the emphasis placed on human rights by colonized peoples during the initial stages of the UN decolonization process).

[44] *See, e.g.*, "Statement by the Bangladesh Delegation" (Nov. 23, 1995) doCip Doc. 034_AS01 (on file with author) (arguing Bangladesh is an indigenous people, and so, the Declaration would also protect the nation of Bangladesh).

[45] *Id.*

[46] Kymlicka, *supra* note 35, at 282.

[47] *Id.* at 78.

[48] Will Kymlicka, *The Internationalization of Minority Rights*, *in* CONSTITUTIONAL DESIGN FOR DIVIDED SOCIETIES: INTEGRATION OR ACCOMMODATION? 133 (Sujit Choudhry ed., 2008).

> As a result, there is anxiety that such minorities are irredentist—that is, that they wish to redraw international boundaries so as to unite (or reunite) the territory where they live with their adjacent kin-state. Indeed, it is often assumed that they would collaborate willingly with their kin-state if it militarily invaded the country in order to claim this territory, as, indeed, some have done at various times in the twentieth century.

Matters were complicated by the broader geopolitical interests of the time, due to the work of the working groups coinciding with the Cold War. The United States and other Western states emphasized individual freedom and used human rights as a means to embarrass the Soviet Union particularly during President Carter's administration when the President made human rights a platform of his administration.[49] And so during the 1970s, the US State Department was critical of the Communist Sandinista government of Nicaragua due to human rights failings, while violations by the US allies—Honduras and Guatemala—were not condemned.[50]

The United States supported the extension of the indigenous rights movement beyond the North, to the Asian region.[51] This provided the United States with the opportunity to criticize the Soviet states and Communist bloc countries for neglecting the human rights of their indigenous peoples.[52] It also diverted attention from the Northern states. To extend the indigenous rights movement beyond the North meant there would be no directed focus—as had been the case in the early years of the Declaration negotiations—on the decolonization model and the plight of Northern indigenous peoples. Asian states were also likely to oppose any reference to self-determination if there was the prospect of the Declaration applying to their states or at least support a reference to territorial integrity.

In response, in the working group and the UN Sub-Commission on Human Rights, the Soviet Union and China criticized the United States for its seizure of Indian lands and called for land redistribution measures.[53] The

[49] Richard A. Falk, Human Rights Horizons: The Pursuit of Justice in a Globalizing World (2000).

[50] *Id.* at 61.

[51] *See* "General Statement by Leslie A. Gerson, Deputy Assistant Secretary of State, United States Department of State" (1998) doCip Doc. 021_as03 (on file with author) (The United States was "concerned by statements from regional groups that have suggested the need for a definition of the indigenous groups which would exclude their own groups of indigenous people. Such insistence on a narrow definition would in our view de-rail the process altogether. In this regard we do not believe that the focus of the Declaration should be the privileging of historically prior inhabitants.").

[52] Sanders, *supra* note 30, at 415.

[53] *Id.*

Soviet Union also offered political asylum to Leonard Peltier—an American Indian Movement activist convicted in 1982 for the murder of FBI agents on Indian lands.[54] China consistently called for recognition of collective rights, which contradicted the US claim that the Declaration should focus only on individual rights.[55]

A significant flashpoint occurred with the appointment of the Cuban member of the working group to complete a study on treaties.[56] Miguel Alfonso Martínez had been given the task to follow-up on some of the recommendations made by the UN Special Rapporteur José Martínez Cobo in the Cobo Report.[57] The report had suggested an additional study on "Treaties between Indigenous Populations and States."[58] Indigenous advocates of the North, led by the Treaty Council, lobbied the working group to undertake the study. In the UN Sub-Commission on Human Rights, which was required to supervise the report and appoint its rapporteur, Canada and the United States strongly opposed Martínez's appointment. It was highly likely that his report would be critical of their states and call for historical inquiry into implementation of treaties. But Martínez was approved. Martínez could see the efforts made to accommodate communities from Asia and Africa in the working group, and he was strongly opposed to their inclusion. According to Martínez, neither the Asian nor the African situations qualify for the usage of the term "indigenous peoples." "[I]n post-colonial Africa and Asia," he states, "autochthonous groups/minorities/ethnic groups/peoples . . . cannot . . . claim for themselves, unilaterally and exclusively the 'indigenous' status in the United Nations context."[59]

According to Martínez, several historical points distinguished the claims of settler-state indigenous peoples. First, he noted the brutality of colonization in the settler states, specifically:[60]

[54] *Id.*

[55] *See, e.g.*, "Statement of China" (1998) doCip Doc. 023_as02 (on file with author) ("The Chinese delegation believes that indigenous peoples have not only individual rights but also collective rights").

[56] *Study on Treaties, Agreements and Other Constructive Arrangements Between States and Indigenous Populations: Final Report by Miguel Alfonso Martinez, Special Rapporteur*, UN Commission on Human Rights, 51st Sess., U.N. Doc. E/CN.4/Sub.2/1999/20 (1999) [hereinafter *Study on Treaties*].

[57] José Martínez Cobo, *Study of the Problem of Discrimination Against Indigenous Populations: Final Report*, UNESCOR, U.N. Doc. E/CN.4/Sub.2/1986/7/Add.4 (1986).

[58] *Id.* at paras. 388–92.

[59] *Study on Treaties*, *supra* note 56, at para. 88.

[60] *Id.* at para. 175.

> The inherent nature of the colonial undertaking, the exploitative, discriminatory and dominating character of its "philosophy" as a system, the methods employed and the final results it had on very dissimilar societies mark the difference.

Second, unlike indigenous peoples of the settler states, he notes that most Asian, African, and Middle Eastern states have undergone decolonization.[61] Finally, treaties mark another distinction, and few could be found in Asia or Africa.[62]

Martínez suggests that cases relating to any of the Asian, African, and European continents should be handled in forums other than the working group, preferably at the (then) newly established working group on minorities.[63] Martínez insisted on a "clear-cut distinction between indigenous peoples and national or ethnic minorities,"[64] but refrained from providing his own definition of indigenous peoples, or minority rights. The basic distinction, from his perspective, ultimately related to the different historical trajectories of, on the one hand, "territorial expansion by indigenous nations into adjacent areas" (for example, like Bengalis in the Chittagong Hill Tracts of Bangladesh) and, on the other hand, "organized colonization, by European powers, of peoples inhabiting, since time immemorial, territories on other continents."[65] Martínez sought to emphasize the particular shock of conquest and its effects over centuries on indigenous peoples of the settler states. The term "indigenous peoples" should thus only be reserved for cases of the latter kind.

For Martínez, some of the blame for the blurring of the differences between indigenous peoples and "minorities" could be laid at the feet of the UN, for having merged the two categories in official publications such as "The Rights of Indigenous Peoples" (Fact Sheet No. 9), prepared by the UN Centre for Human Rights.[66] The fact sheet referred to indigenous peoples in both the classic case of colonization from afar and those cases where "dominant neighbouring peoples have expanded their territories" onto indigenous lands. The UN secretary of the working group and the manager of

[61] *Id.* at para. 68.
[62] *Id.* at paras. 78 and 79.
[63] *Id.* at para. 90.
[64] *Id.* at para. 68.
[65] *Id.* at paras. 71–73.
[66] The Rights of Indigenous Peoples (Fact Sheet No. 9), UN Centre for Human Rights, Geneva, 1990.

the indigenous peoples' program in the Office of the High Commissioner for Human Rights was Julian Burger who had, prior to joining the UN, championed the cause of indigenous peoples in Asia while working for the Anti-Slavery Society. The indigenous peoples' program established the "UN Voluntary Fund for Indigenous populations," which financed both Northern and Southern indigenous advocates. There was, then, a broad perception that the UN administration responsible for indigenous rights was supportive of a global approach to indigenous peoples.

Asian indigenous activists were highly critical of the Martínez report, calling it "colonial" and "racist,"[67] while Asian states commended the "excellent and scholarly" report.[68] The report encouraged Asian governments to demand a definition that would exclude Asian indigenous peoples. It also aggravated an increasingly tense situation between indigenous advocates of Asia and those of the North who had lobbied for the study. The report clearly indicated that the Northern movement would be better off without the Asian movement in the working group.

With the end of the Cold War, the focus shifted from ideology to culture. In the early 1990s, human rights began to be critiqued by Asian states as a result of the inherent bias due to its Western origins. Under the banner of "Asian values," they extolled new civilization outlooks positing the Western system of human rights as individualistic and out of step with the East's emphasis on communitarian values.[69] Against this, critics argued that human rights were not necessarily the preserve of the West and that Asian values were being used to divert attention from internal human rights violations.[70]

[67] *Report of the Working Group on Indigenous Populations on Its Sixteenth Session*, UN Commission on Human Rights, 50th Sess., U.N. Doc. E/CN.4/Sub.2/1998/16 (1998).

[68] Several Asian states commended the Report, *see* "Statement of Bangladesh" (1989) doCip Doc. 211081_1 (on file with author) (commending Martinez for his scholarly work); *see also* "Statement by the India Delegation" (1991) doCip Doc. 200170_1 (on file with author) (commending "the excellent preliminary report on treaties" at 200170_2).

[69] The Asian regional preparatory meeting for the Vienna Conference on Human Rights. *See Report of the Regional Meeting for Asia of the World Conference on Human Rights*, UN World Conference on Human Rights, U.N. Doc. A/CONF.157/ASRM/8, at 38 (1993) (adopting the Bangkok Declaration, which included the statement: "while human rights are universal in nature they must be considered in the context of a dynamic and evolving process of international norm-setting, bearing in mind the significance of national and regional particularities and various historical, cultural and religious backgrounds").

[70] Sally E. Merry, *Human Rights Law and the Demonization of Culture (and Anthropology Along the Way)*, 26:1 PoLAR Polit. Leg. Anthropol. Rev. 55 (2003).

2.3 Asian Indigenous Peoples and the Human Rights Model

In response to the objections of Asian states, Asian indigenous advocates and the anthropology NGOs sought to distinguish Asian indigenous peoples from other (typically more acculturated and powerful) minority groups who sought secession or strong forms of regional autonomy. Instead of calling for strong forms of self-determination like Northern indigenous peoples, Asian advocates emphasized human rights and culture. With culture and not independence as the priority, a line was drawn between Asian indigenous peoples and other more controversial militant and separatist movements like the Tamil, the Uighur, and the Tibetan movements. According to this view, Asian indigenous peoples were the "harmless" communities of remote, mountain, and hilltop areas seeking cultural survival in the face of unrelenting Western development and culture.

There were other practical reasons for emphasizing human rights and culture. This allowed Asian indigenous peoples to show their common cause with indigenous peoples of the settler states. Asian indigenous advocates could not rely on the same prior-sovereignty justificatory arguments that supported the decolonization model. These communities are not first peoples—this being too difficult to establish with millennia of migration and movement of peoples across South Asia. However, there were many other commonalities—as the anthropology NGOs highlighted—in terms of denial of basic human rights, culture, and land, particularly with the indigenous peoples of Latin America.

This human rights strategy can be seen in the 1995 publication, "Indigenous Peoples of Asia," edited by an international lawyer, Benedict Kingsbury, and anthropologists, Andrew Gray (then director of IWGIA) and R.H. Barnes.[71] Each chapter deals with a different South Asian country; however, all describe culturally distinctive groups occupying remote, forested, and hilly areas that have been marginalized and exploited by a dominant culture. As Andrew Gray notes of those participating in the working group negotiations on the Declaration, "[e]xamples range from the Indigenous Peoples in India suffering the relocation effects of the Narmada dam to the hill peoples of the Chittagong hill tracts; the Natives of Sarawak and Peninsular Malaysia; the minority peoples of Burma; the hill peoples of Thailand, Laos, Cambodia,

[71] Indigenous Peoples of Asia (R.H. Barnes, Andrew Gray, & Benedict Kingsbury eds., 1995). *See also* Andrew Gray, *On Anthropological Advocacy*, 31:4 Curr. Anthropol. 387 (1990).

and Vietnam; the Aboriginal peoples of Taiwan and the Ainu."[72] These peoples typically did not seek secession but rather "an autonomy that falls short of independence."[73] The issues raised by them related to the effects of development and land displacement, respect for culture, and basic human rights. While not, strictly speaking, first peoples, Asian indigenous peoples could claim to be "prior peoples." To illustrate, the Jumma may not, strictly speaking, have been the *first* to settle in the Chittagong Hill Tracts, but they had firmly settled there *prior* to the more recent influx of Bangladesh settlers.[74]

The editors acknowledged, however, that some Asian minorities did not fit neatly into their Asian indigenous people category. These were ethnic minority groups with a very different agenda seeking independence and self-determination or at least strong forms of autonomy, or variations of these themes. This included communities subject to transmigration by Indonesia—West Papua, Timor Leste (East Timor), and Moluccas Island. This category also included the claims of the Tamil in Sri Lanka, and Nagaland and Jharkhand in India. These groups would attend the working group negotiating the Declaration but also higher-level UN bodies that were more concerned with decolonization. As Andrew Gray notes, "The West Papuans usually make a statement at the Working Group but they also make it clear that their presence at the Working Group should be seen in respect of *human rights*."[75] "However as they feel that their case is one of independence as well as human rights, many believe a higher forum such as the Decolonization Committee would be better for them."[76]

When "Indigenous Peoples of Asia" was published in 1995, the indigenous movement was still emerging within the region. However, the editors noted that despite only "vague indications of a nascent indigenous movement,"[77] it was clear "the concept was present, ready to be deployed and extended to them." As noted by Andrew Gray, "Regardless of whether these people refer to themselves as indigenous, or are even called indigenous, in the context of human rights issues, their definition emerges out of the problems they face and the rights for which they are fighting."[78]

[72] Andrew Gray, *The Indigenous Movement in Asia*, *in* INDIGENOUS PEOPLES OF ASIA 55 (R.H. Barnes, Andrew Gray, & Benedict Kingsbury eds., 1995).
[73] *Id.*
[74] Mohsin, *supra* note 32.
[75] Gray, *supra* note 72, at 55.
[76] *Id.*
[77] Barnes, Gray, & Kingsbury, *supra* note 71.
[78] Gray, *supra* note 72, at 56.

Benedict Kingsbury also made an independent contribution to the debate in an article entitled, "'Indigenous Peoples' in International Law: A Constructivist Approach to the Asian Controversy," published in 1998 ("Asian Controversy Article").[79] In this article, Kingsbury sought to overcome Asian states opposition to local tribal groups self-identifying as such by shifting the emphasis away from, as he put it, historical continuity with first peoples as the primary normative basis of indigenous rights. This emphasis, he noted, was due to the dominance of Northern indigenous peoples in the working group. Instead, Kingsbury stressed the commonalities between Northern indigenous peoples and Asian tribal peoples in terms of "functional matters such as dispossession of land, cultural dislocation, environmental despoliation and experiences with large development projects."[80]

In particular, there were four "essential" justifications for indigenous rights: (1) self-identification as a distinct ethnic group; (2) historical experience of, or contingent vulnerability to, severe disruption, dislocation, or exploitation; (3) long connection with the region; and (4) the wish to retain a distinct identity. These, Kingsbury argued, "establish a unity that is not dependent on the universal presence of historical continuity."[81] Historical continuity, however, should be viewed as a "strong" justification.[82] Thus, the response to Asian states would be that historical continuity was merely one consideration underpinning indigenous rights, but there were many others, including functional elements that were relevant to Asian indigenous peoples.[83]

The obfuscation was fostered by a new definition of indigenous peoples in the ILO Convention 169. The definition of "indigenous peoples" in ILO Convention No. 107 had reflected first peoples' historical experience with its reference to "historical continuity with the populations which *inhabited the country at the time of conquest or colonization*." The ILO Convention No. 169's definition of indigenous peoples retains this but also extends the concept by including groups with "historical continuity with the populations *which inhabited the country at the time of the establishment of present state*

[79] Benedict Kingsbury, *"Indigenous Peoples" in International Law: A Constructivist Approach to the Asian Controversy*, 92:3 AM. J. INT. LAW 414 (1998).

[80] *Id.* at 457.

[81] *Id.*

[82] *Id.* at 455.

[83] However, Kingsbury's approach does not address Asian states' concern that local self-identified indigenous peoples—which could include the controversial independence movements—may simply claim a right to self-determination. *See* Chapter 3.

boundaries." As a result, indigenous peoples are no longer confined to the first peoples of the settler states—but now include tribal peoples living within the boundaries of newly independent states established during the decolonization process such as India, Bangladesh, and Indonesia.

IWGIA, Survival International, and Anti-Slavery played a significant role in promoting the human rights model and extending the concept of indigenous peoples into new regions. IWGIA, in particular, has assumed a lead role in supporting attendance at international meetings and advocating for indigenous rights in new regions. In 2006, a former non-indigenous member of IWGIA, Jens Dahl, was appointed as a member of the UN Permanent Forum on Indigenous Issues.

These NGOs would form close ties with Asian indigenous advocates and actively supported their movement in the form of advice and funding to attend the working group meetings.[84] IWGIA had always prioritized the need to work closely with and for Asian indigenous peoples. Of the bonds made, the most crucial would be the leaders of the Philippines-based Tebtebba and Cordillera Peoples Alliance—the latter being IWGIA's first long-term partner in the Asia region—established in June 1984 by indigenous advocates to challenge the World Bank-funded Chico Dam.[85] IWGIA also established strong links with indigenous advocates of the Chittagong Hill Tracts and helped establish the Chittagong Hill Tracts Commission—a European-based NGO aimed at advancing indigenous rights in Bangladesh.[86] As the international indigenous rights movement grew, so did IWGIA. Today, it is the largest non-indigenous organization working on indigenous rights. Survival International, on the other hand, would play less of a role in the UN, but it would continue to mount campaigns for indigenous peoples of Asia, Africa, and Latin America. Anti-Slavery eventually withdrew from active participation in the international movement. Eventually, Asian indigenous advocates themselves—often with the financial support of the anthropology NGOs—attended the Declaration negotiations.

As we will see, this human rights model would also be used by the emergent African indigenous movement when they sought to participate in the

[84] Sanders, *supra* note 30 at 416 ("[f]our of the European support organisations established a temporary 'Human Rights Fund' to enable indigenous represents to travel to Geneva. In 1987 that fund resulted in much wider representation from Asia, including new delegations from the Philippines, India, and Burma. It also funded representatives from Bangladesh and Indonesia" at 420).

[85] Jens Dahl, IWGIA: A History 62 (2009).

[86] Sanders, *supra* note 30.

Declaration negotiations. And the anthropology NGOs, especially IWGIA, would play a central role in supporting this new movement.

2.4 African Indigenous Peoples and the Human Rights Model

Maasai advocate, Moringe ole Parkipuny, was the first African indigenous advocate to speak in the UN working group.[87] Addressing the sixth session, Parkipuny described the contemporary situation in Africa:[88]

> The environment for human rights in Africa is severely polluted by the ramifications of colonialism and neo-colonial social and economic relationships in which we are compelled to pursue our development and our sovereignty in a global system replete with injustices and exploitation.

For Parkipuny, African states were up against the wall, given the history and impacts of Western colonialism. However, there was a danger that the drive to reinforce national identities would:[89]

> have thrown wide open the door for prejudices against the fundamental rights and social values of those peoples with cultures that are distinctly different from those of the mainstream national population. Such prejudices have crystallized in many African countries into blatant cultural intolerance, domination and persistent violations of the fundamental rights of minorities.

Parkipuny went on to describe two main categories of vulnerable minority peoples who have been subjected to flagrant violations of community and individual rights:[90]

> These are hunter and gatherers, namely the Hadza, Dorobo and Sandawe together with many ethnic groups who are pastoralists. The Maasai of

[87] *See also* International Work Group for Indigenous Affairs, "Newsletter No. 59" (December 1989); *see also* Moringe Parkipuny, *The Human Rights Situation of Indigenous Peoples in Africa*, 4:1 Fourth World J. 2 (1989).
[88] *Id.*
[89] *Id.*
[90] *Id.*

> Kenya and Tanzania are the largest and most widely known of the many pastoral peoples of East Africa. These minorities suffer from common problems which characterize the plight of Indigenous Peoples throughout the world. The most fundamental rights to maintain our specific cultural identity and the land that constitutes the foundation of our existence as a people are not respected by the state and fellow citizens who belong to the mainstream population. In our societies the land and natural resources are the means of livelihood, the media of cultural and spiritual integrity for the entire community as opposed to individual appropriation. The process of alienation of our land and its resources was launched by European colonial authorities at the beginning of this century and has been carried on, to date, after the attainment of national independence. Our cultures and way of life are viewed as outmoded, inimical to national pride and a hindrance to progress. What is more, access to education and other basic services are minimal relative to the mainstream of the population of the countries to which we are citizens in common with other people.

With the increased presence of Asian indigenous advocates in the working group from the late 1980s, increasing numbers of African indigenous advocates also began to participate. Moringe ole Parkipuny, as he notes in his statement, is the trailblazer for this new movement.

What gave rise to the African indigenous movement? The African movement was preceded by mobilization of local minorities against the loss of lands for large-scale commercial farming, mining, game parks, and wildlife reserves to attract tourists.[91] They were facing similar pressures to those of Latin American and Asian indigenous peoples. However, these factors do not explain why advocates like Parkipuny chose the indigenous category as opposed to the minority rights category. As was the case with the Asian indigenous movement, the participation of African indigenous advocates in the working group had been prompted by the anthropology NGOs. IWGIA, in particular, played a leading role in supporting local movements and assisting with the shaping of their claims.[92]

[91] Dorothy L. Hodgson, *Becoming Indigenous in Africa*, 52:3 Afr. Stud. Rev. 1, 56 (2009).

[92] *See* Kealeboga N. Bojosi, *The African Commission Working Group of Experts on the Rights of Indigenous Communities/Populations: Some Reflections on Its Work*, *in* Perspectives on the Rights of Minorities and Indigenous Peoples in Africa 96 (Solomon A. Dersso ed., 2010) (arguing that despite conventional renderings, the concept of indigenous peoples in Africa emerged through external lobbying, particularly through IWGIA, and not through the growth of local movements

In fact, IWGIA was involved in bringing Parkipuny to the working group.[93]

IWGIA commenced work on the African movement during the mid-1980s but accelerated its efforts from the early 1990s,[94] organizing the "Conference on Indigenous Peoples in Africa" in Copenhagen in 1993, which included representatives from select African groups.[95] The object of the conference was to open debate on "whether we are justified in applying the concept of indigenous peoples in Africa."[96] Most of the papers in the published conference proceedings were directed at pastoralist and hunter-gatherer communities. The picture of indigenous peoples in the African context was quite clear. Indigenous peoples in Africa meant the "primitive" tribes categorized as such by colonizing powers and later the independent state. Examples include the Batwa or Twa of Central Africa (Rwanda, Burundi, and Democratic Republic of Congo) who are commonly known as "Pygmies." The other category of pastoral tribes referred to by Parkipuny occupy Eastern and Southern Africa and include the Maasai of Tanzania and Kenya and the San of Botswana and South Africa. Parkipuny was seeking to show common cause with the international movement by employing the human rights model used by Asian indigenous advocates and their supporters. He was advancing this claim in the context of the working group, fully aware that this was the place to be legitimately recognized as "indigenous" for the purposes of the international movement.

IWGIA set to work at sponsoring national, regional, and international workshops to encourage awareness and discussion of the applicability of the concept of African indigenous peoples.[97] It publicized the debates and initiatives in its annual Yearbook and quarterly periodical, *Indigenous Affairs*, and financed the participation of African indigenous activists in the annual meetings of the working group, the UN Permanent Forum on Indigenous

identifying with the cause); *see also* Rachel Murray, *The UN Declaration on the Rights of Indigenous Peoples in Africa: The Approach of the Regional Organisations to Indigenous Peoples*, *in* Reflections on the United Nations Declaration on the Rights of Indigenous Peoples, Studies in International Law v. 30 (Steve Allen & Alexandra Xanthaki eds., 2011) (noting the Working Group "owes it success to the commitment of a key NGO with long-standing expertise in this area, the International Work Group for Indigenous Affairs" at 486).

93 Dahl, *supra* note 14, at 30.

94 *See* E. Waehle, Africa and the Concept of Indigenous Peoples 144–48 (1990) (arguing for the applicability of the concept of indigenous peoples in Africa).

95 Dahl, *supra* note 14.

96 *Id.*

97 *Id.*

Issues, and relevant UN World Summits.[98] IWGIA assisted African indigenous advocates to attend the 1993 Vienna World Conference on Human Rights. It also funded the capacity-building, land rights, and human rights programs of some African indigenous organizations.[99]

In the years following Parkipuny's speech in the working group, African indigenous advocates assumed a visible presence. When the UN Permanent Forum on Indigenous Issues was formed in 2000, it recognized Africa as one of the seven regions within its mandate and there has always been an African indigenous representative on the Forum's panel. The Expert Mechanism on the Rights of Indigenous Peoples has a representative from Africa. James Anaya, in his capacity as a UN Special Rapporteur on Indigenous Peoples, visited and issued reports on indigenous peoples in Namibia,[100] the Republic of the Congo,[101] and Botswana.[102] His predecessor, Rodolfo Stavenhagen, undertook missions to Kenya[103] and South Africa.[104]

Although it was important to secure a foothold in international meetings, above all the working groups, it was clear that very few African states participated in those meetings and a regional campaign was also needed. There were signs of strong resistance to the domestic application of indigenous peoples in Africa, just as there had been in Asia and for much the same reasons: concern about security, unity, exploitation of resources, and foreign interference. African leaders particularly recall their self-description as "indigenous peoples" during their struggle for decolonization and independence against their European imperial rulers, which suggested that these emergent groups might be candidates for self-rule. Thus, there were security concerns with the self-determination framework in the Declaration and the many groups claiming autonomy and independence in Africa. As the African indigenous

[98] *Id.*
[99] *Id.*
[100] *Report of the UN Special Rapporteur on the Rights of Indigenous Peoples, James Anaya, The Situation of Indigenous Peoples in Namibia*, UN Human Rights Council, 24th Sess., Supp. No. 41, U.N. Doc. A/HRC/24/41/Add.1 (2013).
[101] *Report of the UN Special Rapporteur on the Rights of Indigenous Peoples, James Anaya, The Situation of Indigenous Peoples in the Republic of the Congo*, UN Human Rights Council, 18th Sess., Supp. No. 35, U.N. Doc. A/HRC/18/35/Add.5 (2011).
[102] *Report of the UN Special Rapporteur on the Rights of Indigenous Peoples, James Anaya, The Situation of Indigenous Peoples in Botswana*, UN Human Rights Council, 15th Sess., Supp. No. 37, U.N. Doc. A/HRC/15/37/Add.2 (2010).
[103] *Report of the Special Rapporteur on the Situation of Human Rights and Fundamental Freedoms of Indigenous People, Rodolfo Stavenhagen, Addendum: Mission to Kenya*, UN Human Rights Council, 4th Sess., Supp. No. 32, U.N. Doc. A/HRC/4/32/Add.3 (2006).
[104] *Report of the Special Rapporteur on the Situation of Human Rights and Fundamental Freedoms of Indigenous People, Rodolfo Stavenhagen, Addendum: Mission to South Africa*, UN Commission on Human Rights, 62nd Sess., Supp. No. 78, U.N. Doc. E/CN.4/2006/78/Add.2 (2005).

advocate Naomi Kipuri notes, "to many Africans, the common interpretation of the word indigenous is 'home grown,' or 'ours' and 'not foreigners.'"[105] All people of Africa are therefore indigenous to Africa.

Nigeria, for example, had struggled for decades with the Ogoni indigenous movement as most of Nigeria's oil is based in the Niger Delta, a region claimed by the Ogoni. The Ogoni advocate Ken Serowiwa had raised the issue before several meetings of the working group. To demonstrate what was at stake and the measure of concern by some African states, in 1995 he was executed, with five other Ogoni, by the Nigerian military government on charges widely seen as politically motivated. This sparked international outrage and Nigeria's suspension from the British Commonwealth. Additionally, there were also concerns about indigenous claims to land and resources. Botswana had felt the effect of an "indigenous-framed" claim to lands by local San communities when a domestic court decision ruled that the San had aboriginal title to much of the Kalahari game reserve.[106] The case had been supported by Survival International.

At the regional level, from the late 1990s, IWGIA focused on the African Commission with the aim of establishing a working group within the commission on indigenous rights. IWGIA's logic was that:[107]

> if a major human rights body like the African Commission recognizes the existence of marginalized indigenous communities in Africa and initiates a dialogue with African member states on recognition and protection of the human rights of indigenous communities, this will potentially be a major step forward for the advancement of the human rights of Indigenous Peoples in Africa.

Subsequently, IWGIA began to lobby for the Commission to establish a working group. In 2001, the African Commission agreed to establish a group of experts—the "Working Group on the Rights of Indigenous People and Communities in Africa"—to debate the issue, present a report, and make recommendations to the African Commission.[108] The working group

105 Naomi Kipuri, *The UN Declaration on the Rights of Indigenous Peoples in the African Context*, *in* Making the Declaration Work: The United Nation Declaration on the Rights of Indigenous Peoples (Claire Charters & Rodolfo Stavenhagen eds., 2009).

106 Another high-profile case is the South African Constitutional Court's decision, Alexkor Ltd v. Richtersveld Community, [2003] 12 B. Const. L.R. 1301 (S. Afr. Const. Ct.).

107 Dahl, *supra* note 14.

108 Dorothy L. Hodgson, Being Maasai, Becoming Indigenous: Postcolonial Politics in a Neoliberal World 77 (2011) (The whole process of the Working Group, its study, the report, and

included IWGIA as a member—the first occasion in which an NGO had been permitted to join a working group of the African Commission.

The resulting report became the manifesto for the African movement.[109] The key issue was how to identify indigenous peoples in Africa and how to describe their particular human rights. On the issue of definition, the report focused on basic human rights, particularly the right to culture:[110]

> Indigenous Peoples' has come to have connotations and meanings that are much wider than the question of "who came first". It is today a . . . global movement fighting for rights and justice for those particular groups who have been left on the margins of development and who are perceived negatively by the dominating mainstream . . . and whose very existence is under threat of extinction.

The focus instead should be on:[111]

> . . . the more recent approaches focusing on self-identification as indigenous and distinctly from other groups within a state; on a *special attachment to and use of their traditional land* whereby their ancestral land and territory has a fundamental importance for their collective cultural and physical survival as peoples; on an experience of subjugation, marginalization, dispossession, exclusion or discrimination because these peoples have different cultures, ways of life or modes of production than the national hegemonic and dominant model.

To address concerns about the connection between indigenous peoples and self-determination and decolonization, the report argued that indigenous peoples were not seeking self-rule but effective participation in governance and a say in relation to development on their lands. Land rights were key to indigenous peoples of Africa because of their close cultural affinity with ancestral lands and the need for land to sustain their communities.

the subsequent missions of the Commission and Working Group were all supported by IWGIA with financing from the Danish government. As noted by Hodgson, "without this Danish support, it is unlikely that the ACHPR process would have been so thorough and convincing").

[109] IWGIA and the African Commission on Human and Peoples' Rights (ACHPR), *Report of the African Commission's Working Group of Experts on Indigenous Populations/Communities* (2005).
[110] *Id.* at 87.
[111] *Id.* at 92–93.

Like the Asian movement, the emphasis on *human rights and culture* by the emerging African indigenous movement had the benefit of excluding from the new category of indigenous, those groups in Africa seeking secession or strong forms of regional autonomy. The pygmy and pastoral peoples were not seeking independence—unlike the separatist movements in Rwanda and the Democratic Republic of Congo. This separateness offered some means of addressing the security concerns of the African states. The emphasis on human rights and culture also allowed the African movement to show common cause with the movements in the North, particularly the emphasis on connection to land and cultural difference.

The report of the African Commission's working group received criticism from several African states that saw the concept of indigenous as divisive and a foreign imposition.[112] One would have thought that the preparation of the working group's report might have increased states' sensitivity and acceptance of indigenous rights—as the UN working groups had in relation to the drafting of the Declaration. However, there were major shortcomings with the African Commission's working group. Specifically, the meetings lacked profile, were held for short periods (typically 2 days), often before the sessions of the African Commission, and were not attended by large numbers of state representatives. Compared with the drafting of the Declaration, states did not participate in the drafting of the African Commission's report on indigenous populations/communities. Nevertheless, the report had fulfilled an important function in setting out how indigenous peoples were to be understood in the African context, that is, as a category of people deemed "backward" and "primitive" by states and in need of protection of basic human rights and culture.

3 Path to the UN General Assembly

With the door now opened by the Asian and African indigenous peoples' movements, other movements emerged in Russia as well as Eastern

[112] Bojosi, *supra* note 92, at 68 (noting "African governments have been generally dismissive of the report of the Working Groups of experts on Indigenous populations/communities, particularly with respect to the concept of Indigenous Peoples: Ethiopia has been more outright in its criticism, going as far as to question the establishment of the Working Group and the validity of its report. Sudan has cautioned against the bifurcation of populations into indigenous and non-indigenous, arguing that this was a recipe for conflict. Uganda emphasized that all Ugandans were indigenous to Uganda. Kenya preferred the term "minorities," while Zimbabwe preferred the phrase "small Tribal Peoples"").

and Central Europe.[113] As had been the case with the Asian and African movements, IWGIA and other anthropology NGOs supported these movements' participation in the UN working group and other international meetings.[114] Asian, African, and Russian indigenous advocates—with strong support from IWGIA—lobbied hard for their regions to be included within the Permanent Forum on Indigenous Issues mandate.

By the time of the establishment of the Permanent Forum, there were seven official UN indigenous peoples' regions. The Pacific and North America not only covered the CANZUS states but also nations within the Pacific. The Southern movement now included Africa; Asia; Central and South America and the Caribbean; the Arctic; and Central and Eastern Europe, Russian Federation, Central Asia, and Transcaucasia. The second UN working group thus witnessed the true globalization of the indigenous peoples movement. The Permanent Forum's mandate not only anticipated a global movement but also endorsed a human rights model. Its mandate is to "discuss indigenous issues related to economic and social development, culture, the environment, education, health and human rights."[115]

There were advantages to globalization of the movement.[116] The movement gained a greater profile and patronage as well as achieving financial support from international institutions and civil society, largely due to the perception of indigenous peoples as a global issue. However, there was no doubt that this might cause problems. First, it would result in Southern states resisting the self-determination framework in the Declaration. There were real security concerns about minorities in Asian and African states—more so than any other security concerns relating to Northern indigenous peoples.[117] This resistance could potentially lead to indigenous rights in the

[113] Alexandra Xanthaki, *Indigenous Rights in the Russian Federation: The Case of Numerically Small Peoples of the Russian North, Siberia, and Far East*, 26:1 HUM. RIGHTS. Q. 74 (2004).

[114] Dahl, *supra* note 14 (From the early 1990s, IWGIA and others focused on tribal peoples of Russia and helped establish RAIPON. This was facilitated by the fall of the Soviet Union, which allowed local movements to mobilize. IWGIA met with activists in Russia and invited them to attend the working group meetings. The 1990 meeting of the Working Group on Indigenous Populations marked the entry of Russian indigenous peoples onto the international human rights scene. Since then, IWGIA has invited (usually through the Human Rights Fund for Indigenous Peoples) representatives of the Russian indigenous peoples to participate in UN meetings on indigenous issues.).

[115] The Permanent Forum provides advice on these issues to the UN Human Rights Council, as well as to programs, funds, and agencies of the United Nations.

[116] Dahl, *supra* note 14 ("In a global perspective however the Indigenous Peoples from Latin America, Asia, Africa and Russia made the indigenous issue a *global issue* and alliances were created with governments who otherwise never have cared").

[117] Pitty & Smith, *supra* note 39.

Declaration being significantly diluted. Second, there would likely be a shift in focus from the decolonization model toward the human rights model. Asian and African indigenous advocates especially placed marked emphasis on the human right to culture—more so than Latin American indigenous advocates, who could at least appeal to the decolonization model and who were accepted as indigenous peoples by Latin American states.[118]

3.1 The Second Working Group and the No-Change Strategy

Very little progress was made in the first phase of negotiations between 1995 and 2002 as states and indigenous peoples were deadlocked over whether any changes could be made to the Declaration negotiated in the first working group and endorsed by the Sub-Commission on Human Rights (often called the Sub-Commission text). Indigenous advocates of the North led this "no-change" position, particularly the Treaty Council and others who were strong supporters of the decolonization model.[119] In the face of increasingly diverse indigenous participation in the working group, the Global Indigenous Caucus was an important means of maintaining this line. The caucus comprised only indigenous advocates, gathering before and after each working group's daily session. This had been critical in the first working group in order to hammer out strategy and language for the Declaration, especially inclusion of the self-determination framework. However, in the second working group, it was an important means of ensuring that all indigenous advocates, including those of the South, adhered to the no-change position.

The no-change position had the effect in the Declaration negotiations of minimizing changes, as all proposed revisions had to be considered in light of the text produced in the first working group. As noted by Andrea Carmen, the executive director of the Treaty Council:[120]

118 The early statements in the working group by El Salvador, for example, that it had no indigenous peoples was quickly abandoned in the face of the rise of indigenous social movements across Latin America.

119 "Joint Statement of the Indigenous Peoples Caucus" (1996) doCip Doc. 160_a01 and 160_a02. Information provided by NGOs: International Indian Treaty Council, Saami Council, World Council of Indigenous Peoples, Service Peace and Justice in Latin America, UN Commission on Human Rights, 52nd Sess., U.N. Doc. E/CN.4/1995/WG.15/4 (1995).

120 Andrea Carmen, *International Indian Treaty Council Report from the Battle Field: The Struggle for the Declaration, in* Making the Declaration Work: The United Nations Declaration on the Rights of Indigenous Peoples (Claire Charters & Rodolfo Stavenhagen eds., 2009).

> This prevented certain States, and groups of States, from promoting their new and often seriously flawed drafts on an equal footing with the [Sub-Commission text]. This also ensured that the [text] remained the official Text that was presented, referenced, quoted, used and applied in many situations and contexts, including in UN bodies and expert seminars over the years of the negotiations.

Frustrated with states' proposals to amend the Declaration, and the failure of the second working group's Chair to recognize indigenous representatives when they put up their hand to speak, indigenous peoples walked out in protest and issued a statement stressing the need for fair participation:[121]

> First, it must be explicitly recognized that Indigenous Nations and Peoples are equal participants in this Working Group and not "observers" . . . Why else would Indigenous delegations take the time and expense to travel all this way? Merely to observe, while States discuss the international recognition of our rights? No, common sense should tell you we must be fully involved. There should be no decisions or recommendations here which do not have our full and informed consent. Second, in future, Indigenous Peoples must have an equal ability to recommend how the work of this Working Group is to proceed and play a direct role in the development of the agenda and all other decision making processes of this body. Indigenous participants must have equitable input on organizing the work and other procedures.

Indigenous representatives returned only when they were assured that they would be equal participants in reaching consensus on the Declaration's text.[122] The Māori delegation from New Zealand, however, withdrew from

[121] "Joint Statement of the Indigenous Peoples Caucus" (1996) doCip Doc. 164_a02 (on file with author).

[122] Kenneth Deer, *Reflections on the Development, Adoption, and Implementation of the UN Declaration on the Rights of Indigenous Peoples*, *in* REALIZING THE UN DECLARATION ON THE RIGHTS OF INDIGENOUS PEOPLES: TRIUMPH, HOPE, AND ACTION (Paul Joffe, Jackie Hartley, & Jennifer Preston eds., 2010) ("As a result of the walk-out, for which we received considerable international and UN attention, we achieved a ground-breaking and confidence-building victory, ensuring that Indigenous Peoples would be equal participants in reaching consensus on the Text. It also made it clear that the negotiation process would not garner any legitimacy without the participation of Indigenous Peoples" at 11); *see also* Mattias Ahrén, *The UN Declaration on the Rights of Indigenous Peoples—How Was It Adopted and Why Is It Significant?*, *in* THE UN DECLARATION ON THE RIGHTS OF INDIGENOUS PEOPLES (Henry Minde, Asbjorn Eide, & Mattias Ahrén eds., 2007) (". . . throughout the Declaration process state and indigenous peoples representatives would informally participate

the negotiations given "the continued attempts by States to seek substantive amendment."[123] The walk out sent a clear message that the negotiations were not to be dominated by states. It also helped maintain the no-change stance of the North. However, five years into negotiations, indigenous peoples and states were deadlocked. States continued to seek changes to the text and the no-change camp held firm to their position.

3.2 The Positions of States in the Second Working Group

Few states could accept the Declaration prepared by the first working group without change, and the core concern, as always, was the right of indigenous peoples to self-determination and the absence of a reference to territorial integrity.

During the first two sessions of the working group, Australia, as it had done so in the 1991 and 1992 sessions of the first working group,[124] gave self-determination in the Declaration a human rights reading.[125] According to Australia, self-determination was not "a static concept" but rather:[126]

> an evolving right which includes equal rights, the continuing right of peoples to decide how they should be governed, the right of people as individuals to participate fully in the political process (particularly by way of periodic free and fair elections), and the right of distinct peoples within a state to make decisions on and administer their own affairs.

Australia could accept a reference to self-determination on these terms without a reference to territorial integrity, although it sought a reference

on an equal footing in the Working Group on the Draft Declaration. They would be given the floor in turn, and the position of the state and indigenous representatives would carry equal weight" at 86).

[123] *See* Jackson, *supra* note 6 ("The specific catalyst was a rejection by states of an earlier joint resolution tabled before the Working Group that the text was a minimum set of standards which should not be amended. The resolution included article three, and the continued attempts by States to seek substantive amendment or rejection was seen as yet another attempt by them to consign us to a subordinate status," at 28).

[124] *See* "Australia, Speaking Notes on Self-Determination" (1991) doCip Doc. 200175_2 (on file with author); *see also* "Statement by Colin Milner on Behalf of Australian Delegation" (1992) doCip Doc.960255_3 and 960255_4 (on file with author) ("Australia is sympathetic to a reference to self-determination in the draft Declaration" at 960255_4).

[125] *See Information Received from Governments: Australia*, UNESCOR, U.N. Doc. E/CN.4/WG.15/2/Add.2 (1995).

[126] *Id.* at 4.

to the 1970 Declaration on Friendly Relations (which included a reference to territorial integrity but also indicated a right to secession due to abuse of fundamental human rights).[127] However, with the election of the Howard Liberal government in 1996, Australia's position on the right to self-determination changed dramatically. At the 1998 working group session, Australia proposed that self-determination be replaced with "self-management" or "self-empowerment."[128]

New Zealand, Canada, and the United States were not opposed "in principle" to self-determination in the Declaration, provided it was clear that self-determination was to only operate within states and that it would be exercised in a manner that was broadly consistent with current law and policy.[129] The United States drew a distinction between "human rights" and "aspirations" in the Declaration—the latter appeared to be directed at the self-determination framework.[130] The United States argued that such aspirations ought not to be cast as human rights. "Rather the term 'rights' should be reserved for those duties that governments owe their people, the breach of which generally gives rise to a legally enforceable remedy."[131] The United States sought to merge Articles 3 (self-determination) and 31 (self-government) in order to clarify that indigenous peoples have the right of "internal self-determination."[132] Article 3 now stated: "By virtue of that right [to self-determination], they may negotiate their political status within the framework of the nation state . . . ."[133] This was consistent with the United States' long-standing domestic policy of recognition of aboriginal self-government.

[127] *Id.* at 5.

[128] *See* "Australia" (1998) doCip Doc. 131_as01 (on file with author) ("Self-determination has no settled meaning, and for many, it implies the establishment of separate nations or separate laws. Australia considers this interpretation inappropriate to its situation and is thus unable to accept inclusion of the term. Our view is that it would be more productive for the Working Group to look at the use of alternative language in the Declaration which would more accurately express the principle of indigenous peoples having greater opportunities to exercise meaningful control over their affairs" at 131_as12).

[129] *See* "New Zealand" (1998) doCip Doc. 030_as01 (on file with author) (Among the CANZUS states, New Zealand was most explicit about this point: "Subject to any draft Declaration being consistent with domestic understanding of the relationship between Māori and the Crown . . . and respecting the territorial integrity of democratic states and their constitutional frameworks where these meet current international human rights standards, New Zealand could accept the inclusion in the Declaration of a right to self-determination for indigenous peoples" at 030_as02).

[130] *See Information Received from Governments: United States*, UNESCOR, U.N. Doc. E/CN.4/WG.15/2/Add.1 (1995) (noting a distinction between "rights" in the Declaration and references to "rights" which do not currently exist under international law. "It should not be necessary to convert aspirations or objectives into 'rights' in order to call attention to them" at 7).

[131] *Id.*

[132] *See* "United States" (2004) doCip Doc. 194_as01 (on file with author) (Proposing a merger of Article 3 and Article 4: "indigenous peoples have the right of internal self-determination. By virtue of that right, they may negotiate their political status within the framework of the nation-state and are free to pursue their economic, social and cultural development. Indigenous peoples in exercising their right of internal self-determination, have the internal right to autonomy or self-government in matters relating to their local affairs . . ." at 194_as01).

[133] *Id.*

New Zealand adopted the stance that self-determination "must be elaborated clearly in a way which, as a minimum, preserves and recognizes the territorial integrity of States and their constitutional frameworks."[134] New Zealand also objected to the notion of indigenous political autonomy. As the New Zealand Minister of Justice in 1999 explained:

> . . . the terms "autonomy" and "self-government" as used in the draft Declaration seem to suggest forms of responsibility which go beyond what the New Zealand government has indicated it is willing to consider. These terms are normally associated with indigenous people living on reservations and not integrated into the wider community.[135]

Māori were said to be "fully-integrated,"[136] and New Zealand would only commit to exploring ways in which Māori can exercise greater control over their own affairs within the national legal and constitutional system.[137]

Canada could accept a reference to self-determination, provided it was clear that this related to arrangements for self-government to be implemented flexibly through negotiations between governments and indigenous peoples.[138] Canada had, in 1995, released its policy on recognition of aboriginal peoples' inherent self-government through negotiations with the state.[139] If there was a right to external self-determination, for Canada, Australia, and New Zealand, this seemed to be premised on the gross and sustained violation of the human rights of indigenous peoples.[140]

134 "New Zealand" (1997) doCip Doc. 11_as02 (on file with author). *See also* New Zealand (1998) doCip Doc. 030_as02 (on file with author).

135 Douglas Graham, *The New Government's Policy*, in RECOGNISING THE RIGHTS OF INDIGENOUS PEOPLES—MINISTRY OF SOCIAL DEVELOPMENT (Alison Quentin-Baxter ed., 1999).

136 *Id.* at 10.

137 *Id.*

138 "Canada" (1996) doCip Doc. 228_as01 (on file with author) ("Canada accepts a right of self-determination for indigenous peoples which respects the political, constitutional and territorial integrity of democratic states. In that context, exercise of the right involves negotiations between states and the various indigenous peoples within those states to determine the political status of the indigenous peoples involved . . . the right of self-determination is intended to promote harmonious arrangements between states and indigenous peoples. Exercise of the right must therefore involve negotiations between the state and indigenous peoples" at 228_as22).

139 INDIGENOUS AND NORTHERN AFFAIRS CANADA, THE GOVERNMENT OF CANADA'S APPROACH TO IMPLEMENTATION OF THE INHERENT RIGHT AND THE NEGOTIATION OF ABORIGINAL SELF-GOVERNMENT (1995).

140 *See* "Canada" (1996) doCip Doc. 228_as21 (on file with author); *see also Information Received from Governments: Australia*, *supra* note 23; "New Zealand" (1998) doCip Doc. 030_as01 (on file with author) ("New Zealand considers that, consistent with an emerging usage at international law, any right to self-determination included in the Declaration shall not be construed as authorizing or encouraging any action which would dismember or impair, totally or in part, the territorial integrity or political unity of sovereign and independent states, possessed of a government representative to the whole people belonging to the territory, without distinction as to race, creed, or colour" at 030_as02).

The CANZUS states' position on land and resources, treaties, and informed consent continued to reflect positions made in the first working group. CANZUS states expressed concern regarding the right of indigenous peoples to own land "traditionally occupied" with states calling for the right to relate to the land they occupy in the present. Rectification for loss of lands was acceptable, though most opposed the use of the word "restitution" and called for measures of "redress."[141] The right to enforce treaties was acceptable to many; however, CANZUS states called for the issues of redress and implementation to be addressed within domestic states.[142] CANZUS continued to oppose the right of indigenous peoples to free, prior, and informed consent (FPIC) on any legislative or administrative measures, which may affect them, preferring a right to consultation.

The CANZUS states adopted a fairly consistent common position on collective indigenous rights. They were not opposed "in principle" to collective rights but rather sought to make amendments to clarify that these collective rights could not trump individual human rights; or that collective rights should be interpreted consistently with other human rights instruments; or to designate certain group rights as special measures designed to address indigenous disadvantages.[143] CANZUS states also suggested that certain indigenous rights to land and self-governance should accommodate third-party interests. This can be contrasted with other states that expressly opposed collective human rights. Japan argued that collective rights were fundamentally inconsistent with human rights, preferring a basic human rights or minority rights model.[144] In this respect, Japan was joined by France,[145] Argentina,[146] and, toward the end of the Declaration negotiations, the United Kingdom.[147]

[141] "United States" (1996) doCip Doc. 231_as01 (on file with author) (commenting on Article 27, relating to historical rectification for land loss, the United States doubts: "whether restitution is a viable means for resolving such issues in most states. For this reason, we believe that the Declaration should call on states to consider the possibility of negotiated settlements, including restitution, as appropriate" at 231_as08).

[142] *See, e.g.*, "General Statement by Leslie A. Gerson, Deputy Assistant Secretary of State, United States Department of State" (1998) doCip Doc. 021_as04 (on file with author).

[143] *Id.*

[144] *See Information Received from Governments: Japan,* UNESCOR, 1995, UN Doc E/CN.4/WG.15/2/Add.1 ("'Collective rights' stipulated in this declaration . . . cannot be found in international instruments drafted and adopted by the UN in the past . . . Introducing a new category of rights would be overstepping the mandates of the Commission of Human Rights by broadening the scope of the rights claimed" at 2).

[145] "France" (1997) doCip Doc. 15 (on file with author).

[146] *Information Received from Governments: Argentina*, UNESCOR, U.N. Doc. E/CN.4/WG.15/2, at 3 (1995) (Argentina opposed collective rights as detrimental to the enjoyment of individual rights, but nevertheless recognized the collective holding of land rights).

[147] "United Kingdom" (2004) doCip Doc. 197_as01 (on file with author) ("The United Kingdom recognizes that the governments of many states with indigenous populations have granted them various collective rights at the national level in their constitutions, national laws and agreements. The

The United States also consistently opposed the notion of collective human rights[148] and would eventually support the United Kingdom's view that all collective rights in the Declaration were *sui generis* rights, not human rights.

State positions in Latin America varied throughout the negotiations, but broadly there was support for an approach akin to the human rights model in the ILO Convention No. 169. As Chile noted:[149]

> the work of putting the final touches to the text proposed by the Sub-Commission should be guided by the objective of making it as compatible as possible with International Labour Organization Convention No. 169 concerning Indigenous and Tribal Peoples in independent countries, adopted in 1989.

Although some Latin American states, in the early years of the working group, were highly critical of the Declaration, albeit without much specification, Colombia,[150] Bolivia,[151] Guatemala,[152] Mexico, and Ecuador[153] remained

United Kingdom has no objection to this welcome fact being reflected in the Declaration. But it is important that these rights bestowed nationally remain distinct from individual human rights, enjoyed by indigenous people and all others, which are founded in international law and which provide protection to the individual" at 197_as02).

[148] *See Information Received from Governments: United States, supra* note 130 ("[I]nternational law, with few exceptions, protects and promotes the rights of individuals, as opposed to groups" at 7); *see also* "General Statement by Leslie A. Gerson, Deputy Assistant Secretary of State, United States Department of State," *supra* note 51 (Suggesting the working group "follow the approach taken by the Declaration on the rights of persons belonging to National or Ethnic Religious and Linguistic Minorities, which refers throughout to 'persons belonging to minorities . . .' " at 021_as04 and doCip Doc. 021_as05).

[149] *Information Received from Governments: Chile*, UNESCOR, U.N. Doc. E/CN.4/WG.15/2, at 6 (1995).

[150] Colombia supported self-determination viewing it as recognition of a right to political autonomy, *see* "Colombia" (1997) doCip Doc. 005_es01 (on file with author) ("El gobierno de Colombia considera que en la libre determinación de los pueblos indígenas, entendida como esta autonomía interna, se encierra el pleno ejercicio de sus derechos colectivos fundamentales, y la base de su supervivencia étnica" at 005_es01).

[151] According to Bolivia, self-determination in the Declaration did not allow for secession but rather recognized indigenous peoples right to practice their traditions, culture, languages, religion, education, and self-government, *see* "Bolivia" (1997) doCip Doc. 004_es01 (on file with author) ("Mi delegación considera que la libre-determinación de los pueblos indígenas no constituye una secesión, sino el reconocimiento a los pueblos indígenas a practicar libremente sus tradiciones milenarias, se cultura, sus lenguas, su religión, la educación, a practicar libremente el autogobierno como lo practicaron desde siglos" at 004_es01).

[152] According to Guatemala, self-determination had to be exercised within the borders of the united and indivisible state, *see* "Guatemala" (1997) doCip Doc. 004_es01 (on file with author) ("[M]i delegación es la opinión que el articulo 3 de este Proyecto de Declaración debería considerar la libre determinación de los pueblos indígenas dentro del marco de la unidad de la nación y de la indivisibilidad del Estado" at 004_es01).

[153] "Ecuador" (1997) doCip Doc. 004_es01 (on file with author) (supports the adoption of the Draft Declaration in its present form).

highly supportive of the Declaration. However, they all insisted that self-determination was to be exercised within the state. Mexico sought express language that would clarify the scope of self-determination. Later Mexico, Peru, and Guatemala would support the call for no-change to the Sub-Commission text, at least until some change seemed inevitable.[154] However, Argentina opposed any reference to the "right of self-determination"[155] or the term "territories,"[156] while Brazil argued that many of the provisions of the Declaration needed "extensive redrafting" and self-determination was unacceptable.[157] Chile opposed any reference to the unqualified use of "indigenous peoples" and supported the right to "special political representation" but not the right to self-determination or autonomy.[158] Further, while Venezuela supported the "thrust and intent" of Articles 3 (self-determination) and 31 (self-government), it noted that they overlapped and suggested they be merged into one article, to make clear that indigenous peoples have a right to internal self-determination (similar to the United States).[159] Later, these states would soften their critique but express a preference for the human rights model in the ILO Convention 169.

The Nordic states were supportive of most elements of the Sub-Commission text. Denmark accepted Article 3's wording in the Sub-Commission text,[160] although Norway[161] and Sweden[162] sought further

[154] See *Information Received from Governments: Mexico*, UNESCOR, 1995, U.N. Doc. E/CN.4/WG.15/2/Add.1 (1995) (Mexico expressed concerns about self-determination noting "it might be understood, for the purposes of international law, in the same way as in the first Articles of the [International Covenants]. Mexico therefore sought further wording to 'clarify the scope of [Article 3]' or language that confined Article 3 to a right to 'pursue their development'" at 3).

[155] *Information Received from Governments: Argentina*, UNESCOR, U.N. Doc. E/CN.4/WG.15/2 (1995) ("The Argentine Government does not consider the wording of [Article 3] acceptable, nor does it consider acceptable the other implicit references to the 'right to self-determination' elsewhere in the draft" at 3). Argentina thus sought a reference to territorial integrity in the Declaration's preamble and in the text of the Declaration itself. (*Id.*).

[156] "Argentina" (1995) doCip Doc. 008_A01 (on file with author) ("... use of the term 'territories' in several passages of the draft ... is not considered acceptable, as it is applicable exclusively to States ..." at 008_A03).

[157] "Brazil" (1996) doCip Doc. 27 (on file with author).

[158] *Information Received from Governments: Chile, supra* note 149, at 7.

[159] *Information Received from Governments: Venezuela*, UNESCOR, U.N. Doc. E/CN.4/WG.15/2 (1995).

[160] "Denmark" (1997) doCip Doc. 012_as01 (on file with author). (However, Denmark noted that the right to self-determination was to be "exercised 'within' the framework of the States in which they live" at 012_as01.)

[161] "Norway" (1998) doCip Doc. 138_as02 (on file with author) (Questioning "whether it might clarify the issue [of self-determination] to group Article 3 together with related Articles like Articles 31, 19, 20 and 21 and 30 which elaborate on how self-determination can be exercised in different forms" and noting "We do ... support the principle that indigenous peoples have the right to self-determination in accordance with the principles of international law" at 138_as02).

[162] "Sweden" (1998) doCip Doc. 037_as01 (on file with author) ("[Sweden] would like to see the right to self-determination clearly defined within the Declaration itself" at 037_as01).

clarification—with Sweden at one point suggesting that the right to self-determination be clearly defined within the Declaration itself—and Finland preferred an express reference to either internal self-determination or territorial integrity.[163]

Asian states continued to seek a definition of "indigenous peoples" in order to clarify that the Declaration did not apply to Asia. In the working group, they were joined by Ukraine, given the participation of Tartar advocates in the working group sessions in increasing numbers.[164] China, India, and Bangladesh were most persistent.[165] However, from 1998, Asian states would cease their call for a definition of "indigenous peoples," given that it seemed increasingly unlikely due to the strong opposition from both Southern and Northern indigenous peoples. Furthermore, the United States criticized Asian states for attempting to avoid obligations to protect indigenous peoples in their states.[166] Asian states' strategy instead was—as Northern indigenous advocates had feared—to call for qualification of the right to self-determination. Later, once the Declaration was adopted by the UN General Assembly, almost all Asian states would simply deny indigenous peoples existed in their states.

3.3 Path to the UN General Assembly

Five years into negotiations, indigenous peoples and states were deadlocked. States sought changes and the no-change camp held firm to their position.

163 "Finland" (1997) doCip Doc. 014_as02 (on file with author).

164 *Information Received from Governments: Ukraine*, UNESCOR, U.N. Doc. E/CN.4/WG.15/2 (1995) (on file with author) ("First and foremost, the meaning of indigenous peoples and indigenous community or nation . . . is open to question. As no definition of such concepts is to be found in Ukrainian law, a section providing an interpretation of these terms should be included in the draft Declaration" at 11).

165 *See* "Statement by the Chinese Delegation" (1995) doCip Doc. 032_AS01 (on file with author); *see* "Statement by the Indian Delegation" (1995) doCip Doc. 035_AS01 (on file with author) ("My delegation would like to suggest that we should first of all work on the definition [of indigenous peoples]" at 035_AS02); *see* "Statement by the Bangladesh Delegation" (1995) doCip Doc. 036_AS01 (on file with author) ("As it stands, the draft does not sufficiently respond to the question of whether a given group is indigenous peoples or not . . ." at 036_AS01); *see also Information Received from Governments: Japan, supra* note 144 ("It cannot be sufficiently meaningful to draft this Declaration without clearly defining the term "indigenous populations").

166 Compare "General Statement by Leslie A. Gerson, Deputy Assistant Secretary of State, United States Department of State," *supra* note 51 (the United States expressing concern "by statements from regional groups that have suggested the need for a definition of the indigenous groups which would exclude their own groups of indigenous people. Such insistence on a narrow definition would in our view de-rail the process altogether. In this regard we do not believe that the focus of the Declaration should be the privileging of historically prior inhabitants").

However, some indigenous advocates recognized the need for compromise if the Declaration was to have any chance of reaching the UN General Assembly.

The focus on self-determination by Northern indigenous peoples was viewed as extravagant and self-indulgent by some Asian indigenous advocates, given the denial of basic human rights in their home states. As Suhas Chakma, director of the Asian Centre for Human Rights, observed:[167]

> Unfortunately, the Draft Declaration on the Rights of Indigenous Peoples is viewed more in the context of historical injustices rather than preventing recurrence of similar injustices and the need to promote and protect the rights of Indigenous Peoples to preserve their distinctiveness. There will be no progress in the Working Group on the Draft Declaration so long as some radical indigenous representatives construe the right of self-determination in the Draft Declaration as a license to restore sovereignty of their nations, Chairman/Rapporteur provides more importance to these representatives at the cost of the silent majority and some governmental representatives including the only super power, the United States construe these statements as a threat to their territorial integrity. The Working Group on the Draft Declaration is full of "UN made revolutionary" indigenous representatives and ultra-conservative governmental representatives.

The first indication that there might be a split within the indigenous caucus on the no-change position was in the year 2000, at the sixth working group session. At that point, the working group had adopted only two articles, Articles 5 and 43. These articles were not considered controversial as they related to the rights of indigenous individuals. The proposal to consider changes came from outside of the North,[168] led by the Saami Council, Inuit Circumpolar Conference (representing Inuit communities of Alaska, Canada, Greenland, and Russia), Asian indigenous organizations, and

[167] *See* Chakma, *supra* note 7; *see also* Asian and Indigenous Tribal Network, *Written Statement Submitted by the AITPN: The Damp Squib of the International Decade: Adoption of the Draft Declaration on the Rights of Indigenous Peoples*, UN Commission on Human Rights, 60th Sess., U.N. Doc. E/CN.4/2004/NGO/138 (2004) ("It is a delusion to think that Indigenous Peoples cause is advanced by sticking to present stalemate situation. Unless something drastic happens, after the deluge of the International Decade, the WGDD will end up being a damp squib").

[168] *See, generally*, John B. Henriksen, *The UN Declaration on the Rights of Indigenous Peoples: Some Key Issues and Events in the Process*, *in* Making the Declaration Work: The United Nations Declaration on the Rights of Indigenous Peoples 82 (Claire Charters & Rodolfo Stavenhagen eds., 2009).

IWGIA.[169] The Saami Council had always adopted a more pragmatic human rights approach toward indigenous rights. When ILO Convention 169 was drafted, many Northern indigenous advocates opposed it because it failed to adopt the self-determination framework; however, the Saami Council supported it and requested that the Nordic states ratify it.[170]

The North–South divide quickly became a contest between the no-change advocates led by the Treaty Council and the change advocates led by the Saami Council and Asian indigenous advocates and IWGIA. The Inuit Circumpolar Conference and the Nordic Saami Council delivered a joint statement at the sixth session, indicating a willingness to consider changes to the Declaration:[171]

> . . . if such amendments strengthened and/or clarified the text, respected principles of equality and non-discrimination and were in conformity with international legal standards, including the right to self-determination and also otherwise respected the rights of Indigenous Peoples.

This move signaled that there might be acceptance of a qualified right to self-determination through the inclusion of a reference to territorial integrity. The joint statement was met with strong objections from indigenous advocates of the North led by the Treaty Council. Mattais Ahrén notes how the "Inuit Circumpolar Conference and the Saami Council were literally attacked by adherents of the no-change position, who accused the organizations of being sell-outs" and "not truly indigenous."[172]

The division between the change and no-change camps meant the global indigenous caucus was no longer able to operate effectively. Pro-change

[169] The Inuit Circumpolar Conference represented Inuit communities of Alaska, Canada, Greenland, and Russia and had long-standing ties with the Saami Council. R.G. Williamson, *International Combinations, Present and Possible, Between Circumpolar Inuit National Groups: Politics, Problems and Potentials*, 55 Nordic J. Int. Law 68, 70 (1986).

[170] "Statement by Nordic Saami Council" (1989) doCip Doc. 211072_1 ("We share the opinion expressed by some other indigenous NGOs that the adoption of this convention has to be considered as a step forward in the general efforts of developing more positive and adequate universal standards on the rights of indigenous peoples and our member organizations are most likely to recommend the Nordic government to ratify the ILO Convention 169 as soon as possible" at 211072_1).

[171] *Id.*

[172] Ahrén, *supra* note 122, at 88; *see also* Henriksen, *supra* note 168 ("This created severe problems within the Indigenous caucus, and [the ICC and Saami Council] were branded as deserters by many other indigenous organisations. However, other indigenous organizations gradually joined this position when they, too, realized that to hold on to the strict no-change position was infeasible. The no-change group in the caucus began to lose ground" at 82).

indigenous advocates frustrated with their inability to discuss changes to the text in the caucus meetings proposed that it be split into regional caucuses representing the seven UN regions, that is, Africa, the Arctic, Asia, Latin America, North America, the Russia Federation/Eastern Europe, and the Pacific. According to Ahrén, "this would prove imperative, since the small number of indigenous representatives adhering to the no-change position could no longer hold the caucus hostage by blocking discussions on proposed amendments to the Sub-Commission text."[173] The momentum for change was significantly assisted by a workshop hosted by IWGIA in Copenhagen in May 2003, attended by the American Indian Law Alliance, the Inuit Circumpolar Conference, the Saami Council, the Tebtebba Foundation, and IWGIA. According to the Saami advocate Mattais Ahrén, it was here that "key indigenous organizations 'officially' decided to break with the no-change position" and create "an informal core group of relatively like-minded indigenous representatives that would from then on convene, network, consult and strategize on the Declaration process."[174]For the remaining working group sessions, indigenous advocates would operate predominantly through the regional caucuses.[175] The split had the effect of isolating the hard-line no-change activists of the North and the decolonization model.

States sensed an opportunity for advancement. Norway in the 2002 working group proposed a reference to territorial integrity in one of the Declaration's preambular paragraphs—a suggestion praised by some pro-change advocates like the Saami.[176] Moreover, in the 2004 working group session, the Nordic states, together with New Zealand and Switzerland, introduced for the first time a complete new version of the Declaration—known as "CRP 1"—building on Norway's earlier proposal.[177] This version also contained a reference to territorial integrity in the preambular paragraphs. The Saami Council took the lead in supporting the discussion of the CRP 1 text.[178] At the same session, the Saami Council, the Saami Parliamentary Council, and Asian indigenous organization, Tebtebba, presented a new

[173] Ahrén, *supra* note 122, at 96.
[174] Ahrén, *supra* note 122.
[175] *Id.* at 95.
[176] *Id.* at 89–90.
[177] *Id.* at 93–94.
[178] Les Malezer, *Dreamtime Discovery: New Reality and Hope*, *in* Realizing the UN Declaration on the Rights of Indigenous Peoples: Triumph, Hope, and Action 32 (Paul Joffe, Jackie Hartley, & Jennifer Preston eds., 2010).

and complete draft text of the Declaration,[179] which contained a reference to territorial integrity in a preambular paragraph.[180] According to Ahrén, this "encouraged indigenous organizations to become even more active in the constructive negotiations on specific language, not only as respondents to state proposals, but also by taking control over the process by submitting concrete language of their own."[181]

Even within the North, there were indigenous advocates prepared to shift from the hard-line no-change position. They preferred a reference to self-determination without any reference to territorial integrity but were also prepared to accept the need to compromise for the sake of moving out of the deadlock. Many Northern indigenous advocates began to talk about self-determination's connection with human rights, consistent with the human rights model. The inclusion of a reference to territorial integrity in the Declaration would not be inconsistent with the human rights model in that it accepted that self-determination for indigenous peoples would be exercised within the state (though there would be the option of secession for gross abuse of human rights).[182] The decolonization model had achieved the hard work of getting self-determination into the Sub-Commission text. Now, tactically for many Northern indigenous advocates, it made sense to place greater emphasis on human rights.

Despite this shift among indigenous advocates of the North, the Treaty Council and other Northern indigenous advocates stuck to the principle of no-change to the Sub-Commission text. At the 2004 working group session, the Treaty Council, Sioux Nation Treaty Council, and other no-change advocates initiated a hunger strike/prayer fast and occupied the back of the meeting room. They asked for the Declaration to be:[183]

> sent back to the UN Commission of Human Rights with the message that, in 10 years, proposals by States to weaken or amend the text have not gained the consensus of the Working Group effective participants, which includes both States and Indigenous Peoples.

[179] Ahrén, *supra* note 122, at 96.
[180] *Id.*
[181] *Id.*
[182] *Id.*
[183] "Hunger Strike by Indigenous Peoples Representatives at the UN" (2004) doCip Doc. 126_a01 (on file with author) ("We will not allow our rights to be negotiated, compromised or diminished in this UN process").

According to Charmaine White Face, representative of the Sioux Nation Treaty Council and one of the no-change advocates, the fast ended after six days when an agreement was secured from UN officials that if there was no consensus on the Declaration by the end of the 2004 session, the original version of the Declaration would be presented to the UN Commission of Human Rights for approval.[184]

3.4 The Chair's Text and UN Human Rights Council Vote

At the end of the 2004 session, there continued to be no agreement on self-determination. An extra session was secured from the Commission on Human Rights for 2005, but by the end of this final working group session, there was still a lack of consensus on the core issues related to the self-determination framework. At the conclusion of the meeting, the working group Chair, Luis Enrique Chavez, announced that he would prepare a "compromise text" for submission to the UN Commission on Human Rights, based on proposals he had earlier circulated in the working group together with proposals submitted by states and indigenous representatives.[185]

The Treaty Council was strongly opposed to this move.[186] Others accepted that this was the realistic option. According to Ahrén, "The majority of the participants—state and indigenous delegations alike—agreed . . . that the Working Group had come as far as it possibly could."[187]

The text produced by the Chair, called the Chair's text, resulted in some watering down of the self-determination framework in the Sub-Commission text but most significantly, Article 3's right to self-determination was untouched with no reference to territorial integrity.[188] Article 31 on self-government was moved up to become new Article 4, indicating that self-determination would ordinarily be exercised through self-government. The right to "restitution" was now a right to "redress," which met the state

[184] Charmaine W. Face, Indigenous Nations' Rights in the Balance: An Analysis of the Declaration on the Rights of Indigenous Peoples 2 (1st ed. 2013).

[185] *Report of the Working Group Established in Accordance with Commission on Human Rights Resolution 1995/32 of 3 March 1995 on Its Eleventh session*, UN Commission on Human Rights, 62nd Sess., U.N. Doc. E/CN.4/2006/79, paras. 28–30 (2006) [hereinafter *The Eleventh Working Group Report*].

[186] International Indian Treaty Council, *Written Intervention by the International Indian Treaty Council*, UN Commission on Human Rights, 62nd Sess., U.N. Doc. E/CN.4/2006/ (2006).

[187] Ahrén, *supra* note 122, at 104.

[188] *The Eleventh Working Group Report*, *supra* note 185, at Annex.

demands for more flexibility while still leaving open the possibility of restitution.[189] The right to FPIC was retained, although the Chair's text now provided that consultation must be carried out "in order to" obtain consent, which seemed to weaken it.[190] The rights in the Declaration were generally expressed as collective rights.

Under Article 46, the Chair's text introduced a limitation clause on the exercise of the rights contained in the Declaration. Limitations would be permitted where they[191]

> are determined by law and in accordance with international human rights obligations. Any such limitations shall be non-discriminatory and strictly necessary solely for the purpose of securing due recognition and respect for the rights and freedoms of others and for meeting the just and most compelling requirements of a democratic society.

Article 46 also provided that the provisions of the Declaration "shall be interpreted in accordance with the principles of justice, democracy, respect for human rights, equality, non-discrimination, good governance and good faith." With respect to treaties, whereas the Sub-Commission text spoke of conflicts being "submitted to competent international bodies," the new Article 36 only referred to the "indigenous right to recognition . . . and to have States honour and respect such Treaties"—which indicated a domestic remedy.[192]

Many indigenous representatives accepted the Chair's text.[193] At the May 2006 session of the UN Permanent Forum on Indigenous Issues, a joint statement signed by over one hundred indigenous organizations and their supporters called for the Declaration's immediate adoption by the newly established UN Human Rights Council at its upcoming inaugural meeting.[194] While the Chair's text could be improved in certain key areas, the statement

[189] *Id.* art. 27.

[190] *Id.* art. 30. (However, Article 10 asserted that there could be no relocation of indigenous peoples without FPIC.)

[191] *Id.* art. 46.

[192] *Id.* art. 36.

[193] Malezer, *supra* note 178, at 33; Deer, *supra* note 122 ("We were not happy with every aspect of this final text, but it was a compromise. The revised text kept intact the provisions relating to self-determination; our rights to lands and resources; our collective rights; FPIC; and treaties. These were the major provisions we wanted affirmed" at 23).

[194] *The Draft UN Declaration on the Rights of Indigenous People and Millennium Development Goals: Importance of a Human Rights-Based Approach*, UN Permanent Forum on Indigenous Issues, 5th Sess., 2006.

noted that additional meetings would not be useful and could in fact be a setback.

In June 2006, the Human Rights Council met to vote on the Declaration. Before the meeting, a statement issued by proponents of the no-change position was circulated requesting that the Council not consider the Declaration and seeking more meetings to facilitate discussion concerning the Declaration. According to Ahrén, indigenous advocates worked quickly to consult among their regions and supportive states to make clear that this stance was now a marginal position within the international indigenous movement. The Council voted to support the Declaration with only Canada and Russia voting against it.[195]

3.5 The Third Committee of the UN General Assembly

After adoption of the Declaration by the Human Rights Council, it was directed to the Third Committee of the UN General Assembly, which focuses on social, humanitarian, and cultural issues. At the Third Committee session on October 16, 2006, the group of states sponsoring the Declaration (the Sponsor States)—led by Peru, Mexico, and Guatemala—sought to introduce a resolution recommending that the Declaration be referred to the UN General Assembly for adoption at its next session. However, Namibia on behalf of the African Group of States presented a "non-action resolution," which called for a vote on the Declaration to be deferred.[196]

The African Group of States had serious concerns about the Declaration, as set out in a five-page paper entitled, "Draft Aide Memoire African Group"

[195] *Summary Record of the 21st Meeting*, UNHRCOR, 1st Sess., U.N. Doc. A/HRC/1/SR.21 (2006) (adopted June 29, 2006; Azerbaijan, Brazil, Cameroon, China, Cuba, Czech Republic, Ecuador, Finland, France, Germany, Guatemala, India, Indonesia, Japan, Malaysia, Mauritius, Mexico, the Netherlands, Pakistan, Peru, Poland, Republic of Korea, Romania, Saudi Arabia, South Africa, Sri Lanka, Switzerland, United Kingdom of Great Britain and Northern Ireland, Uruguay, Zambia voted in favor; Canada and Russian Federation voted against; and Algeria, Argentina, Bahrain, Bangladesh, Ghana, Jordan, Morocco, Nigeria, the Philippines, Senegal, Tunisia, and Ukraine abstained.).

[196] On the African Group's opposition to the Declaration, and the African movements response specifically, *see* Albert Barume, *Responding to the Concerns of the African States*, *in* MAKING THE DECLARATION WORK: THE UNITED NATIONS DECLARATION ON THE RIGHTS OF INDIGENOUS PEOPLES 170 (Claire Charters & Rodolfo Stavenhagen eds., 2009); *see also* Naomi Kipura, *The UN Declaration on the Rights of Indigenous Peoples in the African Context*, *in* MAKING THE DECLARATION WORK: THE UNITED NATIONS DECLARATION ON THE RIGHTS OF INDIGENOUS PEOPLES 252 (Claire Charters & Rodolfo Stavenhagen eds., 2009).

(Aide Memoire).[197] According to the Aide Memoire, Africa was said to be "still recovering from the effects of ethnic based conflicts"[198] and the absence of a definition in the Declaration would "create tensions amongst ethnic groups and instability within sovereign States."[199] The right to self-determination was said to only apply to "nations trying to free themselves from the yoke of colonialism."[200] Therefore, reference to self-determination in the Declaration could be: "misrepresented as conferring a unilateral right of self-determination and possible secession upon a specific subset of the national populace, thus threatening the political unity and the territorial integrity of any country."[201] The Aide Memoire also expressed concern at the right to FPIC, which "can be interpreted to confer upon a sub-national group a power of veto over the laws of a democratic legislature."[202] The recognition of land rights and treaties was said to conflict with the constitutional provisions of African states.[203] According to indigenous advocates, this move by Africa was due to the lobbying of the CANZUS states frustrated at their inability to make fundamental changes to the Declaration before its advancement to the Third Committee.[204]

New Zealand, Australia, and the United States also voiced their criticism in the Third Committee of the Declaration.[205] New Zealand was particularly critical of the Declaration's reference to self-determination, which it said "could be misrepresented as conferring a unilateral right of self-determination and possible secession upon a specific subset of the national populace."[206] Further:[207]

[197] *See* African Group, *Draft Aide Memoire: African Group, UN Declaration on the Rights of Indigenous Peoples* (New York, Nov. 9, 2006) at para. 2.2, <http://cendoc.docip.org/collect/cendocdo/index/assoc/HASH0110/1b549795.dir/draft_africangroup.pdf> [hereinafter Draft Aide Memoire].

[198] *Id.*

[199] *Id.*

[200] *Id.*

[201] *Id.* at para. 3.0.

[202] *Id.* at para. 6.0.

[203] *Id.* at paras. 7.0 and 8.0.

[204] IPACC, *UN Declaration on the Rights of Indigenous Peoples delayed by Africa Group*, IPACC (May 4, 2007) (As reported by IPACC, "according to certain African diplomats, Namibia had not prepared the 'aide memoire'. Rather it had been prepared by a set of industrialized Anglo-Saxon States which strongly oppose the Declaration and the powers of the new Human Rights Council.").

[205] Rosemary Banks, "Address on behalf of Australia, New Zealand and the United States" (Statement delivered at the 61st Session of the United Nations General Assembly, Oct. 16, 2006), <https://web.archive.org/web/20131108103333/http://mfat.govt.nz/Media-and-publications/Media/MFAT-speeches/2006/0-16-October-2006b.php>.

[206] *Id.*

[207] *Id.*

> [t]he lack of definition or scope of application within the Chair's text means that separatist or minority groups, with traditional connections to the territory where they live—in all regions of the globe—could seek to exploit this Declaration to claim the right to self-determination, including exclusive control of their territorial resources.

The land rights were said to "ignore the contemporary realities in many countries with indigenous populations"[208] by threatening rights to lands now "lawfully owned by other citizens,"[209] and the redress provisions were simply "unworkable and contradictory."[210] The Declaration also undermined the universality of human rights and was discriminatory by providing "human rights that are denied to other groups within the same nation-state."[211]

The African Group resolution to defer a vote on the Declaration was adopted by the Third Committee and so the Declaration would not be considered by the General Assembly until the September session in 2007.[212] Indigenous activists immediately denounced the Third Committee's decision and were highly critical of the African Group's position. In a press statement entitled "Africans deny Inuit and Saami Human Rights," the Saami Council and Inuit Circumpolar Conference expressed their outrage, noting that the African states were not acting alone in this mission but "were aided and abetted by the deceitful work of Canada, Australia, New Zealand and the United States."[213] IWGIA,[214] Amnesty International, and other human rights NGOs also were highly critical of the African Group.[215] On December 13, only a month after the Third Committee vote, a Botswana court ruled that the Kalahari were not to be displaced from their ancestral lands in the Central Kalahari Game Reserve. IWGIA immediately issued a press release

[208] *Id.*

[209] *Id.*

[210] *Id.*

[211] *Id.*

[212] *Working Group of the Commission on Human Rights to Elaborate a Draft Declaration in Accordance with Paragraph 5 of General Assembly Resolution 49/214 of 23 December 1994*, UN Commission on Human Rights, 61st Sess., U.N. Doc. A/C.3/61/L.18/Rev.1 (2006).

[213] Inuit Circumpolar Council and Saami Council (Artic Caucus), Press Release, "Africans Deny Inuit and Saami Human Rights" (Nov. 28, 2006).

[214] IWGIA, Press Statement, "IWGIA's Statement: UN General Assembly Fails to Bring Hope to World's Indigenous Peoples" (Nov. 30, 2006), <http://www.iwgia.org/iwgia_files_publications_files/IA_4-06_Statement1.pdf>.

[215] IWGIA, Public Statement, "UN Declaration on the Rights of Indigenous Peoples: Human Rights Organizations Condemn Efforts to Block Vital Human Rights Instrument" (Nov. 30, 2006), < http://olddoc.ishr.ch/hrm/archive/CHRWG/WGDDIP/AI_CanadaQuakers_30Nov.pdf>.

noting its expectation that the ruling will "encourage African governments to endorse the UN Declaration on the Rights of Indigenous Peoples."[216]

The prospect of further negotiations presented a major challenge for indigenous advocates. A "global indigenous peoples' caucus steering committee," representing the seven indigenous regions that had emerged during the working group meetings, was established in New York to address the General Assembly politics.[217] Although the split between the change and no-change advocates in the working group sessions had led to the end of the global caucus meetings, universal agreement remained that all regions needed to work together to address the African states' strong opposition to the Declaration.[218] The indigenous advocate Les Malezer was appointed as the convener of the steering committee.

In the UN offices of Geneva, indigenous advocates knew the state representatives and were experienced in working within the human rights bodies of the UN, including the working group, UN Office of the High Commissioner of Human Rights, and the UN Human Rights Council. Further, Geneva-based state representatives participating in working group negotiations were experts on human rights. But in New York, in the UN General Assembly, the emphasis shifted from human rights to *realpolitik*. State representatives were not well versed in indigenous rights issues. Moreover, there was no formal means for indigenous advocates to engage directly with states—particularly African state representatives and those capable of influencing them.[219] Indigenous advocates had struggled in the past to be involved in key decisions relating to the Declaration, but in the two working groups they had maintained a meaningful key role in negotiations. However, now indigenous activists were working from the margins. They could seek meetings directly with states but from November 2006 onward, negotiations on the Declaration were largely conducted between states—that is, Mexico, Peru, and Guatemala, as the Sponsor States, and African states.

[216] IWGIA, Press Statement, "The High Court Ruling in Botswana Is a Milestone for the Recognition of Indigenous Peoples Rights in Africa" (Dec. 13, 2006), <http://www.iwgia.org/iwgia_files_publications_files/IA_4-06_Statement2.pdf>.

[217] Malezer, *supra* note 178, at 33.

[218] *Id.*

[219] Ahrén, *supra* note 122, at 111 (". . . throughout the Declaration process, indigenous representatives were treated as equal partners. This changed however . . . after the Third Committee's decision to defer deliberations on the Declaration. From then on, the Declaration process was predominantly a state affair.").

The Global Indigenous Caucus issued statements at the May 2007 Permanent Forum on Indigenous Issues meeting aimed at countering the concerns raised by African states in the Aide Memoire.[220] These statements played down self-determination's connection with decolonization and emphasized its connection with human rights.[221] However, it was the African indigenous movement that responded with a strong human rights reading of the Declaration. In the form of a "Response Note" to the Aide Memoire, African indigenous advocates (signed by several African experts on indigenous rights)[222] argued:[223]

> there is no one single indigenous community in Africa that is claiming statehood or threatening its country with secession. On the contrary, these peoples or communities are claiming aspects of the right to self-determination that do not threaten national boundaries, including the right to full participation in national life, the right to local self-government, the right to be consulted and to participate in the making of certain laws and programmes, the right of recognition and appreciation of their traditional structures along with the freedom to enjoy and promote their cultures. These variant aspects of the right to self-determination are different from secessionist demands that threaten the territorial integrity of States.

The implication was that a "strong form of self-determination" was for Northern indigenous peoples not African indigenous peoples. In the African context, the Declaration was about affirmation of human rights and culture.[224] The absence of a definition in the Declaration was addressed by

[220] Les Malezer, "Address by the Chair of the Indigenous Caucus on the UN Declaration on the Rights of Indigenous Peoples" (Statement delivered at the UN Permanent Forum on Indigenous Issues, May 18, 2007), http://cendoc.docip.org/collect/cendocdo/index/assoc/HASH0125/679be446.dir/PF07les140.pdf

[221] *Id.*

[222] IPACC, "Response Note to the Draft Aide Memoire of the African Group on the UN Declaration on the Rights of Indigenous Peoples" (Mar. 21, 2007), <https://www.iwgia.org/en/resources/publications/4016-response-note-to-"the-draft-aide-memoire-of-the-african-group-on-the-un-declaration-on-the-rights-of-indigenous-peoples"-presented-by-an-african-group-of-experts,-21-march-2007.html> (This group was comprised of mostly African human rights activist-lawyers who had participated in the growth of the regional movement.).

[223] *Id.* at para. 3.4.

[224] *Report of the African Commission's Working Group of Experts on Indigenous Populations/Communities* (New Jersey: Transaction Publishers; Banjul, Gambia: ACHPR; Copenhagen: IWGIA, 2005) (The Report also quoted the African Commission's position on self-determination in Africa: "In Africa, the term 'indigenous peoples or communities' is not aimed at protecting the rights of the 'first inhabitants that were invaded by foreigners.' Nor does the concept aim to create a hierarchy among national communities or set aside special rights for certain people. On the contrary, within the African context the term 'indigenous peoples' aims to guarantee equal enjoyment of rights and freedoms to some communities that have been left behind" at 4).

re-emphasizing the concept of African indigenous peoples as those pushed to the margins of social life due to their perceived cultural difference.[225]

With the help of IWGIA, members of the group of African experts traveled to New York to meet with African diplomatic missions to advance their arguments in the Response Note.[226] The African Commission on Human and Peoples Rights produced an advisory opinion asserting, as it had done in its earlier report on indigenous peoples in Africa, that indigenous peoples ought to be understood in terms of human rights and culture.[227]

Despite these lobby efforts, the African Group of States submitted a proposal to the President of the UN General Assembly to substantially revise the Declaration by making over thirty amendments.[228] These called for changes that would remove the self-determination framework from the Declaration and reduce it to an instrument aimed at human rights and minority rights. In relation to self-determination, the words "right to self-determination" were replaced with "right to participate in the political affairs of the State."[229] The proposal contained the "right to define who constitutes indigenous people in their respective countries or regions taking into account its national or regional peculiarities."[230] Each of the rights of concern to the African Group of States—including rights to traditional lands and restitution—was now expressed to be "subject to national laws."[231] The large number and nature of the amendments by the African Group left many skeptical about any chance of ever reaching a consensus between states and indigenous peoples.

A real shift in momentum did not occur until indigenous activists began to accept the reality that there would need to be further changes made to the Declaration to address the principal concerns of the African Group of States. In May 2007, the Sponsor States advised the Global Caucus Steering Committee that they were in negotiations to see if an acceptable agreement could be achieved between the Sponsors States and the African Group leading to final adoption of the Declaration. By the end of August 2007, Mexico advised the Steering Committee that the negotiations had resulted in a proposal. The African Group would require changes to the text, most

225 IPACC, *supra* note 222.

226 Albert Barume, *Responding to the Concerns of the African States*, *in* Making the Declaration Work: The United Nations Declaration on the Rights of Indigenous Peoples 175 (Claire Charters & Rodolfo Stavenhagen eds., 2009).

227 African Commission on Human and Peoples' Rights, Advisory Opinion on the United Nations Declaration on the Rights of Indigenous Peoples 33 (2007).

228 *See* Letter from the African Group to the President of the General Assembly (May 10, 2007).

229 *Id.*

230 *Id.*

231 *Id.*

significantly a reference to territorial integrity. The initial Article 46(1) text had stated: "Nothing in this Declaration may be interpreted as implying for any State, people or group or person any right to engage in any activity or perform any act contrary to the Charter of the United Nations." The following additional phrase was added: "or construed as authorizing or encouraging any action which would dismember or impair totally or in part, the territorial integrity or political unity of sovereign and independent States."[232]

In addition, the African Group of States secured the addition of a complete and new paragraph in the Declaration's preamble on national and regional particularities:[233]

> Recognizing also that the situation of Indigenous Peoples varies from region to region and from country to country and that the significance of national and regional particularities and various historical and cultural backgrounds should be taken into consideration.

African states sought to emphasize that the self-determination framework was really for indigenous peoples of the North, not the African states. Otherwise, all key provisions, including those relating to land and resource rights, self-determination, FPIC, and treaties, remained intact. This included an agreement by the African Group of States to vote against any amendments proposed on the floor of the UN General Assembly by other states (that is, CANZUS states and supporters).

For indigenous advocates, this was a difficult pill to swallow. The Global Indigenous Caucus Steering Committee referred the amendments to the

[232] This included a reference to the Charter of the United Nations in the preamble of the Declaration, and the deletion of the whole fifteenth paragraph of the preamble, which recognized that "Indigenous Peoples have the right freely to determine their relationships with States in a spirit of coexistence, mutual benefit and full respect." This would have stood in tension with the right to territorial integrity. A third amendment added the Vienna Declaration and Programme of Action to the international instruments mentioned in paragraph 18 of the preamble, because the Vienna Declaration refers to States' territorial integrity.

[233] An earlier version had contained additional language noting that states had the "prerogative to define who constitutes indigenous people in their respective countries." But this was abandoned due to strong objections from indigenous advocates. Other amendments were to Article 8(2)(d), which requires states to "provide effective mechanisms for the prevention of, and redress for, forced assimilation." The following words were deleted from the article: "by other cultures or ways of life imposed on them by legislative, administrative or other measures." Article 30(1) was watered down by deleting the requirement that military activities only take place on Indigenous Peoples' lands and territories when justified by a "significant threat to" the public interest. In Article 32(2), the pronoun "their" was deleted before the words mineral, water, or other resources on lands, territories, and natural resources.

seven indigenous regional caucuses. There was clear reluctance to accept the reference to territorial integrity. However, given the limited options available to indigenous peoples, there was general acceptance of the changes, provided other key provisions in the self-determination framework remained intact.[234]

3.6 The UN General Assembly's Adoption of the Declaration

On September 13, 2007, Peru introduced the resolution to adopt the Declaration in the UN General Assembly:[235]

> Today, the General Assembly faces the enormous responsibility and challenge of bridging a significant gap in the area of promoting and protecting human rights: the protection of Indigenous Peoples. As attested by the various human rights protection mechanisms, such peoples are among the most vulnerable groups.

Noting the twenty-five-year process by which the Declaration had traveled through the UN, including the negotiations between the African Group and Sponsor States during the preceding twelve months, Peru said it was:[236]

> convinced that the changes do not undermine the substantive aspects of the protection of Indigenous Peoples and, at the same time, that they guarantee adoption of the Declaration at the present session.

Peru then called upon all states to adopt the draft resolution without a vote.[237] However, the representatives of Australia, New Zealand, and the United States requested a recorded vote on the draft resolution.

The CANZUS group of states all voted against the Declaration.[238] All CANZUS states underscored the Declaration's non-binding status.[239] Their

234 Malezer, *supra* note 178, at 34.

235 UNGAOR, 61st Sess., 107th Plen. Mtg., U.N. Doc. A/61/PV.107, at 10 (2007) (Statement of Peru delivered by Mr. Chávez); *see Draft Resolution—United Nations Declaration on the Rights of Indigenous Peoples*, UNGAOR, 61st Sess., U.N. Doc. A/61/L.67 (2007) [hereinafter GA Declaration vote record].

236 *Id.* at 10 (Statement of Peru delivered by Mr. Chávez).

237 *Id.*

238 *Id.*

239 *Id.*

principal objection remained self-determination. Australia noted its "long expressed dissatisfaction"[240] with the references to self-determination in the Declaration. According to Australia, self-determination was related to "decolonization" and "the break-up of States into smaller States" or "where a particular group within a defined territory is disenfranchised and is denied political or civil rights."[241] Australia could accept "the full and free engagement of indigenous peoples in the democratic decision-making processes in their country," but not "a concept that could be construed as encouraging action that would impair, even in part, the territorial and political integrity of a State with a system of democratic representative Government."[242] Australia also expressed concern that "the declaration places indigenous customary law in a superior position to national law."[243]

Canada and New Zealand expressed no specific concern regarding self-determination. Canada noted that it had concerns about a reference to "self-government without recognition of the importance of negotiations,"[244] which reflected its earlier statements. New Zealand noted its opposition to indigenous peoples having any rights that others do not have,[245] which suggested that it was not supportive of the self-determination framework.

The United States, however, continued to offer its construction of self-determination in the Declaration as a *new* right specific to indigenous peoples:[246]

> It was not the mandate of the Working Group (nor was it within its power) to qualify, limit, or expand the scope of the existing legal obligations set forth in common article 1, and it was never the intent of States to do so. Instead the mandate of the Working Group was to articulate a new concept, i.e., self-government within the nation-state. It is not the same concept as the right contained in common article 1.

240 *Id.* at 11.
241 *Id.*
242 *Id.*
243 *Id.* at 12.
244 *Id.*
245 *Id.* at 14.
246 *Id.* at 15. *See also* the Statement of the United Kingdom delivered by Ms. Pierce noting that Article 3 of the Declaration was understood as "separate and different from the existing right of all peoples to self-determination in international law, as recognized in common article 1 of the two International Covenants." (*Id.* 21).

References in the Declaration to "Indigenous Peoples being free and equal to all other peoples" and affirmation of "the fundamental importance of the right to self-determination of all peoples" were:[247]

> not intended to imply that the existing right of self-determination is automatically applicable to Indigenous Peoples *per se* or to indicate that Indigenous Peoples automatically qualify as "peoples" for purposes of common article 1.

The United States (joined by the United Kingdom) also rejected the indication in the Declaration that indigenous rights were collective human rights.[248] Rather, "the rights set forth in this declaration are collective rights of Indigenous Peoples as first peoples and are in a distinct category from human rights, which are held by all individuals."[249] The United Kingdom acknowledged that these collective rights could be seen in the domestic laws of states and that accounted for their inclusion in the Declaration.

In relation to land rights, CANZUS states objected to the provisions on lands and resources because, as Australia put it, "they could be read to require recognition of indigenous rights to lands without regard to other legal rights existing in land, both indigenous and non-indigenous."[250] On FPIC, CANZUS states argued that the right was "unworkable" on a practical level as it would give a subset of the population a veto power over the legitimate decisions of a democratic and representative government.[251]

The United States' objections to the redress measures were blatantly self-interested. The goal of the states in the working group, according to the United States, was "to encourage just, transparent and effective mechanisms for redress for actions taken by states *after* endorsing the declaration."[252] The United Kingdom also noted that it understood the Declaration "does not propose to have any retroactive application on historical episodes."[253] For the

[247] *Id.* at 15.

[248] *Id.* Several states that voted in favor of the Declaration noted their reservations about collective human rights; for example, Sweden was of the firm opinion that individual human rights prevailed over the collective rights (not collective human rights) in the Declaration and stressed the principle of territorial integrity (*Id.* at 24).

[249] Robert Hagen, USUN Press Release, "Explanation of vote by Robert Hagen, U.S. Advisor, on the Declaration on the Rights of Indigenous Peoples, to the UN General Assembly, Sept. 13, 2007" (2007).

[250] U.N. Doc. A/61/PV.107, *supra* note 142, at 11 (Statement of Australia delivered by Mr. Hill).

[251] *Id.* at 14.

[252] Robert Hagen, *supra* note 249.

[253] *Id.* at 22.

United States and the United Kingdom, there would be no inquiry into historical takings of lands, violation of treaty rights, and so forth.

In relation to Asian states, Bangladesh noted its disappointment that indigenous peoples had not been defined or identified in clear terms and decided to abstain in the vote.[254] India,[255] Indonesia,[256] and Pakistan[257] observed that while there was no definition in the Declaration, they understood the term to mean indigenous peoples as outlined in ILO Convention 169, that is, the description of indigenous peoples as first peoples in settler states. India noted that self-determination only applied to "peoples under foreign domination" and noted the reference to territorial integrity in Article 46.[258] Therefore, the Declaration had no application to their states. Myanmar[259] and Thailand[260] did not raise any concerns over the lack of a definition but emphasized the reference to territorial integrity in the Declaration. Both the Philippines and Nepal noted their domestic recognition of indigenous peoples and their rights, although the Philippines acknowledged the reference to territorial integrity[261] and Nepal emphasized that the Declaration was not binding but provided "guidelines" for the promotion of indigenous rights.[262]

Latin American states, except Colombia, voted for the Declaration. However, several Latin American states emphasized that self-determination was to be exercised within the state and would not interfere with the sovereignty or political unity of states (Mexico,[263] Brazil,[264] Suriname).[265] Likewise, most African states present in the General Assembly voted for the Declaration (Nigeria, Burundi, and Kenya abstained), although most African states that spoke endorsed the principle of territorial integrity and/or said the Declaration would operate consistently with constitutional frameworks and other national laws of states. Nigeria noted that its abstention was due to the

[254] *Id.* at 22–23.
[255] See, UNGAOR, 61st Sess., 108th Plen. Mtg., U.N. Doc. A/61/PV.108, at 1–2 (2007).
[256] *Id.* at 3–4.
[257] *Id.* at 4.
[258] *Id.* at 2.
[259] *Id.* (Myanmar gave self-determination a human rights reading noting "indigenous peoples residing in a sovereign State that have already attained self-determination have the right to participate in the political affairs of the State in accordance with the provisions of national laws" at 2).
[260] U.N. Doc. A/61/PV.107, *supra* note 235, at 25.
[261] *See* U.N. Doc. A/61/PV.108, *supra* note 255, at 5.
[262] *Id.* at 3.
[263] U.N. Doc. A/61/PV.107, *supra* note 235, at 23.
[264] *Id.* at 25.
[265] *Id.* at 27.

issue of territorial integrity, self-determination, and the control of lands, territories, and resources.[266]

The Nordic states also endorsed the Declaration and encouraged implementation. However, Norway and Sweden gave self-determination (or in Finland's case, the whole Declaration)[267] a human rights reading, with Norway noting the right: "requires that indigenous peoples have full and effective participation in a democratic society and in decision-making processes relevant to the indigenous peoples' concern."[268] Sweden also rejected the notion of collective human rights.[269]

4 Conclusion

Many indigenous advocates heralded the Declaration's adoption by an overwhelming majority of member states as a "breakthrough" achievement for the international indigenous movement. And clearly, it was a long and difficult negotiation spanning over more than two decades. However, it is clear that all states endorsing the Declaration did so with many hedges and qualifications. Between April 2009 and December 2010, each of the CANZUS states all reversed their opposition to the Declaration and endorsed it, although their formal substantive positions had not altered.[270]

However, at the time of their endorsement of the Declaration, the United States, Canada, and New Zealand emphasized the "human rights" in the Declaration while also characterizing the self-determination framework as new and "aspirational" (this had been the approach of the United States in the early years of the second working group). According to the United

[266] U.N. Doc. A/61/PV.108, *supra* note 255, at 6.

[267] *Id.* at 9.

[268] *See* U.N. Doc. A/61/PV.107, *supra* note 235, at 22. *See also* Statement of Sweden: "A large part of the realization of the right to self-determination is without doubt possible to ensure through article 19, which deals with the duty of States to consult and cooperate with indigenous peoples." (*Id.* at 24).

[269] *Id.*

[270] Jenny Macklin, "Statement on the United Nations Declaration on the Rights of Indigenous Peoples" (Speech delivered at the Australian Parliament, Canberra, Apr. 3, 2009), <un.org/esa/socdev/unpfii/documents/Australia_official_statement_endorsement_UNDRIP.pdf>. Pita Sharples, "UNPFII Opening Ceremony New Zealand Statement" (Speech delivered at the United Nations Permanent Forum on Indigenous Issues, New York, Apr. 19, 2010). Canada, Indigenous Affairs and Northern Development Canada, "Canada's Statement of Support on the United Nations Declaration on the Rights of Indigenous Peoples" (Ottawa: IANDC, June 29, 2011), <caid.ca/CanSupUNDec2010.pdf>.

States, self-determination is "different from the existing right in international law."[271]

This new aspirational concept of self-determination was said to be "consistent with the United States existing recognition of, and relationship with, federally recognized tribes as political entities that have inherent sovereign powers of self-governance."[272] This indicated that this new meaning of self-determination was a reflection of legal practice in the United States, that is, state practice of recognizing limited powers of indigenous self-government.

New Zealand's endorsement also followed this line. The Declaration affirmed accepted international human rights while also expressing "new, and non-binding, aspirations."[273] New Zealand referred to the new aspirations no less than six times in its short statement of support. The aspirational elements of the Declaration were to be defined within the bounds of New Zealand's existing "legal and constitutional frameworks."[274] As an example of these aspirational elements, New Zealand cited "restitution of traditionally held land and resources," which New Zealand had addressed through its "distinct," well-established domestic processes for resolving Treaty claims.[275] Canada adopted a similar line to New Zealand and the United States, focusing on its human rights commitments while also noting the Declaration's aspirational and non-legally binding status. Canada, like New Zealand, noted the Declaration was to be interpreted "in a manner that is consistent with [Canada's] Constitution and legal framework."[276] Australia's approach was to give the Declaration's self-determination framework a human rights reading, while speaking of the Declaration as a whole as non-binding and aspirational.[277] All statements of support, therefore, sought to read down the self-determination framework and preserve the status quo, through a

[271] The White House, Press Release, "Announcement of US Support for the United Nations Declaration on the Rights of Indigenous Peoples, Initiatives to Promote the Government-to-Government Relationship & Improve the Lives of Indigenous Peoples" (Dec. 16, 2010), <achp.gov/announcement-us-support-united-nations-declaration-rights-indigenous-peoples>.

[272] *Id.*

[273] NZ, Hansard, Ministerial Statements: UN Declaration on the Rights of Indigenous Peoples—Government Support, Apr. 20, 2010 (Simon Powers).

[274] *Id.* ("In moving to support the Declaration, New Zealand both affirms those [human] rights and reaffirms the legal and constitutional frameworks that underpin New Zealand's legal system. Those existing frameworks, while they will continue to evolve in accordance with New Zealand's domestic circumstances, define the bounds of New Zealand's engagement with the aspirational elements of the Declaration.")

[275] Sharples, *supra* note 270.

[276] Indigenous Affairs and Northern Development Canada, *supra* note 270.

[277] Macklin, *supra* note 270 ("While it is non-binding and does not affect existing Australian law, it sets important international principles for nations to aspire to" at 3).

combination of emphasizing human rights, characterizing the self-determination framework as aspirational, and noting that ultimately the framework would be determined domestically by the state.

The CANZUS states' persistent efforts to read down and limit the nature and extent of these international rights demonstrate states concern about their implications for the domestic development of indigenous rights The right to self-determination poses a real threat to states by challenging existing state sovereignty and calling for the restoration of indigenous peoples' inherent prior sovereign rights. This is the reason why indigenous advocates struggled through various means, including the no-change strategy, to keep the Sub-Commission text. Contrary to the argument made by Karen Engle, indigenous advocates did not give up on "strong forms of self-determination," despite the pressures placed upon Northern advocates to shift to a human rights model. The decolonization narrative has to be remembered and used in advocacy planning and activities, least it be subsumed by the human rights model. Human rights as is clear from the speech given by Les Malezer after the Declaration's adoption is the conventional means of reading the Declaration. But that doesn't have to be the case moving forward.

Asian and African states, with a few exceptions, simply do not accept that the Declaration is relevant to their states. They continue to seek an international definition that clarifies this point. As we will see in Chapter 4, initiatives like a UN General Assembly proposal to enhance participation in UN meetings have been undermined by Asian states' opposition to local movements. Central and South American states, almost all of which have special laws recognizing indigenous rights, still prefer to refer to the rights set out in the ILO Convention 169. Due to indigenous activists' persistence in the North and South, reforms continue to emerge through state laws and policies. In the Northern states, for example, treaties continue to be negotiated, and states and indigenous activists are engaged in discussion on major reforms including constitutional reform. What I argue in the next chapter is that these moves would benefit from the decolonization reading of self-determination. I also argue that more progress would be made in the South on the basis of a human rights reading of the Declaration. What I call for is a new mixed-model interpretation of the Declaration that incorporates both the decolonization and human rights models.

3
The Declaration and the Mixed Model Interpretative Approach

In Chapters 1 and 2, I demonstrated that the politics behind the drafting of the UN Declaration on the Rights of Indigenous Peoples involved a continual and unresolved struggle between proponents of different models of interpreting the Declaration. In the main, the decolonization model used by advocates from the North competed with the human rights model used by advocates from the South and also preferred by states. Now that the Declaration has been adopted by an overwhelming number of states, ultimately including the CANZUS states, what are the implications of the historical narrative I have established for the implementation of the Declaration?

In this chapter, I argue that the existing normative models informing the interpretation of the Declaration are all unsatisfactory. I criticize the one-note human rights model proposed as historically accurate by Karen Engle,[1] a variation on which is advanced by James Anaya.[2] I also critique the accounts of Will Kymlicka[3] and Patrick Macklem,[4] which feature decolonization as the sole normative idea animating the Declaration. This model in effect excludes Southern indigenous peoples, especially Asian and African movements, from legitimately claiming the rights in the Declaration.

Instead, I argue for a new mixed-model interpretation of the Declaration that incorporates both the decolonization and human rights models. The benefits of this bifurcated reading of the Declaration are that it enables both the Northern and Southern indigenous movements to gain the rights they seek from the Declaration. The mixed model is supported by the political history of the Declaration negotiations as outlined in this book. It is also supported by legal and political theory justificatory arguments. First, the

[1] *See generally*, Karen Engle, The Elusive Promise of Indigenous Development: Rights, Culture, Strategy (2010).
[2] *See generally*, S. James Anaya, Indigenous Peoples in International Law (2004).
[3] *See generally*, Will Kymlicka, Multicultural Odysseys: Navigating the New International Politics of Diversity (2007).
[4] *See generally*, Patrick Macklem, The Sovereignty of Human Rights (1st ed. 2015).

The UN Declaration on the Rights of Indigenous Peoples. Andrew Erueti, Oxford University Press. © Oxford University Press 2022. DOI: 10.1093/oso/9780190068301.003.0004

mixed model is justified by the widely shared understandings of the interpretative community associated with the Declaration negotiations, the relevant interpretive community not being limited to states as it tends to be assumed for the purposes of treaty interpretation.[5] Second, drawing on Thomas Franck's legal theory of legitimacy, I argue that the mixed model is imbued with legitimacy because it meets the criteria of pedigree, coherence, determinacy, and adherence. The model thus has a strong normative pull for states and other non-state actors.

1 One-Note Interpretations of the Declaration

1.1 Human Rights Models

As discussed in the Introduction, Karen Engle rejects most indigenous advocates' characterization of the Declaration as a "breakthrough" achievement for the international indigenous movement, seeking to establish instead that (1) partway through the negotiations, indigenous advocates made a pragmatic choice to give up on "strong forms of self-determination" (that is, secession or independence)[6] and (2) began to articulate their claims in human rights terms, particularly the human right to culture.[7] This leads to a focus on maintenance of a way of life/tradition through land, heritage, and development.[8]

This strategy was a response to resistance to such strong forms of self-determination by states, and to a focus on human rights and culture by Latin American indigenous advocates.[9] This is a mistake, she argues, because it results in indigenous peoples giving up on the bigger rewards that may be gained from the self-determination project.[10] Engle's advice to the international indigenous movement is to shift "away from the acceptance and deployment of static and essentialized notions of culture and to raise questions about whether the right to culture—and perhaps human rights more generally—is up to the task of the major economic and political restructuring

[5] *See* section 2.2 of this chapter.
[6] Engle, *supra* note 1, at 3.
[7] *Id.*
[8] *Id.* at 6.
[9] *Id.* at Chapters 2 and 3 (she also adds that indigenous advocates enjoyed some successes with cultural rights before international law and regional human rights bodies).
[10] Samuel Moyn, The Last Utopia: Human Rights in History (2010).

that many advocates (if covertly) seem to seek."[11] Courtney Jung similarly sees the claims of the indigenous rights movement as based in culture and, like Engle, seeks to encourage indigenous advocates to focus instead on structural injustice.[12]

Although Engle's argument is that a human rights model is what emerged from the politics of the negotiations, she singles out James Anaya as "perhaps the strongest *proponent* of self-determination as a human right."[13] Anaya has indeed played a key role in the shift within the indigenous movement toward a human rights model and rejects "historical sovereignty" arguments that call for recognition of indigenous statehood based on the illegitimate denial of indigenous peoples' prior sovereignty.[14]

According to Anaya, self-determination as a precept of international law has always been fundamentally grounded in human rights, and especially rights to freedom and equality. In its "substantive" sense, self-determination promotes governmental legitimacy by serving as an ongoing standard to evaluate how governing institutions are constituted and how they continue to operate. Self-determination also operates in a "remedial" sense for deviations from the substantive elements of self-determination. The decolonization process represents a remedy for a "sui generis" violation of the substantive right of peoples to self-determination.[15] But self-determination's remedial prescriptions will not always require decolonization. The remedy will depend on the nature of the violation of the substantive right to self-determination. Thus, "the substantive elements of self-determination apply broadly to benefit all segments of humanity, that is, all peoples"; however, "self-determination applies more narrowly in its remedial aspect."[16]

In the specific case of indigenous peoples, Anaya argues that while there are historical similarities between the indigenous experience and "classic colonialism," the violations experienced by indigenous peoples are distinct. In particular, he points to the contemporary absence of "formal colonial structures."[17] Thus, rather than independence as a remedy, the rights in the

[11] Engle, *supra* note 1, at 10.

[12] Courtney Jung, The Moral Force of Indigenous Politics: Critical Liberalism and the Zapatistas (2008).

[13] Engle, *supra* note 1 at 98.

[14] *See, e.g.*, James Anaya, *Divergent Discourses about International Law, Indigenous Peoples, and Rights over Lands and Natural Resources: Toward a Realist Trend*, 16 Colo. J. Intl. Envtl. L. & Pol'y. 237 (2005).

[15] Anaya, *supra* note 2, at 104.

[16] *Id.*

[17] *Id.* at 110.

Declaration and the ILO Conventions may require change in the political order but independence would be a course of last resort (in those cases of gross abuse of human rights).[18]

Contrary to Engle, Anaya's human rights model delivers much more than rights to land and culture. Anaya's model, in theory, supports the self-determination framework and could lead to significant political autonomy for indigenous groups *vis-à-vis* the state.[19] However, by viewing the right to self-determination in the Declaration as grounded in human rights, Anaya's account obscures the connection between self-determination in the Declaration and anti-colonialism. The human rights model is directed at equality, property rights, and autonomy and relies on the state to provide these remedies, whereas the decolonization model challenges existing state sovereignty and is directed at a nation-to-nation relationship.

The narrative of the drafting of the Declaration that I developed in Chapters 1 and 2 contradicts Engle's account in two principal ways. First, it disagrees that "strong forms of self-determination" were abandoned in favor of the human rights model. While it confirms that many adopted the human rights model and some placed emphasis on the right to culture, the narrative also establishes that the decolonization model was, in fact, consistently maintained throughout by the Treaty Council and other prominent indigenous advocates of the North. Although Engle notes that not all advocates abandoned their commitment to a strong form of self-determination,[20] she de-emphasizes this internal struggle among Northern indigenous advocates and the continued assertion of a decolonization model right up to the Declaration's adoption by the UN General Assembly. She also does not register the full extent of the pressures placed upon Northern advocates to give up the decolonization model.

In contrast, I argue that it is the decolonization model that created the self-determination framework in the Declaration. Adapting their domestic, historical sovereignty claims to the UN standard-setting process, advocates of the North sought recognition of the right to self-determination. They had been battle-hardened by their advocacy experience in their home states and were positioned at the more radical end of the domestic indigenous advocacy movement. They sought the advice of experts in international law, and

[18] *Id.* at 109.

[19] Anaya, *supra* note 2, at 106–10, 150–56.

[20] Engle, *supra* note 1 ("some indigenous groups, primarily in the former British colonies, long insisted on keeping open the possibility of external self-determination" at 73).

many soon became experts themselves, basing their argument on their particular experience of colonization and settlement by the British. They were prior sovereigns and (excepting Australia) this status was recognized in their treaties, which were international in character. These advocates of the North did not seek independence, although recognition of the right to self-determination without qualification indicated that they had the option of independence. Human rights were important—it was clear that indigenous peoples occupied the margins of life in their home states, but human rights were most important as a means of supporting their decolonization model.[21]

As I have shown, in the Working Group on Indigenous Populations, it was extremely difficult to have the right to self-determination included in the Declaration. Yet, this was achieved. Not only did Northern indigenous advocates manage to secure recognition of the right to self-determination without reference to territorial integrity in the first working group, they also managed to achieve this in the second working group. Northern advocates like the Treaty Council insisted on no-change to the text produced by the first working group and approved by the Sub-Commission on Human Rights (especially self-determination without any reference to territorial integrity). They walked out in protest when the chair did not recognize their right to speak, and sought input into the working group agenda and the appointment of an indigenous chair. They sought to maintain the no-change line through the Global Indigenous Caucus meetings, even though there was mounting pressure from states as well as Asian and African indigenous advocates and their supporters (including IWGIA) to break from the no-change position. The advancement of the decolonization model through the UN-sponsored treaty seminars and hunger strikes was all aimed at shoring up the decolonization model, securing the self-determination framework, and keeping territorial integrity out of the Declaration.

Second, not only was the decolonization model maintained, the account of the drafting history that emerged in Chapters 1 and 2 showed that although Engle is correct that the decolonization model was replaced as the dominant model by an emphasis on human rights, she misses a crucial element that led to the shift because she confines her analysis to the settler states. As she notes, Latin American indigenous advocates seemed to prefer human rights and culture. Latin American advocates were slow to participate in the emerging

[21] Moyn, *supra* note 10, at 85. *See also* Roland Burke, Decolonization and the Evolution of International Human Rights (2010).

international movement given the difficulties many advocates faced with mobilization under repressive political regimes.[22] When they did participate, however, their focus, as she shows, tended not to be political independence but issues of cultural autonomy and basic human rights.[23] However, as is clear from Chapter 2, it is the participation of indigenous peoples of Asia and later Africa that saw a particular emphasis on human rights and culture in the Declaration negotiations. These factors established common cause with indigenous peoples of the North. Asian and African indigenous peoples could not credibly advance the decolonization model. They can only benefit from alternatives to the decolonization model. Also, Asian and African (as well as Latin American) indigenous peoples were not as interested in historical injustices as they were with contemporary struggles.

Because it is the Asian and African movements that led to the heavy emphasis on human rights and culture and because they are not featured in Engle's narrative (apart from a few oblique references), she misses a pivotal North–South tension. Engle overstates Northern indigenous advocates' emphasis on human rights and culture. The greatest emphasis came from the Asian and African movements. As a result, there was more pressure on Northern indigenous peoples to shift from the decolonization model than Engle records. Recall that it was Asian and Saami indigenous advocates that led the break from the no-change strategy in the second working group. Also, this pressure to shift came from not only Southern indigenous peoples but also Southern states that were concerned about the implications of self-determination for internal security issues. African and Asian states sought a definition of indigenous peoples that clearly excluded minorities in their states. But they did not succeed. Instead, these Southern states imposed their definition of indigenous peoples (directed at the historical experience of indigenous peoples in the settler states); and/or emphasized human rights

[22] Raidza Torres, *The Rights of Indigenous Populations: The Emerging International Norm*, 16 Yale J. Intl. L. 127, 144 (1991) (Writing about the first Working Group, Torres notes, "Guatemalan Indians currently do not emphasize the right of self-determination as strongly as indigenous groups in other countries. In part, this is because they face the more immediate challenge of countering widespread murders by the government. In addition, because Indians form the majority of the Guatemalan population and because they are dispersed throughout the country, it is impracticable to advance the cause of a separate Indian state within Guatemala. The Guatemalan government is sensitive to any threats to the country's territorial integrity, especially given its struggle against leftist groups. Indian demands for substantial autonomy are perceived as threats to the state and are likely to result in more repressive policies." On the other hand, Torres notes how: "In contrast to Guatemala's Indians, the Miskito Indians of Nicaragua have enjoyed greater political autonomy throughout most of the twentieth century.").

[23] Engle, *supra* note 1; Jung, *supra* note 12.

and culture; and/or sought an express reference to territorial integrity in the Declaration.

Eventually, as we saw in Chapter 2, Northern indigenous peoples themselves could see the merit of Anaya's human rights model. This created tensions between the no-change advocates advancing the decolonization model and those Northern advocates who preferred a more pragmatic approach.

What, then, are the implications of this alternative history and, in turn, this alternative reading for the current implementation of the Declaration? It is clear that the human rights model has become the prominent means of reading the Declaration. Because Engle fails to accord real weight to the connection between the self-determination framework in the Declaration and the decolonization model, she is too quick to dismiss the model's relevance in the implementation era. The resistance within the Northern indigenous movement to the human rights model help us to see that the decolonization model is still there and able to do the work she wants it to do. CANZUS states were all too aware of, and concerned about, the right to self-determination in the Declaration and the decolonization model. The United States, for example, when voting against the Declaration in the UN General Assembly emphatically asserted that the reference to self-determination in the Declaration was never meant to "qualify, limit, or expand the scope of the existing legal obligations set forth in common article 1."[24] Even the reference to territorial integrity was not enough to assuage the CANZUS states' concerns with the self-determination framework. When CANZUS states endorsed the Declaration, they all continued to read down the effects of the framework.

The inclusion of the self-determination framework and the decolonization model has significant normative implications. Ultimately, it means that the state is required to engage with indigenous peoples to determine the terms of their co-existence. Self-determination in the Declaration relates to this nation-to-nation relationship. In particular, as I elaborate in Chapter 4, the decolonization model has two implications for implementing the self-determination framework. First, the decolonization model shows that the first priority should be negotiation between indigenous peoples and the state about their relationship in the contemporary state. Second, until those

[24] Robert Hagen, USUN Press Release, "Explanation of vote by Robert Hagen, U.S. Advisor, on the Declaration on the Rights of Indigenous Peoples, to the UN General Assembly, September 13, 2007" (2007), <http://www.fns.bc.ca/info/UNDeclaration/Stmnts%20Made%20by%20States%20Before%20and%20After%20the%20Vote/United%20States.pdf>

reforms occur, the model can be used as a means for influencing the debate about the nature and extent of indigenous rights by highlighting the importance of political autonomy and territorial rights for indigenous peoples.

In Engle's analysis of indigenous rights, the abandonment of a decolonization model in the drafting of the Declaration serves as a critical counterpoint to the human rights model that, she argues, carried the day. While a decolonization model addresses her criticisms of the latter, she does not argue for it outright. It is important to note, though, that a decolonization model would foreclose African and Asian participation in the international indigenous rights movement. These Southern indigenous movements can only appeal to the human rights model and would therefore resist any return to a single note decolonization model.

For Latin America, there could be some potential for asserting a decolonization model given its history of colonization and settlement by European powers. To this extent, there are parallels with the historical experience of Northern indigenous peoples. However, key ingredients to the decolonization model are absent in Latin America, especially nation-to-nation treaty-making and a long-standing political relationship with the state. Engle seems to assume that there was some potential for Latin American advocates to press for "strong forms of self-determination."[25] At the same time, she also seems to accept that the particular history of the North—especially treaty-making—indicates that Northern indigenous peoples have greater claims to strong forms of self-determination.[26] But, as we have seen, the decolonization model was not pursued by Latin American indigenous advocates. Instead, the emphasis was on land, consultation, and revitalization of culture.

1.2 Historical Injustice Models

One alternative to the human rights model might be to exclude Asian and African movements from the international movement altogether by relying on a single-note decolonization model directed at Northern indigenous peoples or more broadly at indigenous peoples of the settler states. Such an approach can be seen in Patrick Macklem's book *The Sovereignty of Human Rights*.[27] Macklem approaches the question of which types of groups might

[25] Engle, *supra* note 1, at 78.
[26] *Id.* at 52–55, 78–82.
[27] Macklem, *supra* note 4.

be considered indigenous peoples in international law by looking for the answer in international law itself.

Macklem is especially critical of the constructivist model that Benedict Kingsbury develops in his article on the Asian controversy,[28] whereby the concept of "indigenous peoples" (and indigenous rights) in international law can be seen as sourced in a variety of justifications, some historical and others contemporary and functional in nature. In an attempt to address Asian states' strong opposition to the domestic application of indigenous peoples, Kingsbury argued that the concept of indigenous peoples ought to be underpinned by a more expansive range of justifications than the historical arguments used by indigenous peoples of the settler states. Instead, the concept should include other more functional notions, like dispossession of land, cultural dislocation, environmental despoliation, and experiences with large development projects.[29] Macklem's objection was that such a broad range of justifications for indigenous rights makes it easy for all types of cultural communities to self-identify as indigenous. As Macklem notes:[30]

> Kingsbury's approach, unless supplemented by an explanation of the normative significance of international indigenous rights, risks conflating different forms of international legal protection into an undifferentiated concern about the disruption or exploitation of diverse communities of value. Numerical minorities, cultural minorities, national minorities, religious communities, linguistic communities, impoverished majorities—are we all indigenous peoples now?

Pointing to Kingsbury's essential attributes of self-identification, experience of severe disruption, and so on, Macklem questions why these factors ought to merit international legal protection in the form of indigenous rights "as opposed to more generic human rights, such as minority rights and rights to cultural protection as well as those that protect civil, political, social, and economic interests."[31] Macklem's point seems to be that the self-determination framework must be based on something more distinctive than a history of displacement.

[28] Benedict Kingsbury, *'Indigenous Peoples' in International Law: A Constructivist Approach to the Asian Controversy*, 92:3 AM. J. INTL. L. 414 (1998).
[29] *Id.* at 457.
[30] Macklem, *supra* note 4, at 160.
[31] *Id.*

Macklem approaches the problem of recognition of indigenous peoples by considering the distinction made between legal and political recognition of states in international law. He draws on Hans Kelsen's observation that there can be *political* recognition in the form of actions like the establishment of diplomatic relations.[32] However, for recognition to be *legal*, states must meet the criteria prescribed by international law itself. Likewise, Macklem notes, a *political* movement may self-identify as an indigenous people but it must meet certain criteria determined by international law in order to possess the *legal* status of indigenous peoples and thereby access indigenous rights in international law.[33]

According to Macklem, these criteria for legal recognition derive from the nature and purpose of indigenous rights.[34] Macklem gleans this purpose from his review of the legal history of international indigenous rights during the twentieth century, that is, the protection of "indigenous workers" in colonies by the International Labour Organization in the 1920s, to the promulgation of ILO Conventions 107 and 169, up to its most contemporary expression in the UN Declaration on the Rights of Indigenous Peoples.[35] The object of these protections, according to Macklem, is to address the wrongs established by international law, in particular indigenous peoples' "historic exclusion from the distribution of *sovereignty* initiated by colonization that lies at the heart of the international legal order."[36] Given this purpose, "Indigenous peoples in international law," Macklem argues:[37]

> . . . are communities that manifest historical continuity with societies that occupied and governed territories prior to European contact and colonization. They are located in States whose claims of sovereign power possess legal validity because of international law's refusal to recognize these peoples and their ancestors as sovereign actors. What constitutes indigenous peoples as international legal actors, in other words, is the structure and operation of international law itself.

[32] *Id.* at 133–41. *See* Hans Kelsen, *Recognition in International Law: Theoretical Observations*, 35:4 Am. J. Intl. L. 605, 605–17.

[33] Macklem, *supra* note 4, at 156–62.

[34] *Id.* at 135.

[35] *Id.* at 141–56.

[36] *Id.* at 162.

[37] *Id.* at 135.

This, of course, describes the historical experience of indigenous peoples of the settler states. However, as is apparent from Chapters 1 and 2, the purpose of indigenous rights has not always been consistent. The targeted category of "indigenous peoples," as well as the aims of international standards and their underlying justifications, has always shifted. The ILO protections for "indigenous workers" of the 1920s were aimed at forced labor and workers conditions for colonial populations.[38] The ILO Conventions 107 and 169 were aimed at both "indigenous peoples" and "tribal peoples"—the former being indigenous peoples of the settler states and the latter tribal peoples of Asia, Africa, and Middle East.[39] The intention of ILO Convention 107 was to assimilate indigenous peoples.[40] Admittedly at the time, this was the benevolent approach, but it would be a stretch to describe ILO Convention 107 as a remedy for the denial of sovereignty. The ILO Convention 169 shifted the focus from integration toward the promotion of indigenous rights, but again, mostly rejected historical considerations and directed its attention toward contemporary basic rights and cultural autonomy.[41] Again indigenous peoples were defined separately from tribal peoples, but little turned on this—the Convention was directed at fundamental human rights and rejected calls by Northern indigenous peoples to recognize the range of rights in the self-determination framework.[42] Both the ILO Convention 107 and ILO Convention 169 were thus directed at basic human rights.

As we saw in Chapters 1 and 2, the Declaration itself—and this is the most significant international development—was initially directed at the anticolonialist claims of Northern indigenous peoples, but it also came to be directed at the human rights concerns of Southern indigenous peoples. This indicates that the Declaration is serving two purposes, not one.

[38] Luis Rodríguez-Piñero, Indigenous Peoples, Postcolonialism, and International Law: The ILO Regime (1919–1989) (2005) (noting "the ILO's definition of 'indigenous workers' [in the Forced Labour Convention] . . . applied, first and foremost, to 'indigenous populations' of . . . *dependent* territories; in other words, to the populations living under a legal status of dependency in conditions of formal colonialism" at 47).

[39] *See* Chapters 1 and 2.

[40] *Convention (No. 107) Concerning the Protection and Integration of Indigenous and Other Tribal and Semi-Tribal Populations in Independent Countries*, June 26, 1957, 328 U.N.T.S. 247, art. 2(1) (entered into force June 2, 1959) ("Governments shall have the primary responsibility for developing co-ordinated and systematic action for the protection of the populations concerned and their progressive integration into the life of their respective countries.").

[41] *See* Chapter 2.

[42] *Id.*

Macklem's reading of the nature and purpose of international indigenous rights comes close to the decolonization model detailed in this book. However, unlike Macklem, I see this as a project confined to indigenous peoples of the North, whereas he sees it as directed at indigenous peoples of the settler states. In my view, Macklem's argument has greater force and resonance in the context of Northern indigenous peoples' experience of treaty-making, treaty-breaking, and international law's refusal to recognize their sovereign status. Implicit in his argument is the idea that indigenous peoples were akin to nations and candidates for sovereignty, but international law after a period of recognition of their nationhood—for purely political, self-serving motives—refused to recognize them as sovereign legal actors.[43] Once the colonizing power had the upper hand, international law doctrines of "terra nullius" and "discovery" were deployed under international law to deny their sovereign status. This nation-to-nation historical experience is difficult to find outside of the North. Indigenous peoples of Latin America would struggle to meet this notion, as would indigenous peoples in Thailand, Nepal, Indonesia, and the Philippines. Moreover, indigenous peoples in Asia and Africa live in states that have enjoyed decolonization. In other words, they have been provided with a remedy, albeit it is the state as a whole that benefits.[44]

Will Kymlicka also advocates an approach that sees indigenous rights as directed at the settler states.[45] He is critical of the move by minorities to re-invent themselves as indigenous peoples. The reasons are clearly due to the weak nature of minority rights:

> [i]f they come to the international community under the heading of national minority, they get nothing other than generic Article 27 [minority] rights; if they come instead as "indigenous peoples," they have the promise of rights to land, control over natural resources, political self-government, language rights and legal pluralism.[46]

For Kymlicka, these minorities (including Asian and African indigenous peoples) are politically opportunistic: self-identifying as indigenous peoples

[43] Macklem, *supra* note 4, at 138–41.

[44] Macklem notes his argument does not "necessarily preclude international law from recognizing indigenous peoples in Africa or Asia" (*Id.* at 162). However, he is aware of the extension of the international indigenous movement to the South (and how Kingsbury has justified this), and his argument seems to be aimed at redirecting attention once more on the indigenous peoples of CANZUS and Latin America.

[45] Kymlicka, *supra* note 3.

[46] *Id.* at 168.

for not only stronger standards of protection than minority rights but to gain greater publicity, and access to international funding and support.[47] Kymlicka's argument is that there ought to be different standards for different types of peoples.[48] For indigenous peoples, there are the standards in the Declaration that promote self-government and territorial rights based on the decolonization-based model of indigenous rights.[49] Kymlicka thinks this is the underlying justification of indigenous rights.[50] These standards are differentiated from those that could be established for "immigrant groups, or for other types of groups with unique histories and needs, such as Roma and Afro-Latinos."[51]

The aim of both Macklem's and Kymlicka's approaches, then, is to counter the obfuscation caused by Kingsbury's constructivist model, developed in the context of the Asian controversy, by providing greater clarity about the normative basis of the most significant indigenous rights in the Declaration. Macklem and Kymlicka are aware that the normative argument does not match the legal right and that indigenous peoples of Asia and Africa have self-identified as indigenous to access the rights in the Declaration. And they seek to remedy this by redirecting attention to the historical experience of the settler states. Their approach also addresses the definition issue in the Asian and African context by simply stating that indigenous rights in international law are for the indigenous peoples of the settler states.

However, I don't see the Declaration as directed at the settler states. Nor do I see the need to establish different normative texts to meet the needs of different categories of people. Rather, as I argue below, the Declaration is a global initiative, although different aspects of the Declaration can serve different types of peoples.

2 Mixed-Model Interpretations of the Declaration

2.1 States' and Kingsbury's Mixed Models

As detailed in Chapter 2, at the time of their endorsement of the Declaration, the United States, Canada, and New Zealand emphasized the "human rights"

[47] *Id.* at 168.
[48] *Id.* at 300.
[49] *Id.* at 281.
[50] *Id.*
[51] *Id.* at 301.

in the Declaration while also characterizing the self-determination framework as new and "aspirational."[52] However, according to CANZUS states, the aspirations in the Declaration are ultimately to be determined by states within their respective legal system and practices. This approach is not the one-note human rights method of interpreting the Declaration (which was Australia's method when it endorsed the Declaration).[53] There is no single model underpinning indigenous rights here. Instead, the model mixes basic human rights and aspirations with the latter's content comprising domestic laws and policies relating to indigenous peoples. Thus, according to this "States' mixed-model," indigenous rights will vary from state to state, disconnected from any international context and determined according to the discretion of the state. In doing so, this approach disconnects the right to self-determination in the Declaration from the decolonization model, or indeed, the human rights model.

Benedict Kingsbury's model continues with this mixed notion; some rights in the Declaration are human rights and others aspirational. As we saw in Chapter 2, according to Kingsbury's "Asian Controversy" article, while initially indigenous rights were strongly connected to the decolonization model—or as he put it, "historical continuity with first peoples"—matters shifted with the inclusion of Asian indigenous peoples.[54] Asian indigenous peoples shared Northern indigenous peoples' concern about "functional matters such as dispossession of land, cultural dislocation, environmental despoliation and experiences with large development projects."[55] These "establish a unity that is not dependent on the universal presence of historical continuity."[56]

Therefore, Kingsbury argued, it was best to see indigenous rights in the Declaration as grounded in a wide range of justifications graduating from "relevant" to "strong" and "essential" justifications. Historical continuity with first peoples would not be an essential justification but a relevant one. The

[52] The White House, Press Release, "Announcement of US Support for the United Nations Declaration on the Rights of Indigenous Peoples, Initiatives to Promote the Government-to-Government Relationship & Improve the Lives of Indigenous Peoples" (Dec. 16, 2010) at para. 3, <https://web.archive.org/web/20130521061949/http://usun.state.gov/documents/organization/153239.pdf>.

[53] Jenny Macklin, "Statement on the United Nations Declaration on the Rights of Indigenous Peoples" (Speech delivered at the Australian Parliament, Canberra, Apr. 3, 2009), <http://www.converge.org.nz/pma/AustDecl0409.pdf>.

[54] Kingsbury, *supra* note 28.

[55] *Id.* at 457.

[56] *Id.*

essential justifications as we saw in Chapter 2 were (1) self-identification as a distinct ethnic group; (2) historical experience of, or contingent vulnerability to, severe disruption, dislocation, or exploitation; (3) long connection with the region; and (4) the wish to retain a distinct identity.[57]

This method was meant to address strong opposition by Asian states to indigenous rights, specifically the historical continuity justification. The response to Asian states would be that this was merely one justification underpinning indigenous rights, but there were many others also applicable, including elements that were germane to Asian indigenous peoples. This approach did not see specific indigenous rights as being sourced in specific justificatory argument. The self-determination framework was not based on historical continuity with first peoples. Rather, *all* of the indigenous rights in the Declaration—one catch-all category—have their basis in a range of justifications, including historical continuity but also the four essential justifications outlined above. As Macklem notes, this leads to conceptual confusion about the basis of indigenous rights. All of the rights may flow from all of these justifications, or some from some—we are not sure which from Kingsbury's argument.[58] On the contrary, as we saw in Chapter 1, the self-determination framework in the Declaration is the result of the anti-colonialism arguments (including historical continuity) advanced by advocates of the North.

Kingsbury's mixed model also failed to address Asian states concerns with self-determination—if anything, it made matters worse by obfuscating the clear connection North indigenous peoples sought to make between self-determination and the decolonization model. Now all Asian indigenous peoples could claim a right to self-determination, even though they could not advance the decolonization model.

In a later article on indigenous rights—"Reconciling Five Competing Conceptual Structures of Indigenous Peoples' Claims in International and Comparative law"—Kingsbury explores the indigenous rights justifications in more detail.[59] The five conceptual structures said to underpin indigenous

[57] *Id.* at 455.

[58] Admittedly my mixed model does this to some degree. While it separates human rights from the self-determination framework, it admits, for example, both a human rights and decolonization reading of self-determination. Self-determination in the human rights sense would include, say, greater local autonomy for Southern indigenous peoples. However, under Kingsbury's mixed model, there is nothing to stop Southern indigenous peoples claiming stronger forms of self-determination, whereas my model sees this as the right of the North on the basis of the decolonization model.

[59] Benedict Kingsbury, *Reconciling Five Competing Conceptual Structures of Indigenous Peoples' Claims in International and Comparative Law*, 34:1 NYUJ INTL. L. & POLIT. 189 (2001).

rights comprise four "established categories" of human rights, minority rights, self-determination, and historic sovereignty, and a distinct, "emerging conceptual category of indigenous peoples."[60] Kingsbury surveys the use of these categories in domestic and international indigenous rights advocacy as well as standard setting in international law.

Historic sovereignty is dismissed by Kingsbury as too radical and impractical.[61] Likewise, in his view, self-determination as the realization of an end state (or the decolonization model):[62]

> is not viable as an express formulation for a U.N. Declaration on the Rights of Indigenous Peoples to be adopted by states, nor does it embody the current preoccupations of most internationally active indigenous peoples.

According to Kingsbury, "most of the groups participating in the international indigenous peoples' movement . . . expect to continue in an enduring relationship with the state(s) in which they presently live."[63] Thus, self-determination in the Declaration is best seen in relational terms as promoting an enduring relationship between indigenous peoples and state governments. As Kingsbury notes, the "Declaration provides much of the material from which the concept of self-determination may be reconstructed in relational terms."[64]

For Kingsbury, "indigenous peoples" as a distinct category offered the most promise of a program that extended beyond the existing established categories and the Declaration embodied such an approach.[65] In his view, the Declaration comprised not only renovated human rights but also new, extensive aspirations:[66]

> While many of the provisions of the [Declaration] apply or restate human rights norms or other principles of international law to reflect particular concerns and experiences of indigenous communities, other provisions depart from this pattern to express specific aspirations and self-understandings of indigenous groups, often couched as "rights."

[60] *Id.* at 190.
[61] *Id.* at 237.
[62] *Id.* at 223.
[63] *Id.* at 221.
[64] *Id.* at 226.
[65] *Id.* at 237.
[66] *Id.* at 237–38.

Examples of the aspirations include the right not to be subjected to ethnocide and cultural genocide, the right to maintain and strengthen their distinctive spiritual and material relationship with their traditional lands, and the right to autonomy or self-government.[67] Therefore, many of the Declaration provisions are adaptations of human rights, while others are not—and here Kingsbury is essentially speaking about the self-determination framework.[68] However, it is not clear what underlies the aspirations that comprise the distinctive category of indigenous peoples. Unlike the mixed model proposed by New Zealand, Canada, and the United States, Kingsbury does not seek to confine the content of these aspirations to the particularities of the domestic domain. What is clear is that the aspirations are not based on decolonization. In the "Asian Controversy," historical continuity plays a role as a justificatory basis—though it is mixed up with others. However, in "Reconciling Five Competing Conceptual Structures," as we have seen, self-determination in the sense of decolonization is rejected as too controversial as a justificatory basis.

If the aspirations are not based on the decolonization model, what is their basis? According to Kingsbury, it seems to be a combination of state "legal practice" and the generic notion of "wrongful deprivation, above all, of land, territory, self-government, means of livelihood."[69] This he describes as "the most powerful argument for a distinctive legal category based on special features of indigenous peoples."[70] In other words, "The appeal is thus to history and culture."[71] Therefore, we come back to Kingsbury's broad-ranging four "essential criteria" that he refers to in the "Asian controversy" article. In terms of the Declaration, Kingsbury's five conceptual categories collapse into two: (1) human rights and (2) culture and history. Thus, Kingsbury's mixed

[67] *Id.* (According to Kingsbury, other normative features of this aspirational Indigenous category are "restitution of traditional lands and territories; historically grounded and culturally grounded entitlements and responsibilities with regard to natural resources, religious sites, and spiritual or guardianship relationships with particular land, water, mountains, etc.; entitlements and responsibilities based on treaties or other agreements to which the indigenous people is party; certain constitutional arrangements for participation and political structures for membership and self-government; duties in relation to ancestors and future generations; continuance of certain kinds of economic practices; and perhaps entitlements and responsibilities in relation to traditional knowledge" at 240).

[68] *Id.* While Kingsbury includes the right to self-determination in his first category of human rights/general principles of international law, as we will see, in his view self-determination in the Declaration is clearly relational, that is, it is to be exercised within the state. Thus, it is like a human right and not a legal right connected with decolonization (*Id.* at 226).

[69] *Id.* at 244.

[70] *Id.*

[71] *Id.*

model—by basing the aspirations in broad justifications linked to "history and culture"—decouples the self-determination framework from its decolonization roots resulting in greater emphasis on functional, human rights issues as the basis of all indigenous rights.

2.2 A Mixed-Model Interpretative Approach

Whereas the Northern indigenous movement initiated the UN-based activity that led to the adoption of the UN Declaration on the Rights of Indigenous Peoples, it was the project's extension to the Southern movement—the Declaration's globalization—that provided it with significant momentum. While Engle emphasizes the great material cost of this globalization for the North and Macklem and Kymlicka focus on the normative dissipation of indigenous rights' *raison d'etre*, all three argue against a focus on human rights and thus necessarily exclude the Southern movement.

In contrast, I offer an account of the Declaration that seeks fully to reflect and respect the impact of both Southern and Northern indigenous peoples. On this account, the political history of the Declaration led it to carry two normative strands. At the same time, mine is not the mixed model advanced by Kingsbury or, say, the United States. These seek to divide the Declaration into two components: basic human rights adapted to the situation of indigenous peoples, and aspirations (the self-determination framework) disconnected from the decolonization model.

Instead, I propose that the Declaration be read as containing two normative themes for different categories of peoples. On the one hand, the Declaration can be read as an instrument for Northern indigenous peoples. It contains the self-determination framework, which is supported by their decolonization model. It also contains the adaptations of human rights—the right to equality, education, religion, and land, for example. These latter rights, too, have the potential to be read with the decolonization lens, or they could simply be read as adapted human rights.

On the other hand, the Declaration as a whole can be read as a human rights instrument as adapted for Southern indigenous peoples.

The benefit of this model is that it is not a zero-sum game for the Northern and Southern movements. Both get what they want from the Declaration. This interpretation of the Declaration enables indigenous peoples of Africa and Asia (as well as Latin America) to access the rights in the Declaration that mean the most to them and are grounded in their particular experience. These include the rights to practice and revitalize their cultural traditions and customs (Article 11); the right to manifest, practice, develop, and teach their spiritual and religious traditions, customs, and ceremonies (Article 12); and the right to determine and develop priorities and strategies for exercising their right to development (Article 23).

However, the self-determination framework—the right to self-determination, self-government, historical redress, treaty rights, and FPIC—resulted from the decolonization model. Indigenous peoples are first peoples, prior to the state, and entitled to recognition of their inherent sovereign status. For indigenous peoples of the CANZUS states, this interpretative approach highlights the normative power of the decolonization model and demonstrates that the self-determination framework is in the Declaration to address their specific circumstances. Northern indigenous peoples would, of course, claim the basic human rights outlined in the Declaration. These are important to them, albeit their *first priority* was decolonization and self-determination. Thus, under this mixed model, the decolonization model can be applied to counter the trend among states to subject the Declaration to a human rights model.

This reading of the roots of self-determination diverges sharply from conventional renderings, and it has important implications for domestic implementation. According to Anaya, self-determination is ordinarily a human right to be exercised within the confines of the state in various forms, from self-government to participation in public life.[72] Anaya rejects the possibility of independence, excepting secession as a last resort due to gross human rights abuses (as provided for in the penultimate paragraph of the 1970 Friendly Relations Declaration).[73] My reading of self-determination indicates that indigenous peoples have the option of independence should there be no agreement with the state about their terms of co-existence. The difficulty, of course, is Article 46's reference to territorial integrity, inserted due to pressure from the African Group of States. It provides that "nothing in this Declaration may be interpreted as implying . . . any right to engage in any

[72] Anaya, *supra* note 2, at Chapter 3. *See also* Hurst Hannum, *Rethinking Self-Determination*, 34:1 VA J. Intl L. 1 (1993) (Hannum notes the new "post-colonial era" for self-determination "in which international law guarantees to individuals and non-colonial peoples a much broader range of human rights, including meaningful self-determination but excluding a right to independent statehood" at 67).

[73] Anaya, *supra* note 2.

activity . . . which would dismember or impair, totally or in part, the territorial integrity or political unity of sovereign and independent states."[74]

On the one hand, it could be argued that this last-minute insertion of a reference to territorial integrity in the Declaration should not detract from the long-standing connection that Article 3 has with the UN decolonization program and that, as I have shown, was kept alive by Northern indigenous peoples. This would account for the CANZUS states' continual efforts after their endorsement of the Declaration to read down the self-determination framework despite the inclusion of states' right to territorial integrity. Territorial integrity is not sacrosanct—as is clear by the assertion in the 1970 Friendly Relations Declaration that territorial integrity is subject to the maintenance of representative government. On this argument, independence remains an option although, of course, an end-state was never the goal of most indigenous advocates participating in Declaration negotiations. The goal was to fundamentally re-adjust indigenous-state relations.

On the other hand, even if external self-determination is not available through Article 3, at the very least it requires that: first, states engage with indigenous peoples on a nation-to-nation basis to negotiate their terms of co-existence. Typically, this would occur in the context of constitutional reform; that is, some higher law within the state. However, it would typically be supplemented by various statutory and policy reforms. The Declaration's right to self-determination is still imbued with strong decolonization overtones, and the close association between self-determination and anti-colonialism remains and that will help at least to fill out and give meaning to self-determination as applied domestically; second, if there is no agreement and the right to self-determination is not fulfilled, then indigenous peoples can avail themselves of the right to independence under the penultimate paragraph of the 1970 Friendly Relations Declaration.[75] In other words, the 1970 Declaration would confer external self-determination on Northern indigenous peoples if their right to self-determination as specified in the Declaration is violated. Thus, it is the 1970 Declaration that performs this function, not the Declaration on Indigenous Peoples Rights.

[74] *United Nations Declaration on the Rights of Indigenous Peoples*, GA Res 61/295, UNGAOR, 61st Sess., Supp. No. 49, U.N. Doc. A/RES/61/295, art. 46 (2007).

[75] However, it is not clear in international law that this creates an additional legal category to classic colonialism. *See Accordance with International Law of the Unilateral Declaration of Independence in Respect of Kosovo (Kosovo Opinion), Advisory Opinion* 2010 I.C.J. Reports 403, at para. 79; *see also Reference re Secession of Quebec*, (1988) 2 S.C.R. 217, at para. 135.

2.3 Northern Indigenous Peoples: Toggling between the Human Rights and Decolonization Models

To be clear, indigenous peoples in CANZUS states may deploy the human rights model in their domestic advocacy efforts. This may be necessary just as a matter of pure expediency in some circumstances because of state resistance to reforms or an interim strategy until the state undertakes reforms to give full effect to the right to self-determination. As we have seen, the human rights model is much more palatable to states and NGOs. It taps into the widely respected, pervasive, and institutionally supported human rights program internationally and domestically. The universalistic quality of human rights and especially the notion of equality and fairness for all irrespective of background is broadly accepted. The human rights model makes sense to international human rights NGOs, like Human Rights Watch and Amnesty International. There is evidence of this model being used widely by indigenous peoples. Certainly, in any project, advancing indigenous rights on the basis of the human rights model is better than not advancing the Declaration at all. So, for example, in a claim to traditional lands, or discrimination in social services like child welfare, policing, or criminal court processes, advocates could appeal to the Declaration's human rights model.

However, in other instances, it would be the decolonization model that comes to the fore to support a claim or the two models could be advanced alongside each other. For example, a claim by Northern indigenous peoples to traditional lands in Article 26 of the Declaration may be advanced as a claim grounded in human rights—indigenous tenure systems deserve equal recognition with state-derived tenures. However, in the North, because of the decolonization model, Article 26 has self-determination connotations. The right in the land is based not only on the right to equality but prior sovereignty. This indicates that the indigenous right to land is more than a property right but has governmental elements. While courts in aboriginal title claims to date have excised any such governmental elements from land claims determinations, preferring to leave such matters to state-indigenous peoples' political negotiations, there is nothing to be lost by advancing a claim on these terms and thereby at least acculturating courts to the decolonization model. I discuss this more fully in the case study on aboriginal lands claims in Chapter 4.

With regard to the self-determination framework, including the specific right to self-determination, again I expect that the human rights model will continue to be used by some, perhaps most Northern indigenous peoples. However, this model is a thin model normatively and should—like the land rights example—be supported or replaced by the decolonization model where feasible. For example, in asserting a right to FPIC, the self-determination model provides more robust support normatively than a human rights model. The model can counter claims that FPIC should translate as a right to free, prior, and informed consultation.

2.4 Southern Indigenous Peoples and the Human Rights Model

Indigenous peoples of the South will continue to make claims to, say, FPIC, although such claims would be based on the relatively thin human rights model. A full right to FPIC in the thicker normative sense will be more difficult to justify than a right to informed consultation. Indigenous peoples of the South may claim a right to self-determination itself, in the human rights sense of promoting the right to effective participation in public life and local autonomy. The thicker meaning of self-determination—including the right to negotiate terms of co-existence in a territory—applies to indigenous peoples in the Northern states where historic sovereignty is a historic fact and part of the discourse and practice of indigenous rights. Nevertheless, secession remains a possibility in the South in cases of gross abuse of human rights under the 1970 Declaration on Friendly Relations.

It must also be emphasized that Southern indigenous peoples have access to a broad range of robust rights in the Declaration—compared to the limited minority rights contained in the UN Declaration on the Rights of Minorities. As we saw in Chapter 2, minority rights were seen by states as sources of insecurity and destabilization because they could be used by collectives to assert independence or autonomy.[76] The UN Charter, the UDHR, and the first regional human rights treaties make no reference to minority rights.[77]

[76] Will Kymlicka, Multicultural Odysseys: Navigating the New International Politics of Diversity 323 (2007).

[77] *Charter of the United Nations*, June 26, 1945, Can. T.S. 1945 No. 7 (entered into force Oct. 24, 1945); *Universal Declaration of Human Rights*, *supra* note 56. *Convention for the Protection of Human Rights and Fundamental Freedoms*, Nov. 4, 1950, 213 U.N.T.S. 221 (entered into force Sept. 3, 1953). OAS, Conference of American States, *American Declaration on the Rights and Duties of Man*, OEA/Ser.L/V/II. 82/Doc.6/Rev.1 (1948). *American Convention on Human Rights*, Nov. 22, 1969, 1144 U.N.T.S. 123 (entered into force July 18, 1978).

The UN Declaration on the Rights of Minorities contains only nine articles and adapts basic rights like equality to minority groups and seeks to protect cultural rights such as language and culture.[78] To compare the Declaration on the Rights of Minorities with the Declaration on the Rights of Indigenous Peoples on matters of local political autonomy, for example, the former protects minority rights of assembly and to establish and maintain their own associations, whereas the latter—aside from the rights to self-determination and self-government—refers to the right "to maintain and strengthen [indigenous peoples] distinct political, legal, economic, social and cultural institutions";[79] and the right "to determine the structures and to select the membership of [indigenous peoples] institutions in accordance with their own procedures."[80] In relation to education, the Declaration on the Rights of Minorities compels states to "take measures in the field of education, in order to encourage knowledge of the history, traditions, language, and culture of the minorities existing within their territory."[81] The Declaration provides, "Indigenous peoples have the right to establish and control their educational systems and institutions providing education in their own languages, in a manner appropriate to their cultural methods of teaching and learning."[82] There are in total in the Declaration—if we exclude the self-determination framework—forty rights that seek to protect Southern indigenous peoples, all grounded in the notion of indigenous autonomy. In Central and South America, indigenous peoples can now draw on the rights contained in the American Declaration on the Rights of Indigenous Peoples (American Declaration).[83] However, this lacks the normative weight of the UN Declaration because of the limited role of indigenous advocates in its making. It does however contain significant rights including the right to self-determination,[84] although this, like the UN Declaration, is subject to the states' right to territorial integrity[85] and all rights in the American Declaration are

[78] UN General Assembly, *Declaration on the Rights of Persons Belonging to National or Ethnic, Religious and Linguistic Minorities*, Feb. 3, 1992, A/RES/47/135 [hereinafter Declaration on Minorities].

[79] *United Nations Declaration on the Rights of Indigenous Peoples*, GA Res 61/295, UNGAOR, 61st Sess., Supp. No. 49, U.N. Doc. A/RES/61/295, art. 5 (2007) [hereinafter The Declaration].

[80] *Id.*, art. 33(2). Apart from the self-determination framework, *see also* arts. 18, 20(1), 34.

[81] Declaration on Minorities, *supra* note 78, art. 4(4).

[82] The Declaration, *supra* note 79, art. 14(1).

[83] *American Declaration on the Rights of Indigenous Peoples*, AG/RES. 2888 (XLVI-O/16), 3d Sess. (2016).

[84] *Id.*, art. 3.

[85] *Id.*, art. 4.

subject to a general limitation clause.[86] The American Declaration adopts many of the rights in the UN Declaration and contains new rights that are specific to the Americas, such as rights relating to indigenous peoples in "voluntary isolation or initial contact."[87] What is noticeably absent in the American Declaration is any measure for historical redress, like Article 28 of the UN Declaration that recognizes a right of redress for lands, territories, and resources that have been taken from indigenous peoples without their FPIC, or Article 11 that guarantees redress for the taking of cultural, intellectual, religious, and spiritual property.

2.5 Clarification of the Meaning of Indigenous Peoples in International Law

The mixed method of interpreting the Declaration—founded on the political history of the movement and the struggle between the North and South—helps to illuminate who is an indigenous people for the purposes for international law. Determining with some degree of precision just what type of collectives qualify as indigenous peoples for the purposes of international law is one of the most vexed issues for indigenous advocates, states, and commentators. The energy put into the question is vast due largely to the rights at stake. If a sub-state group can with legitimacy claim to be an indigenous people, then that group's members access not only the significant standards of protection but access to international funding and support. This is most evident to date in relation to the indigenous movements that have been formed in the Asian and African regions. Many attempts to address the question of definition are doctrinal and legal in nature, focusing on international texts and commentary on the meaning of peoples, nations, First Nations, aborigines, and minorities. Some review the political history of the Declaration negotiations and/or apply a textual interpretive approach while offering little guiding indicia apart from those grounded in the definition offered in the Cobo report[88] or the ILO Convention 169.[89]

[86] *Id.*, art. 36.

[87] *Id.*, art. 26.

[88] José Martínez Cobo, *Study of the Problem of Discrimination Against Indigenous Populations: Final Report*, UNESCOR, U.N. Doc. E/CN.4/Sub.2/1986/7/Add.4 (1986).

[89] *See, e.g.*, Joshua Castellino and Cathay Doyle, *Who Are Indigenous Peoples? in* The UN Declaration on the Rights of Indigenous Peoples: A Commentary (Jessie Hohman & Marc Weller eds., 2018).

Kingsbury's constructivist model was an attempt to bridge the divide between the North and South by extending the range of justifications typically deployed for indigenous claims-making—historic sovereignty—to those made by indigenous peoples of Asia.[90] However, as we have seen, this had the effect of obfuscating the connection between specific justifications and resulting norms.

It is the political history of the internal divisions in the international movement, cleaved from North to South, that allows us to develop a clearer understanding of indigenous peoples for the purposes of international law. Clearly, in the early years of the Declaration negotiations, indigenous peoples referred to peoples of the settler states. We saw in Chapter 2 that collectives formerly known as tribal peoples or minorities joined the international movement—first by accessing the ILO monitoring mechanism for ILO Convention No. 107 and then through their participation in the UN working groups negotiating the Declaration. Aided by international NGOs, particularly IWGIA, these groups developed a particular idea of *indigenous* for the purposes of their participation in the Declaration negotiations. These movements placed particular emphasis on their marked cultural difference and experience of marginalization and discrimination as minorities because this established common cause with indigenous peoples of the North and enabled them to distance themselves from other more threatening minorities seeking independence.

Thus, the contours of the meaning of indigenous peoples in the South are determined by the specific issues raised in their claims, that is, cultural difference and a history of marginalization within the state. This was the criteria established by the hill-tribes, pastoralists and hunter-gatherer communities of the South. This emphasis on cultural difference is, as we have seen, a double-edged sword. While it gives entry to the movement, it also limits the nature and extent of their claims and forces them to fit within essentialized identities. Nevertheless, despite all these efforts by Asian and African indigenous advocates and their supporters to give clarity to the meaning of indigenous peoples, Asian and African states continue to oppose the domestic application of the international concept of indigenous peoples, concerned about the impact of the self-determination framework.

[90] *Convention (No. 169) Concerning Indigenous and Tribal Peoples in Independent Countries*, June 27, 1989, 28 I.L.M. 1382 (entered into force Sept. 5, 1991).

3 The Case for the New Mixed Model

A mixed-model interpretation of the Declaration might best reflect the political history of its negotiations. It might also offer the best fit with the kinds of rights found in the Declaration. But how, precisely, does that translate into a legal justification for this model? Those who favor a return to the decolonization model could argue that Southern indigenous peoples, particularly Asian and African movements, are not bona fide indigenous peoples and entered the negotiations at a later stage attracted to the legal protection for human rights described in the Declaration. On the other hand, it could be argued that the human rights model adequately meets the needs of both the North and South, and the decolonization aims are unrealistic and merely symbolic. In response to this, I advance two arguments. The first locates the meaning of the Declaration in the "interpretive community" that gave rise to the text, where that community extends to the full range of participants whose interaction generated shared understandings. I argue that the "interpretive community" associated with the Declaration negotiations and its implementation shared, and continue to share, a set of assumptions, expectations, and knowledge that support my mixed-model interpretation of the Declaration. The second focuses on the argument that according to criteria set by Thomas Franck, the mixed model has significant legal legitimacy.

It has to be said at the outset that irrespective of the legal quality of the mixed model, it has political legitimacy because both the Northern and Southern indigenous movements contributed toward the Declaration's making. Compared to other standard-setting processes, the Declaration is held up as the exemplar of a fair and inclusive process and this, in turn, is said to bestow the Declaration with legitimacy and authority. It is clear that the Northern indigenous advocates' active role in negotiations secured the inclusion of the self-determination framework in the Declaration. Their historical experience of exclusion by colonizing powers and international law's complicity in sanctioning colonization made this essential. The full story of the Declaration's making must recognize the contribution made by Southern indigenous peoples. Their advocates provided arguments that formed an empirical basis to support the inclusion of the human rights in the Declaration. The issues raised by the South tended to underscore the urgency of the project. The sheer numbers of indigenous peoples in the South provided a compelling case for immediate action. Both the North and South made important contributions to the Declaration and justify the application of the mixed-model method so as to give due recognition to their respective contributions.

3.1 The "Interpretive Community" Associated with the Declaration

Principles of treaty interpretation in international law, strictly speaking, attend directly only to the negotiating positions taken by states Moreover, non-binding declarations do not benefit from any established alternative principles of interpretation.

It could be argued that the advocacy of one model or another by indigenous peoples (and others) during the negotiations is legally relevant because it informed how *states* understood what ideas had been captured in the Declaration. Such an argument would analogize the interpretation of a non-binding declaration to the interpretation of a treaty—perhaps even bolstered by the view that the Declaration elaborates on existing treaty obligations in the International Human Rights Covenants and elsewhere as applied to indigenous peoples. It would be entirely consistent with principles of treaty interpretation in which only states' positions count directly, but those positions can indirectly reflect any number of non-state inputs from lobby groups, experts, and affected parties regarding the meaning of the text being negotiated. Such an argument, however, would be deeply at odds with the legitimacy derived from the participation, and specifically the recognized status as participants, of indigenous peoples in the drafting of the Declaration.

In this section, I offer an alternative to the analogy with treaties that privileges states. Building on an "interpretive communities" theory of treaty interpretation found in international law scholarship, I argue that the "interpretive community" associated with the negotiation and implementation of the Declaration shared and continue to share a set of assumptions, expectations, and knowledge that support my mixed-model interpretation of the Declaration. The idea of treaty communities is not reflected in the law of treaties as such, although it has important affinities with the use of travaux preparatoires (Article 32) and the relevance of subsequent practice (Article 31(3)), for example, in the Vienna Convention on the Law of Treaties.[91]

[91] *Vienna Convention on the Law of Treaties*, May 23, 1969, 1155 U.N.T.S. 331, art. 32 (entered into force Jan. 27, 1980).

According to Ian Johnstone, interpretive communities are basically composed of all those closely associated with the negotiation and implementation of an international treaty. Johnstone refers to a set of concentric circles with an inner group of government officials (diplomatic representatives to the UN, for example) involved in the actual negotiation of the treaty, and a second circle of experts engaged in professional activities related to the norms in the treaty including international lawyers, NGOs, and academic critics.[92]

The idea of interpretive community, which originated as an idea about literary interpretation, sees "interpretive authority as residing in neither reader nor text but in the community of experts and interested participants engaged in the field of practice in which the interpretive dispute arises."[93] In international law, the interpretive community is an attempt to address particular shortcomings with international law, especially the criticism that all international law is interpreted by states to serve their own interests, and that international law lacks an authoritative, impartial adjudicator of interpretation disputes.[94] The concept rejects both (i) purely subjective readings of a treaty (whether by states or, say, civil society) and (ii) a supposedly objective textual approach whereby the meaning can be extracted from a text by a reader who employs the correct process. The notion is that this community "through the process of formulating, negotiating, adopting, and applying rules, come to share a set of assumptions, expectations, and a body of consensual knowledge."[95] Thus, "good arguments can be distinguished from bad."[96]

The approach is particularly compelling given the collaborative nature of treaty making. The "interpretive community" indicates that no one member of the community can simply offer its view and say that is the only answer for all time. It is the broader community that determines the persuasiveness of any position.[97] And states have buy-in to this process because ultimately

[92] *See* Ian Johnstone, *The Power of Interpretive Communities, in* Power in Global Governance (Michael Barnett & Raymond Duvall eds., 2004) [hereinafter Johnstone, "The Power of Interpretive Communities"].

[93] Ian Johnstone, The Power of Deliberation: International Law, Politics and Organizations 35 (2011).

[94] *Id.* at 380–93.

[95] *Id.* at 41.

[96] Johnstone, "The Power of Interpretive Communities," *supra* note 92, at 189.

[97] *Id.* ("[i]nternational law is an intersubjective enterprise. Interpretation is the search for an intersubjective understanding of the legal norm at issue: the interpretative task is to ascertain what the law means to the parties to a treaty or subjects of the law collectively rather than to any one of them individually" at 192).

they prefer to base their decisions in *law*, and not some politically motivated position, as this protects their reputation and self-interest in reciprocity and stability in international law.[98]

In the context of the Declaration, Johnstone's theory of treaty communities requires some adaptation. The Declaration is not a treaty, but nonetheless it resulted from a comprehensive exercise in norm creation and is an international rights instrument that is widely considered to possess significant normative force.[99] A further important difference in the context of the Declaration negotiations was that the "inner circle" of norm creators was not confined to government officials as is typically the case with standard setting. Northern indigenous peoples sought to ensure their equal participation in the negotiations as if they were states. Once the change was instituted, Southern indigenous peoples likewise were able to engage in negotiations in this open manner. As a result, the leaders of movements in Johnstone's second circle made their way into the inner circle and once there participated alongside states almost as equals. This counters criticisms that interpretive communities can be overly technocratic, comprising "elite" officials and experts.[100] While on the indigenous side there certainly were indigenous and non-indigenous scholars and lawyers involved in negotiating the Declaration, there were also indigenous leaders and community members, NGOs, and activists. And that remains the case in the context of implementation of the Declaration.

It is Johnstone's insights about the shared understandings of the interpretive community that are most useful for the mixed model advanced in this book. By the time the Declaration was brought before the UN General Assembly, there was a widely held view that the Declaration contained two distinct normative models aimed at different movements. And this continues to be the case in the implementation era following the Declaration's adoption by the UN General Assembly. Those closely associated with the Declaration negotiations appreciated that the self-determination framework was in the Declaration due to Northern advocates' emphasis on the decolonization model. This was the shared view despite the increasing prominence of the human rights model. It was also widely understood that

[98] *Id.* at 188.

[99] Making the Declaration Work: The United Nations Declaration on the Rights of Indigenous Peoples (Claire Charters & Rodolfo Stavenhagen, eds., 2009).

[100] Johnstone, "The Power of Interpretive Communities," *supra* note 92, at 53.

the decolonization model was not directed at independence but that this was an option if states and indigenous peoples failed to negotiate their fair terms of co-existence.

Indeed, the mixed model can be witnessed at the very beginning of the contemporary movement at the 1977 Geneva Conference.[101] This was well before the rise of the Asian and African indigenous movements, but it was well attended by Latin American indigenous advocates who spoke more of human rights and culture than their North American counterparts, who emphasized self-determination and decolonization. The model declaration produced at this conference thus referred to two types of indigenous peoples—Article 1 described "Indigenous Nations" as those who:[102]

> shall be accorded recognition as nations, and proper subjects of international law, provided the people concerned desire to be recognized as a nation and meet the fundamental requirements of nationhood, namely,
> a. having a permanent population;
> b. having a defined territory;
> c. having a government; and
> d. having the ability to enter into relations with states.

This definition captured the US indigenous peoples' experience as "domestic, dependent nations" and their aims of independence. However, it had little meaning for Central and South American indigenous peoples who at the time were struggling for recognition of basic human rights. The Declaration thus referred in Article 2 to "Indigenous Groups" who could not meet the requirements of nationhood yet were "subjects of international law" and entitled to the protections of the Declaration provided they had "bonds of language, heritage, tradition, or other common identity."[103]

In addition, the mixed model is reflected in the first working group Chair's explanatory comments on the first draft of the Declaration. Erica-Irene Daes noted that Article 3 would "ordinarily be interpreted as their right to negotiate freely their status and representation in the State in which they

[101] International Indian Treaty Council, *International NGO Conference on Discrimination Against Indigenous Populations-1977-In the Americas*, 1:7 Treaty Council News (1977).

[102] *Draft Declaration of Principles for the Defense of the Indigenous Nations and Peoples of the Western Hemisphere*, UNESCOR, U.N. Doc. E/CN.4/Sub.2/L.684, at Annex IV (1978).

[103] *Id.* at 25.

live."[104] But she also gave self-determination a human rights reading noting that "[o]rdinarily, it is the right of the citizens of an existing, independent State to share power democratically" or more strongly that gross human rights abuses could result in independence (here, Daes was referencing the 1970 Declaration on Friendly Relations).[105] It could be argued that the dual reading of self-determination seeks to accommodate the competing demands of Northern indigenous peoples and states. However, Daes was clearly aware of the tensions between the North and South and their different objectives. Her mixed reading of self-determination, I argue, also accounts for these differences.

Of course, as we saw in Chapter 1, the right to self-determination itself has always been the subject of dual interpretations. President Woodrow Wilson saw self-determination in "human rights terms" as supporting "democratic self-government" and "internal self-determination."[106] On the other hand, Lenin and Soviet political leaders saw self-determination as an anti-colonial project. Later, the issue arose during the negotiations on common Article 1 in the International Human Rights Covenants, the 1960 Declaration on the Granting of Independence, and the 1970 Declaration on Friendly Relations. Decolonization leaders sought recognition of human rights through self-determination but also viewed self-determination as a path to independence, while Northern states emphasized its human rights qualities.[107]

Focusing on the interpretive community associated with the Declaration negotiations, it is clear that indigenous peoples and states accepted a mixed model. Asian and African indigenous advocates accepted that the "strong self-determination claims" related to the situation of Northern indigenous peoples (as did the anthropology NGOs responsible for introducing them). The African Commission Working Group, which lobbied for African indigenous peoples' participation in the Declaration negotiations, advanced a mixed model.[108] Generally, Latin American indigenous advocates did not pursue strong forms of self-determination seeing this as the preserve of the North. However, as discussed below, the mixed model is not the main model

[104] Erica-Irene A. Daes, *Explanatory Note Concerning the Draft Declaration on the Rights of Indigenous Peoples*, UN Commission on Human Rights, 45th Sess., U.N. Doc. E/CN.4/Sub.2/1993/26/Add.1 (1993).

[105] *Id.*

[106] Antonio Cassese, Self-Determination of Peoples: A Legal Reappraisal 50–51 (1998).

[107] *Id.* Moyn and Roland Burke, Decolonization and the Evolution of International Human Rights (2010).

[108] *See* IWGIA and the African Commission on Human and Peoples' Rights (ACHPR), *Report of the African Commission's Working Group of Experts on Indigenous Populations/Communities* (2005).

used by Northern indigenous advocates. And this, as I argue below, is due to the dominant human rights model.

States involved in the negotiations also accepted these positions. China, India, and Bangladesh consistently insisted that self-determination was for the North—as did African states. To an extent, this was a political strategy by states wary of international scrutiny and concerned about local secessionist movements. However, it was also because these states saw indigenous peoples and self-determination as suited to the particular historical circumstances of the North. Latin American states saw the Declaration as affirming basic human rights like the ILO Convention 169 and this view is reflected in local reforms. That no doubt accounts for why all Latin American states have endorsed the Declaration. Their statements at the time of the UN General Assembly adoption of the Declaration make clear that it is the human rights that are of most significance in Central and South America.[109]

The Northern states opposed the domestic application of the decolonization model. Yet, they all understood its connection with the self-determination framework. They had witnessed the shift from a human rights and minority rights model in the early stages of the Declaration negotiations and the emergence of the self-determination framework. These states were consistently exposed to the decolonization model advanced by Northern indigenous advocates. The CANZUS states repeatedly said that self-determination could be read as conferring a unilateral right of self-determination and possible secession.[110] However, there was no ever-present threat of secession by indigenous movements—not compared to the threats faced by many Asian and African states.[111] Instead, the Northern states fully appreciated that the inclusion of a right to self-determination in the Declaration would have weighty normative implications domestically.

At the same time, there was a shared understanding that the Declaration also met the core concerns of Southern indigenous peoples through the human

[109] *See, e.g.*, UNGAOR, 61st Sess., 107th Plen. Mtg., U.N. Doc. A/61/PV.107, at 23 (2007) (Statement of Brazil delivered by Mr. Tarragô) (Latin American states emphasized that self-determination was to be exercised within the state and would not interfere with the sovereignty or political unity of states).

[110] *See, e.g.*, Rosemary Banks, "Address on behalf of Australia, New Zealand and the United States" (Statement delivered at the 61st Session of the United Nations General Assembly, Oct. 16, 2006), <https://web.archive.org/web/20131108103333/http://mfat.govt.nz/Media-and-publications/Media/MFAT-speeches/2006/0-16-October-2006b.php>.

[111] Roderic Pitty & Shannara Smith, *The Indigenous Challenge to Westphalian Sovereignty*, 46:1 Aust. J. Polit. Sci. 121 (2011).

rights set out in the Declaration. Asian and African states continue to oppose local application of indigenous peoples, but that is largely due to the threat posed by minorities with secessionist ambitions. The right to self-determination is seen as too dangerous. However, they ought to be more willing to accept a human rights application of the Declaration. Thus the mixed model helps address Asian and African objections to domestic application of the Declaration.

The mixed model is now applied in practice by indigenous advocates seeking implementation of the Declaration, including Southern indigenous advocates and international institutions. For example, James Anaya, in his capacity as the UN Special Rapporteur on the Rights of Indigenous Peoples, advanced the human rights model in Southern states (for example, his reports on the Democratic Republic of Congo and Asia), and directed his attention at groups commonly accepted by the movement to be indigenous in Asia and Africa (the culturally distinctive and marginalized, Batwa, San, Massai, etc.). Yet, he adjusted his approach and applies both human rights and decolonization-type models when working on Northern states (for example, his New Zealand and Canadian reports).[112] Likewise, his successor Vicky Tauli Corpuz also placed greater emphasis on self-determination in her reports on Canada and the United States compared to those on Latin America and Africa.[113]

3.2 The Legal Legitimacy of the Mixed-Model Interpretative Method

In this section, I advance a legal theory justification for the inclusion of both a decolonization and human rights model in the Declaration that is based on Thomas Franck's arguments on legitimacy.[114] According to Franck, there are four "indicators"—pedigree, determinacy, coherence, and adherence—that determine the degree to which a rule, or a system of rules, or a process for

[112] *See, e.g., Report of the Special Rapporteur on the Rights of Indigenous Peoples, James Anaya, The Situation of Indigenous Peoples in Canada,* UN Human Rights Council, 27th Sess., U.N. Doc. A/HRC/27/52/Add.2 (2014).

[113] *Report of the Special Rapporteur on the Rights of Indigenous Peoples on Her Mission to the United States of America,* UN Human Rights Council, 36th Sess., U.N. Doc. A/HRC/36/46/Add.1 (2017).

[114] THOMAS FRANCK, FAIRNESS IN INTERNATIONAL LAW AND INSTITUTIONS (1995) [hereinafter Franck, Fairness in International Law]. *See also* Thomas Franck, *Legitimacy in the International System*, 82 AM. J. INTL. L. 705 (1988).

making or interpreting rules, has legitimacy in international law and, as a result, possesses normative pull for states to comply with the rule or process. Some rules or processes are more or less legitimate than others to varying degrees, and thus accordingly exert varying degrees of compliance pull. The question here is the degree of legitimacy of the mixed-model method of interpreting the rights in the Declaration assessed against Franck's criteria.

Starting with the criteria of pedigree, this refers to the depth of the rule's roots in a historical process. It is clear that the mixed model has a long history in the context of the Declaration negotiations over twenty-five years. But the notion of a mixed-model construction of the right to self-determination reaches back much further to the inter-War years. Determinacy refers to the rule's ability to communicate the content with clarity. Indeterminate normative standards make it harder to know what conformity is expected, which in turn makes it easier to justify non-compliance. The mixed model as an interpretive framework assists determination of the rights in the Declaration. For example, a contentious issue on FPIC, covered in the case study on FPIC below, is whether the right to FPIC calls for consent or merely consultation. Many businesses, like extractive industry operating in indigenous territories, prefer a constrained reading of FPIC—what Nathan Yaffe describes as a "thin, liberal notion of consent"[115]—or assume an obligation to consult only. Scholars argue that the general limitation of indigenous rights in Article 46(2) of the Declaration means any right to consent may be limited in specific circumstances. These types of readings may be consistent with a human rights model. However, as I argue below, in the North, a decolonization model would indicate that the requirement is consent, not consultation, and that limitation clauses like Article 46(2) need to accommodate FPIC's normative grounding in decolonization. With the right to self-determination, the mixed model also clarifies that there are different considerations in any deliberation about the requirements for a remedial right to secession under the penultimate paragraph of the 1970 Declaration on Friendly Relations. For Southern indigenous peoples, the Declaration will be invoked in cases of gross abuses of human rights. For Northern indigenous peoples, the 1970 Declaration would confer external self-determination if their self-determination as understood in the context of the decolonization model is violated. The mixed model thus provides greater clarity about the effect of

[115] Nathan Yaffe, *Indigenous Consent: A Self-Determination Perspective*, 19:2 Melb. J. Intl. L. 709 (2018).

specific norms in the Declaration by matching them up with their respective justificatory basis.

Coherence is that quality of a rule which permits it to be seen holistically: that is, as part of a rule context in which the parts gather compliance pull from the purpose and meaning of a larger whole. A rule will still lack a measure of legitimacy if the rule is so at odds with other applicable rules as to establish cognitive dissonance in the audience to which it is addressed. In other words, the given rule must be seen as being in a certain kind of harmony with the network of related previously existing rules of which it is apart. In terms of coherence, it is clear that both the decolonization and human rights constructions of the Declaration are in keeping with the pre-existing rules of international law. The human rights model clearly is connected to the human rights system in international law. The decolonization model also has a connection with the body of laws and practices that emanated during the decolonization movement in the post-war years. The inclusion of a reference to territorial integrity in the Declaration further ensures coherence between the Declaration and the pre-existing law relating to self-determination. As we have seen, if a right to independence is to be invoked that would occur under the 1970 Declaration on Friendly Relations.

The mixed model has coherence, too, in that it promotes clarity about who is indigenous for the purposes of the Declaration and allocates indigenous rights on a fair basis. Coherence requires that "like cases are treated alike" in the application of the rule. This aspect of coherence is similar to the idea of consistency, but Franck draws a distinction between coherence and consistency. Consistency refers to the treatment of two or more subjects in the same way, whereas coherence allows differing treatment of the various subjects provided the differing treatment is connected to "some rational principle of broader application." Thus, the mixed model promotes coherence by recognizing that indigenous peoples of the North and those of the South should be treated differently on the basis that the justifications underlying their claims differ. To merge both groups under a human rights model, in fact, promotes dissonance by obfuscating the conceptual basis of each group's rights. What would be incoherent is to limit indigenous peoples to the human rights model. That would not be treating like case alike. There is, then, inconsistency in that within the large concept of indigenous peoples, some are treated differently from others. But there is coherence.

According to Franck, adherence means "the vertical nexus between a single primary rule of obligation and a pyramid of secondary rules governing the creation, interpretation and application of such rules by the community."[116] The legitimacy of each primary rule depends in part on its adherence to the secondary rules or processes. Rules are better able to pull toward compliance if they are demonstrably supported by the procedural and institutional framework within which the community organizes itself. Franck refers to national constitutions and their function in producing legitimate primary rules through a clear process. As noted above on the matter of coherence, both the human rights and decolonization models are grounded in well-established principles in international law.

4 Conclusion

The normatively mixed account of the Declaration is truest to its political history and can also be justified in terms of legality and legitimacy. But it is not the dominant model in international law. In Chapter 4, I focus on how the mixed model could be applied in this implementation era. In the South, the mixed model will assist local movements in their struggle for recognition of indigenous rights. The mixed model ought to address Central and South American states' ambivalence toward, and Asia's and Africa's outright objection to, indigenous rights while also emphasizing the salience of the human rights model in the Declaration for Southern indigenous peoples.

In the North, the challenge for the mixed model proposed is how to avoid the risk of the decolonization model being subsumed by the human rights model. The human rights model reigns supreme. The mixed-model reading offered by Benedict Kingsbury in particular—which sought to accommodate the movements of the North and South but under the generic categories of "history and culture"—has facilitated this process by de-emphasizing the connection between the decolonization model and the self-determination framework. James Anaya and Karen Engle are part of a self-fulfilling prophecy. Anaya's human rights model has provided the main platform for his work as (former) UN Special Rapporteur on the Rights of Indigenous Peoples. The more Engle argues that the Northern indigenous groups resiled from strong claims to self-determination and embraced a human rights model, the less likely they are to use the decolonization model. However, Engle overstates Northern indigenous advocates' emphasis on human rights

116 Franck, Fairness in International Law, *supra* note 114, at 41.

and culture by reading the political history too starkly. Anaya seems to favor human rights for its broad appeal and utility.

It is possible for the Declaration to contain competing narratives without one collapsing into the other. Indeed, as Martti Koskenniemi argues in *From Apology to Utopia*, there is a perennial tension in international law between utopian and apologetic models—one necessarily borrows from the other but neither is ever submerged in the other.[117] The utopian model refers to the ideal of international law—the notion, say, of human rights as supranational—while the apologetic model speaks to the realities of international law, that is, international law is simply made by states for states. International lawyers therefore navigate their way between extreme versions of the two poles.[118] To consider this in the context of the Declaration, each of the component parts of the mixed model contains elements of both utopia and apology. The human rights model is based on state practice and what many states have committed to in human rights treaties while also being utopian insofar as human rights impose limitations on the exercise of sovereignty. The decolonization model likewise is utopian in the sense that it extends beyond the current state practice in the North, but is also realist insofar as it involves the negotiation of a social contract after the fact of unjust deprivation of sovereignty. The mixed model is thus both utopian and apologist without being completely one or the other.

A comparison can also be made to the competing interpretative approaches toward constitutions in modern constitutional democracies (for example, the American Constitution, or the Canadian Charter of Rights and Freedoms).[119] There is much at stake, given the special role constitutions play in defining and limiting the authority and powers of government. On the one hand, we have what is commonly known as the "originalist model."[120] According to this model, Constitutions establish—at their point of

[117] Martti Koskenniemi, From Apology to Utopia: The Structure of International Legal Argument (2006).

[118] Frederic Megret, *The Apology of Utopia: Some Thoughts on Koskenniemian Themes, with Particular Emphasis on Massively Institutionalized International Human Rights Law*, *27*:2 Temp. Intl. & Comp. L. J. 484 (2013), <http://www.temple.edu/law/ticlj/fall2013/Megret_TheApologyofUtopia.pdf> (As Megret observes, "human rights adjudication is a constant balancing act-nodding to an eager civil society whilst winking at states that one has understood their concerns . . . The heart of that form of practical knowledge is that international legal reasoning is never so strong as when it navigates adroitly-typically at roughly equal distance-between the twin traps of apology and utopia.").

[119] Charles J.G. Sampford & Kim Preston, Interpreting Constitutions: Theories, Principles and Institutions (1996).

[120] Dennis J. Goldford, The American Constitution and the Debate over Originalism (2005).

creation and for all time—a framework of broadly stated moral and political commitments by which the various branches of government are to function. Emphasis is placed on the intentions of those who created the constitution, or the original public understandings of the words chosen for inclusion in the constitution.

On the other hand is the model of "living constitutionalism."[121] This model sees a constitution as an evolving, living entity that is capable of adapting to changing social circumstances and contemporary moral and political beliefs. Originalists oppose this approach on the basis that it undermines the certainty and neutrality offered by the originalist model. There is the risk that contemporary judges, through their interpretation, will change the constitution to suit their own political inclinations and moral preferences. The point of this example is that there is a continuing contest between the "originalist position" and the "living constitutionalism model," with neither ever being victorious. However, this is due to *persistence* of the originalist position, particularly by those concerned about the rising influence of the courts under the living constitutionalism model. As I discuss in Chapter 4, it is really up to indigenous advocates to draw on the decolonization model. Although it does not have to be used in every case—toggling from a human rights to a decolonization model is possible or they could be advanced together—it should be viewed as the fundamental model.

[121] Ran Hirschl, Constitutional Theocracy (2011).

4
Applying the Mixed-Model Interpretative Approach

1 Introduction

Chapter 3 presented the case for a mixed-model interpretation of the Declaration based on the fact that throughout negotiations two principal strands of argument were emphasized by two different types of social movements. The mixed model thus keeps faith with the Declaration's political history, particularly the diverse and extensive participation of indigenous peoples. Other models tend to obfuscate this history by discounting the differences between the North and South, papering over them, or emphasizing the role of the North.

However, as I note in this chapter, while Southern movements use the human rights model, the Southern states, especially African and Asian states, continue to resist local application of indigenous rights given their connection with the self-determination framework in the Declaration. The exception to this is Latin America where the "indigenous category" is long-established and widely accepted by states. However, these states tend to draw on the standards in the ILO Convention 169 rather than the Declaration. I argue that the mixed model could benefit the Southern movements, particularly the Asian and African movements, by (1) removing state concerns with the self-determination framework and fear of secession movements; (2) recognizing the legal and political legitimacy that these human rights have for Southern indigenous peoples and thus strengthening the obligations owed by Southern states; and (3) hopefully leading to less emphasis on cultural difference by Southern movements—there would be less need to use culture to establish common cause with the international movement and to defuse anxiety held by Southern states over minority security and stability issues. The human rights model would draw attention away from culture toward equality as the fundamental basis of their indigenous rights in the Declaration.

The UN Declaration on the Rights of Indigenous Peoples. Andrew Erueti, Oxford University Press. © Oxford University Press 2022. DOI: 10.1093/oso/9780190068301.003.0005

I also note that ironically even in the Northern states, indigenous rights reforms track the human rights model. Indeed, many indigenous advocates themselves have resiled from the key demands sought in the early years of the movement and hard-won, as I have argued, in the Declaration. But that does not mean that decolonization has been given up completely by domestic movements. What I call for is clearer positioning of the decolonization model as the interpretative model by Northern indigenous advocates domestically and internationally—which generally has not been the case so far. Indigenous advocates need to re-assert the decolonization model to counteract the current emphasis on human rights models (or their correlates). I set out how the decolonization model can make a difference to indigenous advocacy in CANZUS states by considering how it could have influenced the outcome in three case studies. The first concerns aboriginal title litigation in Canada; the second, the recognition of Māori rights to freshwater in New Zealand. I also critique the orthodox human rights reading of the right to free, prior, and informed consent (FPIC) and argue for a mixed-model understanding of FPIC.

2 The Human Rights Model in Asia, Africa, and Latin America

Within the regions of Asia, Africa, and Latin America, the indigenous movements apply the human rights model. They are assisted in this by UN institutions, regional human rights bodies, and international human rights organizations.[1] However, the problem is that Southern states remain opposed to the Declaration—especially African and Asian states.

2.1 Southeast Asia

In Southeast Asia, there have been regular calls by Asian indigenous advocates for the UN Special Rapporteur on Indigenous Rights to carry

[1] The human rights groups that adopted and applied the human rights model and were closely associated with the Declaration negotiations include Amnesty International, Canadian Friends Service Committee (Quakers), International Service for Human Rights, International Work Group for Indigenous Affairs (IWGIA), Kairos: Canadian Ecumenical Justice Initiatives, Netherlands Centre for Indigenous Peoples (NCIV), and Rights & Democracy.

out country field missions to Asian states, but it is not politic for the rapporteur to do so without a government invitation. Since the mandate of the Special Rapporteur was established in 2001, there has been only one mission to Asia—the Philippines, one of the few Asian countries to recognize indigenous peoples.[2] In 2013, the (then) Special Rapporteur, James Anaya, participated in a "consultation" in Malaysia with representatives of indigenous peoples from several Asian states including Bangladesh, India, Indonesia, Japan, and Malaysia.[3] The report was careful to avoid shaming specific states and so directed its criticism toward particular human rights "themes," including the lack of adequate regulatory protections for indigenous peoples' customary rights over land, political participation, socioeconomic conditions, and religious discrimination.[4] The appointment of Vicky Tauli-Corpuz as the first Indigenous Asian UN Rapporteur on Indigenous Rights raised some hopes of greater acceptance of indigenous rights in the region. Yet, there was only a visit to Timor Leste during her six-year tenure and this is a country where basically all of the inhabitants are "indigenous" in a newly independent state formerly under Indonesian rule. Instead, as with her predecessor, Tauli-Corpuz conducted a consultation with Asian indigenous NGOs in Thailand.

Despite application by the Asian indigenous movement of the human rights model, there continues to be state opposition to the domestic application of indigenous rights. Bangladesh, India, China, and Indonesia remain the strongest opponents. Their principal concern continues to be the Article 3 right to self-determination in the Declaration and the self-determination framework. As noted in Chapter 2, most Asian states voted for the Declaration but also argued that there were no indigenous peoples in their states while also endorsing the inclusion of a reference to territorial integrity in the Declaration. As an example of the resistance, in 2010, the Permanent Forum on Indigenous Issues sent a rapporteur to Bangladesh without the government's invitation to investigate continuing disputes over land in the Chittagong Hill Tracts. Bangladesh strongly objected when the Forum's

[2] *Report of the Special Rapporteur on the Situation of Human Rights and Fundamental Freedoms of Indigenous People, Rodolfo Stavenhagen: Mission to the Philippines,* UN Commission on Human Rights, 59th Sess., Supp. No. 90, U.N. Doc. E/CN.4/2003/90 (2003).

[3] *Report of the UN Special Rapporteur on the Rights of Indigenous Peoples, James Anaya, Addendum: Consultation on the Situation of Indigenous Peoples in Asia,* UN Human Rights Council, 24th Sess., Supp. No. 41, U.N. Doc. A/HRC/24/41/Add.3 (2013).

[4] *Id.* at para. 4 (there is a reference to self-determination, but this is said to include issues such as identity, religious discrimination, customary justice, and political participation).

rapporteur presented his report at the 2011 session,[5] asserting that while there may be "ethnic minorities" or "tribals" in the Chittagong Hill Tracts, all citizens of Bangladesh are indigenous peoples.[6] As a result, Bangladesh argued that the Permanent Forum lacked "locus standi" to consider the situation of the Chittagong Hill Tracts[7] and suggested that initiating inquiries such as this could lead to questioning of the Permanent Forum's tenure[8] and mandate.[9]

Several Asian states formally recognize indigenous peoples within their borders. Nepal recognizes indigenous peoples in its constitution, while the Philippines enacted the Indigenous Peoples Rights Act in 1997 (IPRA), providing a process for demarcating traditional lands and instituting a right to FPIC. Japan, while initially opposed to indigenous rights, now officially accepts the Ainu as indigenous peoples.[10] In Taiwan, local tribal peoples are recognized in domestic law as indigenous peoples. However, even these states exhibit ambivalence toward implementing indigenous rights. In Nepal, for example, just who qualifies as indigenous has become a vexed issue, given the preferential treatment accorded to indigenous peoples and the ethnic tensions and political instability following Nepal's civil war.[11] Japan does not recognize the fishing rights of the Ainu and continues to reject the concept of collective rights for the Ainu.[12] Critics argue that the Philippine's IPRA is not implemented.[13]

Asian states' opposition to indigenous rights has seriously impeded the movement as a whole in the context of a proposed UN General Assembly resolution on more effective indigenous participation in the UN. In 2015,

[5] *Study on the Status of Implementation of the CHT Peace Accord of 1997 Submitted by the UN Special Rapporteur*, UN Permanent Forum on Indigenous Issues, Supp. No. 6, U.N. Doc. E/C.19/2011/6 (2011).

[6] *See* "Statement by the Bangladesh Delegation" to the 10th session of the UN Permanent Forum on Indigenous Issues, May 25, 2011, New York.

[7] *Id.*

[8] *Id.* ("We believe, this 'cherry picking' approach might not be beneficial for the Forum in the long run bearing in mind that we have seen the demise of even higher bodies on allegations of selectivity.")

[9] *Id.* at 4, noting that the report was not "related to the mandate of the Forum."

[10] M.V. Okada, *The Plight of Ainu, Indigenous People of Japan*, 1:1 J. Indigenous Soc. Dev. 2 (2012), <http://www.hawaii.edu/sswork/jisd/jisd_i1.html>.

[11] *Special Rapporteur on the Rights of Indigenous Peoples, James Anaya, Addendum: Report on the Situation of the Indigenous Peoples of Nepal*, UN Human Rights Council, 12th Sess., Supp. No. 34, U.N. Doc. A/HRC/12/34/Add.3 (2009).

[12] Erik Larson, Zachary Johnson, & Monique Murphy, *Emerging Indigenous Governance: Ainu Rights at the Intersection of Global Norms and Domestic Institutions*, 33:1 Alt. J. 53 (2008); Richard Siddle, *The Limits to Citizenship in Japan: Multiculturalism, Indigenous Rights and the Ainu*, 7:4 Citizenship Stud. 447 (2003).

[13] Joji Carino, *Indigenous Peoples' Right to Free, Prior, Informed Consent: Reflections on Concepts and Practice*, 22 Ariz. J. Intl. & Comp. L. 19 (2005).

the UN General Assembly asked the President to lead a consultation on the possible measures needed "to enable the participation of indigenous peoples' representatives and institutions in meetings of relevant United Nations bodies on issues affecting them."[14] The object was a "draft text" to be adopted by the General Assembly the following year. This was widely viewed by many in the international movement as an opportunity to open new doors for indigenous advocates, including the possibility of permanent observer state status in the UN General Assembly, like the Vatican. The President of the UN General Assembly appointed four advisers, including two indigenous representatives, to lead consultations with states and indigenous peoples which produced a "compilation of views."[15] However, the whole proposal foundered on the rock of opposition led by India, Bangladesh, and China. These states sought an internationally agreed definition of "indigenous peoples" and the right for their governments to act as effective gatekeepers by determining who if anyone within the nation would qualify as indigenous.[16] India argued that the concept of indigenous peoples "could not be expanded arbitrarily to include societies where diverse ethnic groups had lived together for thousands of years."[17] The representative of Bangladesh said "consultations on the participation of those peoples must remain inter-governmental."[18] After three years of negotiations, the result was a resolution that merely affirmed the existing right of indigenous peoples to participate in the UN and noted that further elaboration of this right will be needed in the future.[19]

2.2 Latin America

Latin America does not expressly reject the Declaration or the indigenous peoples' category in domestic law and policy. Nevertheless, Latin American states tend to favor the ILO Convention 169 over the Declaration and the

[14] *Rights of Indigenous Peoples*, GA Res 70/232, UNGAOR, 70th Sess., U.N. Doc. A/RES/70/232 (2015).

[15] *Compilation of Views on Possible Measures Necessary to Enable the Participation of Indigenous Peoples' Representatives and Institutions in Relevant United Nations Meetings on Issues Affecting Them, and of Good Practices within the United Nations Regarding Indigenous Peoples' Participation*, GA Res A/70/990, UNGAOR, 70th Sess., Supp. No. 49, U.N. Doc. Res A/70/990 (2016).

[16] *Enhancing the Participation of Indigenous Peoples' Representatives and Institutions in Meetings of Relevant United Nations Bodies on Issues Affecting Them*, GA Res 71/321, UNGAOR, 70th Sess., U.N. Doc. A/RES/71/321 (2017).

[17] *Id.*

[18] *Id.*

[19] *Id.*

American Declaration—it seems because most of the Latin American states have ratified the convention, and it does not contain the self-determination framework.[20] The American Declaration was an important achievement for indigenous peoples in the Americas, most significantly because it guarantees a right to self-determination.[21] However, as noted in Chapter 3, there are significant gaps—including the absence of any right to historical redress for lands, resources, and cultural and intellectual property taken without indigenous peoples' consent—and indigenous peoples' participation in negotiations fell well short of the standard set in the UN Declaration negotiations.[22]

Compared to Africa and Asia, there is little threat of self-determination being used by secessionist movements. However, Latin American states are concerned about FPIC.[23] Indigenous peoples have lobbied for consultation laws—or initiated their own consultation processes[24]—and there have been some important reforms. For example, in Peru and Ecuador—both countries with large numbers of indigenous communities—the governments have each enacted regulations on free, prior, and informed *consultation*.[25] Indigenous organizations throughout the Americas often insist on a right to FPIC, not merely the right to consultation, and in support point to the right to FPIC in the Declaration. However, many indigenous advocates seem to be content

[20] Peru was a co-sponsoring state and introduced the Declaration to the UN General Assembly. For example, the Peru and Ecuador regulations refer to the ILO Convention 169 and do not refer to the Declaration even though both countries were regular and active participants in the Declaration negotiations.

[21] *American Declaration on the Rights of Indigenous Peoples*, AG/RES. 2888 (XLVI-O/16), 3d Sess., (2016), art. 3.

[22] When the American Declaration was adopted, the United States noted that it had persistently objected to the text, that it was not legally binding, and did not create new law. Canada took no position on the Declaration given it had not participated in recent negotiations. *Id.* at 2.

[23] Inter-American Commission on Human Rights, *Indigenous and Tribal Peoples' Rights over their Ancestral Lands and Natural Resources: Norms and Jurisprudence of the Inter-American Human Rights System*, 35:2 AM. INDIAN L. REV. 263 (2010).

[24] In Guatemala, for example, in response to mining proposals by corporations and the absence of any official consultation process or efforts at engagement by mining companies, indigenous communities have organized their own *consultas populares*—or local referenda—to decide on whether mining should proceed in their area; *see Report of the Special Rapporteur on the Situation of Human Rights and Fundamental Freedoms of Indigenous People, James Anaya: Observations on the Situation of the Rights of the Indigenous People of Guatemala with Relation to the Extraction Projects, and other Types of Projects, in Their Traditional Territories*, UN Human Rights Council, 18th Sess., Supp. No. 35, U.N. Doc. A/HRC/18/35/Add.3, at 1 (2011); *see also* Amnesty International, "Guatemala: Mining in Guatemala: Rights at Risk," AMR 34/002/2014 (2014).

[25] *See* Peru, *Ley del Derecho a la Consulta Previa a los Pueblos Indigenas u Originarios, Reconocido en el Convenio 169 de la Organizacion Internacional Del Trabajo Ley No. 29785*, 2011, <http://www.minem.gob.pe/minem/archivos/Ley%2029785%20Consulta%20Previa%20pdf.pdf>; and Ecuador, *Ley Organica de Consulta a las Comunas, Comunidades, Pueblos y Nacionalidades del Ecuador Exposicion de Motivos*, 2012.

with a robust framework for consultations given the absence in many cases of any proper form of consultation.

The Inter-American system has developed a body of law that sees indigenous rights as human rights adapted to the indigenous situation. However, rather than seeing the rights as grounded in *equality*, the Inter-American Court sees them as based on "cultural survival."

The breakthrough decision was *Awas Tingni* (2001), where the Inter-American Court recognized that the human right to property in Article 21 of the American Convention included indigenous peoples' collective forms of traditional land tenure.[26] Equality was key to the decision in that the Awas Tingni community's indigenous tenure was viewed as deserving of the same equal protection as non-indigenous tenures.[27] But the human right to culture was also used quite independently as a rationale for recognition of the right to land. As the Court put it:

> The close ties of indigenous peoples with the land must be recognized and understood as the fundamental basis of their cultures, their spiritual life, their integrity, and the economic survival. For indigenous communities, relations to the land are not merely a matter of possession and production but a material and spiritual element, which they must fully enjoy, even to preserve their cultural legacy and transmit it to future generations.

This jurisprudence has been subjected to criticism given its essentialization of indigenous peoples.[28] It is only the most culturally distinctive indigenous peoples that can lay claim to these rights.[29] The difficulty lies in basing

[26] Case of the Mayagna (Sumo) Awas Tingni Indigenous Community v. Nicaragua (2001), Inter-Am. Ct. H.R. (ser. C) No. 79.

[27] S. James Anaya, *Divergent Discourses about International Law, Indigenous Peoples, and Rights over Lands and Natural Resources: Toward a Realist Trend*, 16 COLO. J. INTL. ENVTL. L. & POL'Y. 237 (2005) ("The interpretive method that resulted in the outcome in Awas Tingni arises within a human rights frame of analysis, rather than one that sees indigenous peoples' rights as based fundamentally on a continuity of historical sovereignty.").

[28] *See generally* KAREN ENGLE, THE ELUSIVE PROMISE OF INDIGENOUS DEVELOPMENT: RIGHTS, CULTURE, STRATEGY (2010).

[29] The constraining effect of the human rights model is clear from the Inter-American Court's treatment of the Saramaka claim to natural resources and gold within its territory, *see* Saramaka People v. Suriname (2007), Inter-Am. Ct. H.R. (ser. C) No. 172 (A right to timber was permitted because it was seen as "essential for the survival of their way of life," but not gold as this was not traditionally used by the Saramaka people. The human rights model also leads to the notion that all "cultural communities" in Latin America are indigenous peoples. With the cultural survival of indigenous peoples as the basis of indigenous rights recognition, the Inter-American Court of Human Rights has been able to extend indigenous rights to similarly situated "cultural communities," like the Afro-Caribbean peoples of Suriname. Indeed, the *Saramaka* decision of the Court was about the

indigenous rights in culture and not the human right to equality, which lies at the heart of the human rights model.

2.3 Africa

Likewise, in Africa, the local indigenous movement and supporters continue to assert the human rights model. During his tenure as UN Special Rapporteur, James Anaya carried out visits to the Republic of the Congo in 2011[30] and Botswana[31] in 2010 and Namibia in 2013.[32] His reports followed the cue of the African movements in framing local indigenous identities within the human rights model but with a particular emphasis on the human right to culture. For example, in his report on Namibia, indigenous peoples are characterized as "culturally distinct peoples"[33] who are "disadvantaged relative to other groups in the country."[34] The report focuses on human rights, including rights to lands, exclusion from decision-making processes, health, and education.[35] Anaya's successor Tauli-Corpuz continued with this approach when reporting on her visit to the Congo in 2019 emphasizing the right to culture and human rights.[36]

However, despite the emphasis on human rights, African states remain wary of the Declaration and indigenous peoples' rights. There have been very few reforms in the name of indigenous rights. The Democratic Republic of the Congo endorsed the Declaration in 2007 and has adopted an Indigenous Rights Law—the first of its kind on the African continent—that specifically targets the disadvantaged conditions of indigenous peoples and promotes

rights of an Afro-Caribbean Maroon "tribal people," not an indigenous people. The Saramaka people did not self-identify as an indigenous people. And the Court did not see them as indigenous.).

[30] *Report of the UN Special Rapporteur on the Rights of Indigenous Peoples, James Anaya, The Situation of Indigenous Peoples in the Republic of the Congo*, UN Human Rights Council, 18th Sess., Supp. No. 35, U.N. Doc. A/HRC/18/35/Add.5 (2011).

[31] *Report of the UN Special Rapporteur on the Rights of Indigenous Peoples, James Anaya, The Situation of Indigenous Peoples in Botswana*, UN Human Rights Council, 15th Sess., Supp. No. 37, U.N. Doc. A/HRC/15/37/Add.2 (2010).

[32] *Report of the UN Special Rapporteur on the Rights of Indigenous Peoples, James Anaya, The Situation of Indigenous Peoples in Namibia*, UN Human Rights Council, 24th Sess., Supp. No. 41, U.N. Doc. A/HRC/24/41/Add.1 (2013).

[33] *Id.* at 4.

[34] *Id.* at 1.

[35] *Id.*

[36] *Report of the Special Rapporteur on the Rights of Indigenous Peoples, Vicky Tauli-Corpuz, Visit to the Congo* UN Human Rights Council, 45th Sess., Supp. No. 34, U.N. Doc. A/HRC/45/34/Add.1 (2020).

their collective and individual rights.[37] This includes rights to lands and resources as well as consultation regarding measures that affect indigenous lands or resources. However, this is the exception to the rule.

There have been efforts by NGOs and indigenous advocates to have judicial bodies adopt and apply the human rights model with some successes. For example, the African Commission on Human and Peoples' Rights recognized the land rights of the Endorois indigenous people of Kenya who were forcibly evicted from their lands around Lake Bogoria.[38] The Commission accepted that the human right to property under the African Charter on Human and People's Rights extended to the traditional lands of the Endorois. However, like the Inter-American jurisprudence on land rights (which the African Commission draws on liberally) the Commission bases its decision largely on the right in culture.[39] Kenya continues to reject local application of indigenous rights and has failed to fully implement the African Commission's decision. As noted in Chapter 3, in Botswana, Survival International led a human rights campaign to keep the San on their ancestral lands in the Central Kalahari Game Reserve including judicial proceedings that ruled the San had aboriginal title to much of the Kalahari. However, Botswana has failed to implement the decision.[40]

2.4 The Merit of the Mixed Model in the South

The ambivalence, or outright rejection, of indigenous rights in Asia and Africa is due largely to concern about the connection between the indigenous rights and the self-determination framework. There are security concerns raised by self-determination. In Latin America, states are concerned about the implications of FPIC, and the Inter-American indigenous

[37] Act No. 5-2011: On the Promotion and Protection of the Rights of Indigenous Peoples (Republic of Congo).

[38] *Centre for Minority Rights Development (Kenya) and Minority Rights Group International on behalf of Endorois Welfare Council v Kenya*, Application No. 276/03, African Commission on Humans and Peoples' Rights, Nov. 25, 2009 ["Endorois"].

[39] *Id.* at para. 154 (Referring to jurisprudence on indigenous rights in Latin America created by the Inter-American Court of Human Rights, the *Endorois* decision notes there is a common thread running through all attempts to define indigenous peoples—that is, "indigenous peoples have an unambiguous relationship to a distinct territory" . . . "the linkages between people, their land, and culture.")

[40] Jeremy Sarkin & Amelia Cook, *The Human Rights of the San (Bushmen) of Botswana: The Clash of the Rights of Indigenous Communities and Their Access to Water with the Rights of the State to Environmental Conservation and Mineral Resource Exploitation*, 20 J. Transnat'l L. & Pol'y. 1 (2010).

rights jurisprudence is fixated with culture. The mixed model could, therefore, benefit the Southern movements by removing this cause for concern. It would also emphasize that the human rights in the Declaration owe much to their participation in Declaration negotiations, thus, underscoring the political legitimacy these rights have for the South. The rights are also imbued with legal legitimacy as we saw in Chapter 3. A direct focus on human rights would also reduce Southern indigenous peoples' emphasis on cultural difference.

3 Decolonization Model in the North/CANZUS States

In the CANZUS states, the dominant model is not, strictly speaking, a human rights model. However, the resulting reforms over the course of the last forty years, in effect, reflect the human rights model. That is, most prominent reforms have included processes on consultation and recognition of culture, existing land rights, and economic development. The focus, then, is on recognition of present issues and needs. There are few instances of policies and laws aimed at historical rectification in relation to the suppression of indigenous peoples' political institutions and the taking of territory.

Kirsty Gover has argued that the CANZUS concerns with the Declaration can best be explained by considering their unique approach to addressing indigenous rights claims.[41] She notes that while reforms may be complemented—and in some cases prompted—by legal mechanisms, many of them are deals struck outside of the formal "rights-based" legal process via quasi-political negotiations between the executive branches of states and indigenous peoples. Examples of this "politicization" of indigenous rights include contemporary historical settlements in New Zealand and the contemporary treaty-making process in Canada. This special relationship between indigenous peoples and the State/Crown flows from their historical dealings and is given expression in terms of "trust" or "fiduciary" duties in the United States, or the "honour of the Crown" in Canada and New Zealand. As she puts it:[42]

[41] Kirsty Gover, *Settler–State Political Theory, "CANZUS" and the UN Declaration on the Rights of Indigenous Peoples*, 26:2 Eur. J. Intl. L. 345 (2015).
[42] *Id.* at 347.

> CANZUS states may be reluctant to accede to some expressions of indigenous "rights" in international law, even when domestic agreements give effect to norms that are consistent with such rights, because of the possibility that these could *disrupt* or undermine local bargains, allow *non-discrimination* principles to be used to challenge settled claims, empower settler judiciaries to enforce or refer to those rights at the expense of domestic executive prerogatives and obligations, and in so doing, perhaps bring the discursive processes of bargaining to a premature close. These reforms, especially the settlements, put standard liberal premises (including those associated with the rule of law: non-discrimination, equality, universality, certainty and transparency) under increasing strain. Introducing a indigenous rights/human rights framework in terms of the Declaration threatens to undo these political compacts.

Thus, the CANZUS states are caught in a bind between meeting their commitment to the liberal promise of equality while also seeking to further the legitimacy of the state through the vesting of self-government and property rights in historical communities.[43] By shifting the debate out of a rights-based regime into a political regime, the state has sought to shield indigenous rights from rights-based challenges. The Declaration threatens to import a human rights analysis that can undo all of the work done to give effect to collective-historical rights.

Many of the recent indigenous rights reforms in the North including settlements have been struck in the political domain. This practice reflects a long-standing experience of tribes engaging directly with the Crown through the executive arm of the state.[44] In New Zealand, this makes sense for Māori tribes in that rather than legal or human *rights* their claims are based on an enduring *political* relationship. However, the challenge for Māori is the inequality of bargaining power. Māori rights are not constitutionally protected,

[43] *Id.* at 346.

[44] For comment on New Zealand, *see* Mark Hickford, Lords of the Land: Indigenous Property Rights and the Jurisprudence of Empire (2011) (During the height of decolonization and settlement, the colonial courts typically rejected indigenous claims for relief and deferred to the Executive. In New Zealand, for example, the Treaty of Waitangi was rendered a "legal nullity" by the courts and Māori land rights non-justiciable only three decades after its signing in 1840 but at a time when settlement was in full swing and Māori outnumbered by settler peoples. Indigenous rights in New Zealand remained non-justiciable up until the 1970s when the courts began to adopt a more interventionist role.). *See also* Paul G. McHugh, Aboriginal Societies and the Common Law: A History of Sovereignty, Status, and Self-Determination (2004).

and the courts have normally refused to intervene in any dispute between the Māori and Crown over the content of political settlements.

It was precisely this inequality that motivated indigenous rights leaders in New Zealand to appeal to the UN. The Declaration has made indigenous rights an international issue, and it is clear that domestic legal practice falls well short of the self-determination framework. Both New Zealand and Australia were strongly opposed to forms of political autonomy in the Declaration negotiations, and this is reflected in a well-established opposition to indigenous self-government in domestic law and policy.[45] Indigenous rights to self-government are recognized in Canada and the United States, however. Yet as we will see below, indigenous peoples in these states object to the limited nature of these rights.

Instead of the prospect of the Declaration disrupting local political settlements by importing a rights-based discourse, CANZUS states are concerned about the Declaration's potential normatively to support extensive fundamental reforms through strong forms of self-determination. Throughout the Declaration negotiations, CANZUS states sought to weaken the self-determination framework and insist on a reference to territorial integrity.[46] Ultimately, the Declaration calls for a process of historical rectification. The very issues that prompted the indigenous peoples of the CANZUS

[45] *See* Jenny Macklin, "Statement on the United Nations Declaration on the Rights of Indigenous Peoples" (Speech delivered at the Australian Parliament, Canberra, Apr. 3, 2009), <http://www.converge.org.nz/pma/AustDecl0409.pdf> (As Minister Macklin said, when Australia endorsed the Declaration in 2009, Australia's position in relation to self-determination is that it recognizes the right to participate in public life, self-management, and "the entitlement of Indigenous peoples to have control over their destiny and to be treated respectfully."); *see also* Australia, Commonwealth, Department of the Attorney-General, *Public Sector Guidance Sheets: Right to Self-Determination*, <https://www.ag.gov.au/RightsAndProtections/HumanRights/Human-rights-scrutiny/PublicSectorGuidanceSheets/Pages/Righttoselfdetermination.aspx> (Under the heading "What is the scope of the right to self-determination?," the Guidance Sheet notes: "The Australian Government believes that individuals and groups, particularly Aboriginal and Torres Strait Islander peoples, should be consulted about decisions likely to impact on them. This includes ensuring that they have the opportunity to participate in the making of such decisions through the processes of democratic government, and are able to exercise meaningful control over their affairs. Aboriginal and Torres Strait Islander peoples also have the right to preserve their group identity and culture. The importance of consultation is manifested in the establishment of the National Congress of Australia's First Peoples. Self-determination is widely understood to be exercised in a manner that preserves the territorial integrity, political unity and sovereignty of a country."); in New Zealand's case, this was asserted in the first working group, *see* New Zealand, "New Zealand Statement under Item 5" (July 31–Aug. 4, 1989) doCip Doc. 200284_1 at 8 (on file with author) ("The right to autonomy in matters relating to their own internal and local affairs . . . presupposes a system of Indigenous reserves or separate areas. There is an implication or presumption of segregation which NZ finds unhealthy.").

[46] *See, e.g.*, Robert Hagen, USUN Press Release, "Explanation of vote by Robert Hagen, U.S. Advisor, on the Declaration on the Rights of Indigenous Peoples, to the UN General Assembly, September 13, 2007" (2007) (on file with author) (when the United States voted against the Declaration in the UN General Assembly, it argued that the rectification measures were not retrospective.).

states to approach the UN—matters such as restoration of political power and territories—remain unaddressed. CANZUS states thus are concerned about the large gap between what Northern indigenous peoples are entitled to (the self-determination framework based on anti-colonialism) and what they have obtained through four decades of state reforms (the human rights model and its correlates).

3.1 Australia

In Australia, the most important contemporary breakthrough for Aboriginal peoples was the 1992 High Court decision of *Mabo v. Queensland (No. 2)* ("*Mabo*"), which determined that following annexation of the country by the British Crown, Aboriginal peoples' pre-existing land rights continued to exist under the introduced common law.[47] *Mabo* heralded the rejection of the notion that Australia was *terra nullius*—land owned by no one—on the basis of Aboriginal peoples' supposed backward character. However, native title relates to only existing property rights that have "survived" colonization and settlement. If this title has been "extinguished"—for example, by simple grant of freehold title by the state—or has "expired" due to the effects of European settlement, then the title does not exist and compensation to indigenous peoples whose rights have been extinguished is extremely difficult to obtain.[48]

Efforts to obtain recognition of native title have proven so difficult that Justice Callinan—described by aboriginal scholars Marcia Langton and Lisa Palmer as one of the most conservative members of the Australian High Court[49]—observed that:[50]

> It might have been better to redress the wrongs of dispossession by a true and unqualified settlement of lands or money than by an ultimately futile or unsatisfactory, in my respectful opinion, attempt to fold native title rights into the common law.

[47] Mabo v. Queensland (No. 2), [1992] 175 C.L.R. 1.

[48] *Id.* at para. 68.

[49] *See* Marcia Langton & Lisa Palmer, *Modern Agreement Making and Indigenous People in Australia: Issues and Trends*, 8:1 Aust. Indigenous L. Reporter 1 (2003).

[50] Western Australia v. Ward, (2002) 213 C.L.R. 1 at paras. 398–399 per Callinan J.

Australia has never had a national policy directed at historical rectification relating to self-determination and territories. The *Mabo* decision was not directed at rectification, and the historical and ongoing injustices experienced by Australian Aboriginal peoples provided only a distant backdrop to the decision. Indeed, too much emphasis on history would have suggested the need for more than simple recognition of existing property rights. For the Meriam Islanders who brought the claim, there could be no doubt that underlying the native title claim was a broader issue relating to political autonomy.[51] However, *Mabo* was firmly fixed on continuing occupation rights, not sovereignty.

In Australia, statutory land agreements have resulted in the return of large tracts of land to Aboriginal peoples. The Aboriginal Land Rights (Northern Territory) Act 1976 (ALRA) in the Northern Territory—the state with the largest Aboriginal population—has resulted in approximately half the Northern Territory being held by Aboriginal peoples under a collective form of freehold title. This was an act of reparation for historical taking of the land. Other similar statutory settlements have been followed in all other states. Under this legislation, about 15% of Australia's land mass has been returned to Aboriginal peoples, but there are winners and losers. Not all Aboriginal peoples are covered by these agreements, and they vary in terms of their rationale, aims, and specific rights. In some cases, rather than reparations the agreements are seeking to grant rights to land already occupied by Aboriginal peoples such as "reserves" (Anangu Pitjantjatjara Yankunytjatjarra Land Rights Act 1981). Other agreements allow any aboriginal community—whether they have an ancestral connection to the land or not—to apply for areas of land (for example, Aboriginal Land Rights Act 1983, s 3 (New South Wales)). In all cases, the agreements relate to "Crown land," that is, land now owned by the state. Land in private ownership cannot be claimed. In addition, the statutory agreements are directed at land rights not at the recognition of aboriginal political institutions. Aboriginal rights have not been conceptualized in a more holistic way.

In part, the reason for lack of a clear focus on rectification in these statutory settlements is due to less emphasis on traditional tribes (or "traditional owners" as they are commonly called in Australia) in Australia compared to New Zealand, Canada, and the United States. Native title

[51] B.A. Keon-Cohen, *The Mabo Litigation: A Personal and Procedural Account*, 24:3 Melb. U. L. Rev. 35 (2000).

litigation may be directed at the traditional owners. However, statutory deals like the Aboriginal Land Rights (Northern Territory) Act 1976 relate to great expanses of land and encompass aboriginal occupants irrespective of whether they are the traditional owners or not.

The prospect of native title interests in lands has also resulted in negotiated agreements.[52] These agreements may provide for recognition of land rights, compensation for impacts of projects or access to land, benefit sharing with resource companies, and consultation protocols.[53] However, they are motivated by the notion of lands being subject to existing native title rights—rather than rectification for loss of lands.

Australia has never recognized a right of self-government for Aboriginal peoples. Subsequent to *Mabo*, the Australian courts have been adamant that Aboriginal peoples lost the power to make cognizable laws after the assertion of British sovereignty.[54] Aboriginal scholars have argued that this defies logic. As Marcia Langton notes:[55]

> Aboriginal people have continued to argue that not only customary property rights in land but also ancient jurisdictions survive, on the grounds that, just as British sovereignty did not wipe away Aboriginal title, neither did it wipe away Aboriginal jurisdiction. Aboriginal governance under the full body of Aboriginal customary laws, by the same logic as that that led to the recognition of native title at common law, must, even if in some qualified way, have survived the annexation of Australia by the Crown.

[52] *See* Australia, Commonwealth, National Native Title Tribunal, *Annual Report 2011–2012* (As at June 30, 2012, there were 646 registered Indigenous Land Use Agreements, covering about 1,398,127 km^2 (or approximately 18.1%) of Australia's land mass.).

[53] Marcia Langton, Settling with Indigenous People: Modern Treaty and Agreement-Making (2006).

[54] *See* Members of the Yorta Yorta Aboriginal Community v. Victoria, (2002) H.C.A. 58 at para. 43 ("Rights or interests in land created after sovereignty and which owed their origin and continued existence only to a normative system other than that of the new sovereign power, would not and will not be given effect by the legal order of the new sovereign." Native title, therefore, had to be grounded in custom law that existed prior to the Crown acquiring sovereignty.); *see also* Coe v. Commonwealth (No. 2), [1993] H.C.A. 42, 118 A.L.R. 193 (Chief Justice Mason noted that *Mabo (No. 2)* was "at odds with the notion that there resides in the Aboriginal people a limited kind of sovereignty embraced in the notion that they are 'a domestic dependent nation' entitled to self-government and full rights (save the right of alienation) or that as a free and independent people they are entitled to any rights and interests other than those created or recognized by the laws of the Commonwealth, the State of New South Wales and the common law."); *see also* Walker v. New South Wales, [1994] H.C.A. 64, 182 C.L.R. 45 (where Chief Justice Mason rejected the suggestion that Australian criminal law accommodates an alternative body of law operating alongside it).

[55] *See* Langton and Palmer, *supra* note 49.

Instead, governments have established a series of aboriginal representative structures charged with providing government with advice in relation to aboriginal policy.[56] The Aboriginal and Torres Strait Islander Commission (ATSIC) established in 1990 provided services to Aboriginal peoples and delivered some of the government's indigenous programs and services. But its goal was to "promote indigenous self-management and self-sufficiency."[57] In any event, it was dismantled by the Howard liberal-led government in 1995. A new national representative body—National Congress of Australia's First Peoples—was established in 2010 to formulate policy and act as an advocate for indigenous rights. Membership of Congress was open to Aboriginal and Torres Strait Islander individuals and organizations, but it struggled to engender support from aboriginal communities and was closed in 2019.

The end of the Howard government in 2008 and start of a new left-leaning Labour government resulted in a series of positive reforms aimed at "resetting the relationship,"[58] including the Australian Federal Parliament's apology to Australia's indigenous peoples on February 13, 2008, for "the laws and policies of successive Parliaments and governments that have inflicted profound grief, suffering and loss" on Aboriginal and Torres Strait Islanders.[59] However, rather than address calls for restoration of aboriginal self-government or historical rectification, the crux of contemporary government aboriginal policy is aimed at reducing the significant disadvantages faced by Aboriginal peoples in socio-economic areas such as health and education (called the "Closing the Gap" policy).[60]

Aboriginal activists of the 1970s emphasize the lack of progress made on their original goals. Gary Foley, reflecting in 2012 on the Aboriginal Tent Embassy occupation outside Parliament, noted: "Whilst politicians and

[56] *See also* M. Davis, *NARRM Oration 2012—Aboriginal Women: The Right to Self-Determination*, 16:1 AUST. INDIGENOUS L. REV. 78, 80 (2012) (Megan Davis argues that reforms in Australia have been state-centric, directed at land rights and the creation of institutions, like ATSIC, so that "less attention was paid to how the right to self-determination should be managed internally within Indigenous groups themselves, especially in regard to Aboriginal women, gender equality and violence.").

[57] Aboriginal and Torres Strait Islander Commission Act 1990 (Cth), s 3.

[58] Macklin, *supra* note 45.

[59] Kevin Rudd, Prime Minister of Australia, "The Apology to Australia's Indigenous Peoples" (Address delivered at the Parliament of Australia, House of Representatives, Canberra, Feb. 13, 2008), <http://australia.gov.au/about-australia/our-country/our-people/apology-to-australias-indigenous-peoples>.

[60] *See* Council of Australian Governments, "Closing the Gap in Indigenous Disadvantage" (2008) <https://www.coag.gov.au/closing_the_gap_in_indigenous_disadvantage> (Created in 2008 through an agreement of the Council of Australian Governments (COAG), the Closing the Gap campaign aims to reduce indigenous disadvantage across seven identified "platforms": early childhood, schooling, health, economic participation, healthy home, safe communities, and governance and leadership.).

bureaucrats in Canberra would prefer that people focus on more timid and gentle distractions such as 'reconciliation', ersatz land rights in the form of native title, and a completely meaningless and empty Prime Ministerial 'apology,' the Aboriginal Embassy remains on the lawns of Parliament as a reminder of the truth."[61] The "truth" for Foley was the "basic values of self-determination, land rights and political independence" that for him "continue to this day to be at the heart of Aboriginal-white relations in Australia."[62]

There are currently calls for amendments to the Australian Constitution to repeal measures that enable the Government to enact laws that discriminate on the basis of race and recognize Aboriginal peoples as the first peoples of Australia. An expert panel established by the government to consult with Aboriginal peoples about the proposed reforms reported that many Aboriginal peoples sought recognition of "aboriginal sovereignty."[63] However, any amendment to the Constitution requires a nation-wide referendum and the Expert Panel noted "any proposal relating to constitutional recognition of the sovereign status of Aboriginal and Torres Strait Islander peoples would be highly contested by many Australians, and likely to jeopardize broad public support for the Panel's recommendations."[64] Instead the Panel favored language that expressly prohibits racial discrimination while allowing special measures of Aboriginal peoples.[65] For now the aim is to establish a First Nations Voice that will engage directly with the Australian legislature and government and Local and Regional Voices to engage with local governments.[66]

[61] *See* Gary Foley, *A Reflection of the First Thirty Days of the Embassy*, *in* The Aboriginal Tent Embassy: Sovereignty, Black Power, Land Rights and the State (Gary Foley, Andrew Schaap, & Edwina Howell eds., 2013).

[62] *Id.* at 40.

[63] Expert Panel on Constitutional Recognition of Indigenous Australians, "Recognising Aboriginal and Torres Strait Islander Peoples in the Constitution" (Jan. 2012) at 97, http://www.recognise.org.au/wpcontent/uploads/shared/uploads/assets/3446_FaHCSIA_ICR_report_text_Bookmarked_PDF_12_Jan_v4.pdf ("At almost every consultation, Aboriginal and Torres Strait Islander participants raised issues of sovereignty, contending that sovereignty was never ceded, relinquished or validly extinguished."); *see also* "Recognising Aboriginal and Torres Strait Islander Peoples in the Constitution" at 207 (The Tent Embassy submission to the Expert Panel: "Recognition of Aboriginal Peoples in the constitution must not usurp our continuing Sovereignty. The only resolution of the constitutional issue is by way of negotiated Sovereign Treaties under the supervision of the international community.").

[64] *Id.* at 213 (The Panel held the same views in relation to recognition of a Treaty: "any proposal for a form of constitutional backing for a treaty or other negotiated agreements with Aboriginal and Torres Strait Islander peoples would be likely to confuse many Australians, and hence could jeopardise broad public support for the Panel's other recommendations."); *Id.* at 201.

[65] *Id.* at 231.

[66] Australia, Commonwealth, National Indigenous Australians Agency, *Indigenous Voice Discussion Paper* (2021), <https://apo.org.au/node/310489>.

3.2 Canada

In Canada, reform has focused on land rights, consultation, and social benefits. Major issues remain in relation to poverty, discrimination, housing, and education.[67] However, indigenous scholars and leaders lament the lack of reforms relating to rectification for the loss of aboriginal sovereignty and territories.[68] The 1996 *Report of the Royal Commission on Aboriginal Peoples* called for a comprehensive rectification process under the framework of nation-to-nation treaty negotiations. A new treaty process would "lead the way to reconciliation between Aboriginal and non-Aboriginal people over the next 20 years."[69] These treaties would deal with self-government and the re-distribution of the land and resources required to make self-government viable. The Commission observed:[70]

> Negotiation is the best and most appropriate way to address these issues, and land claims policies should be replaced by treaty processes, primarily under the auspices of regional treaty commissions, with Aboriginal Lands and Treaties Tribunals performing supplementary functions.

However, the Commission's recommendations have not been taken up by Canada. Many of the reforms that have taken place are directed at addressing claims to existing aboriginal rights to land. The decision of *Calder v. Attorney-General of British Columbia*,[71] like *Mabo*, recognized that aboriginal rights survived sovereignty, at least until the rights were legally extinguished. Ever since, Canada has grappled with the prospect of much of the North West Territories, Nunavut, the Yukon, and British Columbia being subject to existing aboriginal rights because there were few historical treaties extinguishing aboriginal rights negotiated in these regions.

[67] *See* S. James Anaya, "United Nations Special Rapporteur on the Rights of Indigenous Peoples, James Anaya, Statement upon Conclusion of the Visit to Canada" (Oct. 15, 2013), <http://unsr.jamesanaya.org/statements/statement-upon-conclusion-of-the-visit-to-canada>.

[68] Douglas Sanderson, *Redressing the Right Wrong: The Argument from Corrective Justice*, 62:1 UTLJ 93 (2012) (Sanderson argues the single greatest mistake committed against Canadian indigenous peoples has been the historical and ongoing suppression of institutions in indigenous communities. However, Canada has focused on recognition of land rights, not restoration of aboriginal self-government.).

[69] Royal Commission on Aboriginal Peoples, Volume 2: Restructuring the Relationship (1996).

[70] *Id.* at 430.

[71] Calder v. Attorney-General of British Columbia, [1973] S.C.R. 313.

In British Columbia, the British Columbia Treaty Commission (BCTC) was established to address existing aboriginal rights in lands through the negotiation of "comprehensive land agreements" or "modern treaties," which extinguish existing aboriginal rights, replacing them with specific rights contained in the treaties. The Nisga'a Treaty, for example, included a cash settlement of $190 million, the creation of the Nisga'a Lisims Government, ownership of 2,000 square km of land, and entitlement to fish stocks and wildlife harvests.[72] But the Nisga'a had to give up all aboriginal title interests. The BCTC process has been criticized for this in particular. As Taiaiake Alfred notes:[73]

> The BCTC process is not about negotiating treaties, which would in fact represent the start of a new relationship between the First Nations and the newcomers to this land. The process is all about assimilation and control; it uses base manipulation of our people's poverty and weakness in an attempt to terminate their freedom and achieve a final degree of control over the futures of Indigenous peoples.

In addition to the BCTC process, there is a "comprehensive claims process" led by the Federal Government that aims to address aboriginal rights in provinces outside of British Columbia. Like the BCTC process, Indian tribes—through direct negotiations—"cede" aboriginal rights in "Comprehensive Land Claims Agreements" in exchange for other benefits. Since 1973, across Canada, twenty-six comprehensive land claims agreements have been concluded and are in effect. These cover approximately 40% of Canada's land mass and affect ninety-five indigenous communities. Almost all of these agreements are in the remote northern areas of Canada (the North West Territories, Nunavut, and the Yukon).[74]

[72] Nisga'a Final Agreement Act, SC 2000; *see also* the Tsawwassen First Nation Final Agreement Act, SC 2008 and the Maa-nulth First Nations Final Agreement Act, SC 2009; *see* BC Treaty Commission, *Negotiation Updates*, <http://www.bctreaty.net/files/updates.php> (The Nisga'a treaty provides the Nisga'a with jurisdiction in their territories over matters that are a mix of federal and provincial powers. So, it is possible to create legislative/jurisdictional space for modern indigenous governments.).

[73] Taiaiake Alfred, *Time to Kill the BC Treaty Process*, 17:12 WINDSPEAKER 4 (2000).

[74] *See Agreement Between the Inuit of the Nunavut Settlement Area and Her Majesty the Queen in Right of Canada* (1992), <http://www.gov.nu.ca/sites/default/files/files/013%20-%20Nunavut-Land-Claims-Agreement-English.pdf> (The Nunavut Land Claims Agreement relates to a major portion of Northern Canada and most of the Canadian Arctic Archipelago. It is one of the most remote, sparsely settled regions in the world, with a population of 31,906, mostly Inuit, spread over a land area of the size of Western Europe. They are comprehensive agreements in the sense that they recognize a broad range of rights.).

There may be elements of reparation in the agreements, but in the main, they are a response to existing aboriginal rights in areas of Canada that are abundant in natural resources, their legal extinguishment, and the creation of new legal rights in "modern treaties." The agreements create certainty for government and private enterprises about the nature and scope of indigenous rights. Arguably, rather than providing a means of reparations for historical wrongs, these treaties, in fact, create new injustices by extinguishing the aboriginal title.

The Canadian government has committed to recognizing Aboriginal peoples' self-government. Recognition of the inherent right of Aboriginal peoples to self-government has been official government policy since 1995.[75] These are reached through "self-government agreements." The self-government policy could be viewed as reparative in nature—the reference to self-government as an inherent right indicates that it pre-dates Canadian sovereignty and has its source in aboriginal law. But the policy says little about the need to recognize self-government in order to address past injustices. Rather, the emphasis lies more with the benefits of control over their lives and economic benefits. Moreover, practically all self-government agreements form part of comprehensive land claim agreements. Of the twenty-five self-government agreements reached to date, almost all of them are attached to a comprehensive land claim agreement.[76]

In other words, the self-government rights are more readily realized in those cases where aboriginal land rights continue to exist. The vast majority of Indian communities, however, exercise self-government under the Indian Act, which offers very limited powers. As Canadian Cree scholar Douglas Sanderson notes, "Because of the Indian Act, Indigenous communities lack meaningful powers of taxation and so have no fiscal capacity to set and pursue ends without asking for Federal money—that means no meaningful choices in education, in health and child care, in policing and housing, and virtually no choice as to the economic, social, or environmental world around them."[77]

Canada has a process for addressing Aboriginal claims of non-compliance by the Canadian state with the terms of historical treaties. The "Specific

[75] Indigenous and Northern Affairs Canada, "The Government of Canada's Approach to Implementation of the Inherent Right and the Negotiation of Aboriginal Self-Government" (1995).

[76] *See* Indigenous and Northern Affairs Canada, "Fact Sheet: Aboriginal Self-government" (Ottawa: INAC, 2015), <http://www.aadnc-aandc.gc.ca/eng/1100100016293/1100100016294>.

[77] Sanderson, *supra* note 68 at 119.

Claims Process" includes a "Treaty Lands Entitlement mechanism," a procedure for settling land debt owed to First Nations who did not receive all of the land to which they were entitled under historic treaties. However, there is no means to pursue issues of consent, coercion, and adequacy of consideration relating to these treaties or any other injustice related to treaty making.

There have been efforts at the federal and provincial levels to establish legislation that will promote implementation of the Declaration and monitor the steps taken to give effect to it. The province of British Columbia and the Canadian federal parliament have enacted legislation that sets out a process to align domestic laws with the Declaration.[78]

3.3 The United States

Self-government and historical redress remain core issues of concern for indigenous peoples in the United States. As noted in the UN Special Rapporteur on Rights of Indigenous Peoples report on the United States: "new measures are needed to advance reconciliation with indigenous peoples and to provide redress for persistent deep-seated problems."[79] This included:[80]

> initiatives to address outstanding claims of treaty violations or non-consensual takings of traditional lands to which indigenous peoples retain cultural or economic attachment, and to restore or secure indigenous peoples' capacities to maintain connections with places and sites of cultural or religious significance, in accordance with the United States international human rights commitments.

The rapporteur also noted concerns about self-government and limitations imposed on indigenous peoples' "powers of tribal regulatory and judicial authorities especially in relation to non-indigenous persons."[81] As noted above, First Nation tribes in the United States possess a measure of sovereignty after being characterized in the early years of settlement as "domestic,

[78] Declaration on the Rights of Indigenous Peoples Act 2019 (British Columbia); United Nations Declaration on the Rights of Indigenous Peoples Act 2021.

[79] *Report of the Special Rapporteur on the Rights of Indigenous Peoples, James Anaya, Addendum: The Situation of Indigenous Peoples in the United States of America*, UN Human Rights Council, 21st Sess., Supp. No. 47, U.N. Doc. A/HRC/21/47/Add. 1, at para. 89 (2012).

[80] *Id.* at para. 90.

[81] *Id.* at para. 52.

dependent, nations."[82] As a result, many tribes, particularly the larger nations such as the Navajo, have their own tribal legislatures and courts. However, Congress retains a "plenary power" to make laws that override Indian jurisdiction, and it has significantly curtailed this jurisdiction.[83]

In addition, it is clear that the United States resists the call for rectification of historical injustices relating to self-determination and territories. Instead, the United States sees the "redress" measures in the Declaration as directed primarily at providing indigenous peoples with access to a legal remedy through the courts. The Announcement of the United States Support for the Declaration noted that "the United States has a well-developed court system that provides a means of redress for many wrongs suffered by U.S. citizens, residents and others—including federally recognized tribes and indigenous individuals and groups."[84] There was acceptance that in "appropriate circumstances" the US Congress might provide redress. However, "The United States will interpret the redress provisions of the Declaration to be consistent with the existing system for legal redress in the United States."[85]

When the United States voted against the Declaration, it argued that the rectification measures were prospective and would not apply to violations committed prior to the General Assembly's adoption of the Declaration. The United States did, in fact, establish a rectification process in 1946—called the Indian Claims Commission—although this has been vilified by many indigenous leaders and scholars. In particular, the Commission could only offer monetary compensation. The Commission had no mandate to restore land to the tribes. And many indigenous peoples struggled to have claims considered by the commission.[86]

3.4 New Zealand

Compared to Canada and Australia, there is comparatively little activity in New Zealand related to common law aboriginal rights.[87] This is due to the

[82] Cherokee Nation v. Georgia, 30 U.S. 1 (1831).

[83] Robert A. Williams Jr., The American Indian in Western Legal Thought: The Discourses of Conquest (1990).

[84] The White House, Press Release, "Announcement of US Support for the United Nations Declaration on the Rights of Indigenous Peoples, Initiatives to Promote the Government-to-Government Relationship & Improve the Lives of Indigenous Peoples" (Dec. 16, 2010) at para. 3, <https://web.archive.org/web/20130521061949/http://usun.state.gov/documents/organization/153239.pdf>.

[85] *Id.*

[86] Ward Churchill, *Charades, Anyone? The Indian Claims Commission in Context*, 24:1 Am. Ind. Culture Res. J. 43 (2000).

[87] *See* Attorney-General v. Ngati Apa, [2003] N.Z.C.A. 117, 3 N.Z.L.R. 643 (Ngati Apa recognized the possibility of the New Zealand foreshore and seabed being subject to Māori customary title. This

fact that most customary title was taken by the Crown either by direct purchase or confiscation following conflict or conversion into freehold titles by the Māori Land Court.[88] However, New Zealand remains the only country among the CANZUS states to adopt a comprehensive historical rectification process.

Since the late 1980s, New Zealand has engaged with Māori in addressing historical grievances under the mantle of the Treaty of Waitangi. The focus has been on addressing the wrongs experienced by iwi (tribes) and hapū (sub-tribes), but principally iwi as the larger tribal grouping. Urban Māori organizations have struggled to participate in the settlement process. Essential to rectification was the establishment of the Waitangi Tribunal in 1975, a commission of inquiry charged with investigating Crown actions that breached the "principles of the Treaty of Waitangi."[89] In 1985, its mandate was extended to inquire into violations dating back to the signing of the Treaty in 1840.[90]

Reports issued by the Waitangi Tribunal contain non-binding recommendations to the government, which typically form the basis of direct negotiations between the iwi claimants and the government regarding redress in the form of settlements (sanctioned by statute).[91] Redress normally takes the form of an apology, commercial redress, and cultural redress. The economic redress has had a significant impact on the Māori economy, estimated in 2018 to be worth $68 billion.[92]

The Crown has settled claims across the country relating to deep sea commercial and traditional fisheries,[93] unjust land acquisitions,[94] Māori interests in forestry,[95] and aquaculture.[96] Ngai Tahu is the largest private landowner

being one of the few areas potentially subject to customary title.); compare MĀORI PROPERTY IN THE FORESHORE AND SEABED: THE LAST FRONTIER (Claire Charters & Andrew Erueti eds., 2008) (The New Zealand government prevented the development of case law by enacting legislation that set out the types of rights that could be claimed in the foreshore).

[88] RICHARD BOAST, MĀORI LAND LAW (2d ed. 2004).

[89] Treaty of Waitangi Act 1975 (NZ), 1975/114, s 6(1).

[90] *Id.*

[91] ANDREW SHARP, JUSTICE AND THE MĀORI: MĀORI CLAIMS IN NEW ZEALAND POLITICAL ARGUMENT IN THE 1980s 77–103 (1990).

[92] Te Ōhanga Māori 2018 (Business and Economic Research Limited, January 2021), https://berl.co.nz/sites/default/files/2021-01/Te%20%C5%8Changa%20M%C4%81ori%202018.pdf.

[93] NZ, "Report of the Waitangi Tribunal on the Muriwhenua Fishing Claim (Wai 22)" June 1988; Treaty of Waitangi (Fisheries Claims) Settlement Act 1992 (NZ), 1992/121.

[94] Ngāi Tahu Claims Settlement Act 1998 (NZ), 1998/97.

[95] Central North Island Forests Land Collective Settlement Act 2008 (NZ), 2008/99.

[96] Waitangi Tribunal, *Ahu Moana: The Aquaculture and Marine Farming Report* (Wai 953, 2002); Māori Aquaculture Claims Settlement Act 2004.

in the South Island. Ngai Tahu and Waikato-Tainui received $170 million in reparations in 1993, but the value of their assets is now well over $1 billion.[97]

Treaty settlements are novel and groundbreaking.[98] And it is clearly a response to the decolonization arguments raised by iwi leaders and young Māori activists.[99]

Treaty settlement negotiations, as noted above, are led by the government under a set of policies and processes largely set by the government. All treaty settlements must be embodied and adopted in legislation ultimately, but there is a strong convention to not overturn or change a settlement.[100] And the courts have tended to refuse requests to scrutinize settlements made in the executive realm. As a result, the treaty settlement process has provided the possibility for innovative political settlements unimpeded by specific legal challenges including *ad hoc* co-governance agreements. At the same time, Māori have struggled to challenge policy or any final settlement over matters like iwi cross claims or allegations of iwi representative bodies lacking a mandate to negotiate a claim.

In addition, treaty settlements are directed at providing economic and cultural but not political redress. There is no recognition of the type of indigenous governance powers exercised in the United States or Canada. Rather, New Zealand policy is directed at "self-management"—as we saw in the statements made by New Zealand in the Working Group on the Draft Declaration.[101] This policy is based on the notion that sovereignty was clearly ceded by Māori to the British Crown. The controversy lies in the distribution of political authority between Māori and the Crown, as set out in Articles 1 and 2 of the Treaty of Waitangi, complicated by the Treaty's three articles

[97] *See* Waikato-Tainui, "Waikato-Tainui Annual Report 2020," waikatotainui.com/wp-content/uploads/2020/11/2020-Waikato-Tainui-Annual-Report-Final-Low-Res.pdf.

Ngai Tahu "Ngai Tahu Annual Report 2020," ngaitahu.iwi.nz/investment/ngai-tahu-annual-reports/2020-annual-report/.

[98] NZ, "Waitangi Tribunal: The Petroleum Report (Wai 796)" May 2003 (However, it is not without its problems. Tribal claimants have objected to the inequality in bargaining power in negotiations and the take or leave it approach to what is on the negotiation table. Rights to water, precious minerals on Māori tribal lands, or royalties resulting from their extraction cannot be included in settlements.); Craig Coxhead, *Where Are the Negotiations in the Direct Negotiations of Treaty Settlements*, 10 WAIKATO L. REV. 13 (2002). (No private land can form part of a settlement. Given much of New Zealand is in private ownership, most treaty settlements are comprised of monetary compensation.)

[99] Sharp, *supra* note 91, at 77–103 (There was support too from non-Māori activists and church groups. This activism was directed at Māori prior-sovereignty, commitments made in the Treaty of Waitangi of 1840—in particular, the guarantee of *tino rangatiratanga* (authority; chieftainship or sovereignty) over lands, villages, and *taonga* (treasures) to Māori.).

[100] C. Charters, *Maori Rights: Legal or Political?*, 26 PLR 231 (2015).

[101] THERESE CROCKER, PRINCIPLES FOR CROWN ACTION ON THE TREATY OF WAITANGI, 1989 (2011).

being written in English and Māori. In the English version under Article 1, "sovereignty" was ceded to the British Crown, while Article 2 guarantees to the "Chiefs and Tribes" of New Zealand "the full exclusive and undisturbed possession of their Lands and Estates, Forests, Fisheries and other properties."[102] Article 3 guaranteed royal protection and the "Rights and Privileges of British Subjects." The Māori version, however, differs. According to Article 1, Māori cede "*kāwanatanga*" to the Crown (a transliteration of "governorship") and under Article 2 Māori are guaranteed their "*tino rangatiratanga*" (that is, their chieftainship or political authority) over their lands, etc. The English version indicates that Māori gave sovereignty to the Crown, while the Māori version with its reference to *tino rangatiratanga* would seem to guarantee the political rights of Māori to self-government. The relationship between Article 1 (sovereignty) and Article 2 (*tino rangatiratanga*) has bedeviled indigenous-state relations ever since. Recently, the question of the intention of Māori and the Crown when negotiating the treaty was taken up by the Waitangi Tribunal in its report, *He Whakaputanga me te Tiriti*.[103] The tribunal's conclusion is that iwi did not cede sovereignty, and under the Treaty, power was to be shared so that *kāwanatanga* gave the Crown power to "control settlers and thereby keep the peace and protect Māori interests accordingly; [while] rangatira [tribal chiefs] would retain their independence and authority as rangatira, and would be the Governor's equal."[104]

While difference of opinion over the meaning of the Treaty continues, within the treaty settlement context, there are increasing measures that seek to give effect to *tino rangatiratanga*, including settlements relating to water and other resources, new autonomous bodies including a Māori Health Authority,[105] and calls for iwi control of child care and protections services for Māori children.[106] The latter social initiatives are spurred on by ongoing negative statistics relating to Māori health and Māori children in state care. A case study on Māori claims to freshwater is set out below. There remain

[102] *See* Treaty of Waitangi Act 1975, Schedule 1.

[103] NZ, "Waitangi Tribunal—*He Whakaputanga me te Tiriti*—The Declaration and the Treaty: the Report on Stage 1 of the Te Paparahi o te Raki Inquiry (Wai 1040)" October 2014.

[104] *Id.*

[105] "Establishment of the New Māori Health Authority Takes First Big Step" (May 7, 2021), https://www.beehive.govt.nz/release/establishment-new-m%C4%81ori-health-authority-takes-first-big-step.

[106] "Ko Te Wā Whakawhiti: It's time for change, A Maori Inquiry into Oranga Tamariki" (Whanau Ora Commissioning Agency, 2020).

ongoing efforts to recognize the Treaty in a higher constitution given that its legal status domestically is unclear.[107]

4 Applying the Decolonization Model

Part of the problem with domestic advocacy in CANZUS states is that many indigenous advocates no longer have political power as their main agenda. They have resiled from their original sovereignty-based positions. There is no longer the degree of emphasis there once was on the restoration of indigenous historical-political institutions and traditional lands and resources. Indeed, the international indigenous advocates always represented the more "radical element" in domestic advocacy. As noted in Chapter 1, the Treaty Council has its origins in the occupation at the Pine Ridge Sioux reservation and the American Indian Movement.[108] The more conservative federally recognized tribes rarely participated in the international movement.

The lack of uptake on stronger forms of self-determination results from a sense of futility when calls for reforms fail to deliver substantive change, and many indigenous advocates are simply locked into the day-to-day struggle of dealing with land claims and access to basic rights to health, education, and livelihood. Yet, self-determination and political autonomy remain important to Northern indigenous peoples. For example, in Australia, there remains a strong call for a treaty between Aboriginal peoples and the state and sovereignty is clearly a high priority for aboriginal leaders.[109] There is a strong call for a First Nations Voice to advise government and the national legislature and that this voice be enshrined in Australia's constitution.[110] Ninety percent of public submissions made on the proposal voice noted that it should have constitutional recognition.[111]

[107] *See Report of Matike Mai Aotearoa: The Independent Working Group on Constitutional Transformation* (2018), https://nwo.org.nz/resources/report-of-matike-mai-aotearoa-the-independent-working-group-on-constitutional-transformation/.

[108] Roxanne D. Ortiz, Indians of the Americas: Human Rights and Self-Determination (1984).

[109] Marcia Langton, *supra* note 53.

[110] *See* The Conversation, "What did the Public say about the Government's Indigenous Voice Co-Design Process" (2021), <https://theconversation.com/what-did-the-public-say-about-the-governments-indigenous-voice-co-design-process-163803.>.

[111] *Id.*

Many indigenous advocates are simply not familiar with the story of the Declaration and the role of Northern indigenous advocates in securing the self-determination framework. They do not appreciate that the self-determination framework is a response to the particular decolonization-type justifications that apply in their backyard. Advocates who arrive at the Declaration for the first time will simply assume that it is to be read and applied in accordance with the human rights models.

In this section, I argue that Northern indigenous peoples need to re-assert the connection between the self-determination framework and the decolonization model in local indigenous rights advocacy projects. Now that the Declaration has been adopted by the CANZUS states, there is an opportunity to reinforce these fundamental goals. Bringing the Declaration "back home" to the CANZUS states provides the means to revisit the motivations and arguments that initiated the international movement. The decolonization model applies in two ways. First, at a meta-level it requires fundamental reform. States must engage with indigenous peoples about their terms of co-existence through, for example, negotiations on the terms of national constitutions. Second, before this process is complete, the decolonization model imbues the right to self-determination with normative weight for the purpose of smaller-scale reforms, for example, in domestic litigation about the content of indigenous rights.

The first case study demonstrates how the decolonization and self-determination framework can influence judicial reasoning in a *case* concerning judicial recognition of aboriginal title in Canada. The second uses the decolonization model to highlight deficiencies in the New Zealand government's response to Māori claims to freshwater in their traditional territories. The third case study presents the case for a decolonization reading of the right to FPIC in the North.

4.1 Proving Aboriginal Title in Canada

The doctrine of aboriginal rights is a means to assert property to natural resources through the common law courts. Aboriginal rights litigation emerged during the 1970s in the CANZUS states.[112] McHugh argues that the

[112] Calder v. Attorney-General of British Columbia, [1973] S.C.R. 313.

judiciary were prodded into action due to the dithering of politicians over how to address land claims.[113] Scholars, legal academics, and indigenous advocates took advantage of the growth of public interest litigation and judicial review to bring claims to lands and resources before the courts. The result was a series of "breakthrough" judicial decisions, including *Calder v. Attorney-General of British Columbia* in Canada in 1973,[114] and the decision of *Mabo v. Queensland (No. 2)* in Australia in 1992,[115] which overturned as discriminatory the common law rule that Australia was terra nullius when sovereignty was asserted over the country. Many of these early decisions said very little about the specific nature of the aboriginal land right.[116] What was significant was the opinion that the rights were legal in nature, after many decades of being characterized by the courts as only political (hence the epithet, "breakthrough"), and unique in that the rights had their origins in precolonial aboriginal life and not the state's property system.

The courts seemed to assume their decisions would provide the basis for political negotiations between indigenous peoples and the state. There were government responses in the form of contemporary treaty settlements in Canada, for example.[117] Yet, little progress was made and disappointment about the content of rights meant that aboriginal rights continued to be litigated. The result, according to McHugh, is a "disfigured jurisprudence" as the courts developed complex evidential standards of proof relating to continuity of connection and the legal extinguishment of aboriginal rights.[118]

[113] P.G. McHugh, *A Common Law Biography of Section 35*, *in* FROM RECOGNITION TO RECONCILIATION: ESSAYS ON THE CONSTITUTIONAL ENTRENCHMENT OF ABORIGINAL AND TREATY RIGHTS (Patrick Macklem & Douglas Sanderson eds., 2016).

[114] Calder v. Attorney-General of British Columbia, [1973] S.C.R. 313.

[115] Mabo v. Queensland (No. 2), (1992) 175 C.L.R. 1.

[116] McHugh, "A Common Law Biography of Section 35," *supra* note 113.

[117] Nisga'a Final Agreement, "Nisga'a Nation–Canada–British Columbia" (opened for signature Apr. 27, 1989).

[118] *See* Paul McHugh, *New Dawn to Cold Light: Courts and Common Law Aboriginal Rights*, 4 NZ L. REV. 485 (2005). For critique of this jurisprudence, *see, e.g.*, Maureen Tehan, *A Hope Disillusioned, an Opportunity Lost? Reflections on Common Law Native Title and Ten Years of the Native Title Act*, 27 UNIV. MELB. L. REV. 523, 556 (2003); Sean Brennan, *Native Title in the High Court a Decade after Mabo*, 14 PUB. L. REV. 209, 212–14 (2003); Noel Pearson, *The High Court's Abandonment of 'The Time-Honoured Methodology of the Common Law' in Its Interpretation of Native Title in Mirriuwung Gajerrong and Yorta Yorta*, 7 NEWCASTLE L. REV. 1 (2003); Kirsten Anker, *Law in the Present Tense: Tradition and Cultural Continuity in Members of the Yorta Yorta Aboriginal Community v Victoria*, 28 MELB. U. L. REV. 1 (2004); Richard Bartlett, *An Obsession with Traditional Laws and Customs Creates Difficulty Establishing Native Title Claims in the South: Yorta Yorta*, 31 UNIV. W. AUST. L. REV. 35 (2003); Greg McIntyre, *Native Title Rights after Yorta Yorta*, 9 JAMES COOK U. L. REV. 268 (2003); Lisa Strelein, *Members of the Yorta Yorta Aboriginal Community v Victoria—Comment*, 2:21 LAND, RIGHTS, LAWS: ISSUES OF NATIVE TITLE 1 (2003); Simon Young, *The Trouble with 'Tradition': Native Title and the Yorta Yorta Decision*, 30 UNIV. W. AUST. L. REV. 28 (2001).

McHugh attributes this result to the focus on property rights by the courts (which were simply unable to accommodate the many dimensions of aboriginal rights claims-making), and especially political authority over territory.[119] It was a mistaken attempt to use private property to address a public end.[120]

The greatest criticism has been of the evidential test for proof of *existing* aboriginal rights. Aboriginal rights law is not restorative or reparative but based on a right that has survived and endured since the assertion of Crown sovereignty. The difficulties, of course, are the many intervening years in which the Crown has displaced indigenous peoples and allocated rights in land and formalized those rights in the form of land grants.

In Canada, the Supreme Court has long recognized aboriginal rights to engage in specific activities like hunting and fishing[121] but did not recognize aboriginal title to exclusive use and occupation of land until the decision of *Tsilhqot'in Nation v. British Columbia*, 2014 SCC 44. The evidential rules for recognition of aboriginal title were originally set out in the Supreme Court decision of *Delgamuukw v. British Columbia* (*Delgamuukw*), which recognized the possibility of aboriginal title but referred the case back to the trial judge due to a technical legal issue.[122] Ultimately the case was settled through a contemporary treaty.[123]

According to the Supreme Court, aboriginal title claimants had to prove that their communities had *exclusive occupation* of the land prior to the assertion of sovereignty. This was because aboriginal title, according to the Supreme Court, is aimed at "the reconciliation of the *prior occupation* of North America by distinctive aboriginal societies with the assertion of Crown sovereignty over Canadian territory."[124] The court made no mention of prior aboriginal sovereignty and how this might provide an alternative justificatory basis for aboriginal title.

The question of what factual circumstances amount to exclusive occupation, however, has been highly contentious. On the one hand, in

119 McHugh, "A Common Law Biography of Section 35," *supra* note 113.

120 *Id. See also* Richard Boast, *Treaty Rights or Aboriginal Rights*, NZLJ 32, 36 (1990), noting "Another criticism [of aboriginal rights] is that the rule forces indigenous claims and indigenous rights into the rather Procrustean bed of an obscure feudal rule of the common law."

121 R v. Van der Peet, [1996] 2 S.C.R. 507.

122 Delgamuukw v. British Columbia, [1997] 3 S.C.R. 1010.

123 Nisga'a Final Agreement Act, *supra* note 72; *see also* Tsawwassen First Nation Final Agreement Act, *supra* note 72; *see also* Maa-nulth First Nations Final Agreement Act, *supra* note 72; *see Negotiation Updates, supra* note 72.

124 Delgamuukw v. British Columbia, *supra* note 122, at para. 81.

Delgamuukw, the state had argued that the standard of occupation must be that set by the common law, which implied the need for evidence of regular and intensive use of the lands.[125] On the other hand, the aboriginal claimants argued that aboriginal title must be established with reference to aboriginal patterns of land holdings.[126] The motivation for this argument was that aboriginal land tenure systems at sovereignty did not always strictly conform to the types of occupation and use that would ordinarily qualify as occupation under the common law. In response, the court decided that both common law and aboriginal "perspectives"—that is, aboriginal law or systems of law—must be taken into account when determining occupation and exclusivity.[127] As a result, through this "dual approach," aboriginal law is used to avoid ethnocentric application of the common law.

Proving aboriginal title has been particularly controversial in relation to Aboriginal peoples who were hunter-gatherer peoples. *The R v. Marshall; R v. Bernard*[128] decision, decided shortly after *Delgamuukw*, concerned two separate appeals from criminal convictions for the logging of timber on state lands without authorization in the adjacent provinces of Nova Scotia and New Brunswick. In each case, the defendants were Mi'kmaq who claimed a logging right on the specific tracts of lands for commercial purposes pursuant to aboriginal title. In the *Marshall* case, the trial evidence showed that at sovereignty the Mi'kmaq were "moderately nomadic" peoples who did not have permanent settlements and "moved with the seasons and circumstances to follow their resources."[129] Nonetheless, the trial judge found that the Mi'kmaq were familiar with their territory and considered all of Nova Scotia to be their territory. In the *Bernard* case, the trial evidence disclosed a similar nomadic existence and connection with territory for Mi'kmaq residing within New Brunswick. The central issues were whether the Mi'kmaq had satisfied the *Delgamuukw* tests of exclusive occupation. The trial courts in each case concluded that exclusive occupation required proof of intensive, regular use of *the specific cutting sites* and that this had not been established in evidence. This has been described by commentators as a "postage stamp" approach to proof of aboriginal title.[130]

[125] *Id.* at paras. 146–47.

[126] *Id.*

[127] *Id.* at 147–48. The Aboriginal perspective could be gleaned in part, but not exclusively, from Aboriginal systems of law (including a land tenure system or laws governing land use).

[128] R v. Marshall; R v. Bernard, [2005] S.C.R. 220.

[129] *Id.* at para. 86.

[130] Kent McNeil, *Aboriginal Title and the Supreme Court: What's Happening?* 69:2 SASK. L. REV. 281 (2006).

On appeal, the Nova Scotia and the New Brunswick courts of appeal ruled that these standards were too strict and that there was no need for the appellants to prove regular use of the cutting sites to establish Aboriginal title. The courts applied what has been described as a "territorial approach" to proof of aboriginal title. In *Marshall*, the court noted:[131]

> The question . . . is not whether exclusive occupation of the cutting sites was established, but whether exclusive occupation of a reasonably defined territory which includes the cutting sites, was established. Insistence on proof of acts of occupation of the specific cutting sites within that territory is, in my opinion, not consistent with either the common law or the aboriginal perspective on occupation.

The Appellate Court in *Bernard* similarly regarded the aboriginal title claim of the Mi'kmaq as a claim to territory rather than as a claim to specific sites. It was only necessary to show that the Mi'kmaq had occupied an area near the cutting site, since "[t]his proximity permitted the inference that the cutting site would have been within the range of seasonal use and occupation by the Mi'kmaq."[132]

On appeal, in *Marshall; Bernard*, the Supreme Court said there was no evidence to support a finding of aboriginal title. According to the court, the "task in evaluating a claim for an aboriginal right is to examine the pre-sovereignty aboriginal practice and translate that practice, as faithfully and objectively as it can, into a modern legal right."[133] If the claim related to aboriginal title—conferring a right to exclusive use and occupation of land—then it was essential that the pre-sovereignty practice demonstrate some correlation with that right.[134] This did not require "absolute congruity" provided "the practices engage the core idea of the modern right."[135] The aboriginal perspective would assist the court's assessment of the true nature of the pre-sovereignty right or practice. In relation to exclusivity, the court did not expressly refer to aboriginal perspectives and law. There was no need to produce evidence of overt acts of exclusion, only "effective control of the land by the group, from which

[131] R v. Marshall, [2003] N.S.C.A. 105 at para. 183.
[132] R v. Bernard, [2003] N.B.C.A. 55 at para. 127.
[133] R v. Marshall; R v. Bernard, *supra* note 128 at para. 48; *see also* Paul Chartrand, *R v. Marshall; R v. Bernard: The Return of the Native*, 55 UNBLJ 135 (2006).
[134] R. v. Marshall; R. v. Bernard, *supra* note 128, at para. 95.
[135] *Id.* at para. 96.

a reasonable inference can be drawn that it could have excluded others had it chosen to do so."[136] Based on these propositions, the court concluded that both trial decisions had correctly ruled that "[i]n each case, they required proof of sufficiently regular and exclusive use of the cutting sites by Mi'kmaq people at the time of assertion of sovereignty."[137]

The court's reasoning was heavily criticized for its approach to proof.[138] According to the aboriginal title scholar, Kent McNeil, instead of adopting the "dual approach" toward determining exclusive occupation, the court had focused on the common law approach and downplayed aboriginal perspectives based on aboriginal law.[139]

As a result, the court adopted the postage stamp approach of the trial court judge; exclusive occupation required proof of intensive, regular use of the cutting sites and this had not been established in evidence.

The issue came before the Supreme Court again in the decision of *Tsilhqot'in Nation v. British Columbia*,[140] which involved a claim brought by the Tsilhqot'in Nation, a semi-nomadic grouping of six bands, in Northern British Columbia, to aboriginal title of a 1,550 square km section of their traditional territory. Legal counsel for British Columbia had argued—citing Kent McNeil's criticisms—that the Supreme Court in *R. v. Marshall; R. v. Bernard* had rejected a territorial approach to title and applied a postage stamp approach that was inconsistent with the dual approach in *Delgamuukw*. In *Tsilhqot'in Nation v. British Columbia*, the court insisted that it had always applied a dual perspective to the question of occupation and exclusivity and had not rejected a territorial approach. Instead, it had held only that there must be "proof of sufficiently regular and exclusive use" of the land in question, a requirement established in *Delgamuukw*.[141] In the court's view, the Tsilhqot'in Nation had established evidence of "sufficiently regular and exclusive use" of the land in question and was entitled to aboriginal title to the land claimed.[142] This apparent softening in approach by the court and the resulting aboriginal title caused a sensation not only in Canada but also in other common law countries. Following the *Tsilhqot'in* case, aboriginal

136 *Id.* at para. 65.
137 *Id.* at para. 72.
138 McNeil, *supra* note 130.
139 R. v. Marshall; R. v. Bernard, *supra* note 128, at para. 298.
140 Tsilhqot'in Nation v. British Columbia, [2014] S.C.C. 44, 2 S.C.R. 257.
141 *Id.* at para. 43.
142 *Id.* at para. 66.

groups with potential aboriginal title claims have significantly enhanced leverage in treaty negotiations.

What are the implications of the decolonization model for this case? First, the decolonization model would highlight how the law of aboriginal title downplays aboriginal sovereignty. Aboriginal title is not based on aboriginal law and sovereignty but on prior *occupation*. Aboriginal law is adopted as a tool to ensure that the common law tests of occupation are modified to accommodate aboriginal perspectives. It would also draw attention to the fact that aboriginal title is not only a proprietary right, it also contains jurisdictional elements. Some law-making function is needed to determine how rights are regulated in relation to aboriginal title, and the obvious answer is aboriginal law.[143] Indeed, the decolonization model would also emphasize that aboriginal sovereignty—not just aboriginal law relating to administration of land—continued post-assertion of Crown sovereignty over Canada, absent any extinguishment or treaty. This would provide greater support for the territorial approach than the notion of the continued existence of aboriginal law relating to land only. In addition, the decolonization model would indicate *another* basis for asserting territorial rights—based on aboriginal laws and the doctrine of continuity, rather than common law aboriginal title.[144]

At the same time, apart from highlighting these shortcomings relating to the proof of aboriginal title in Canada, the decolonization model has much potential for thinking about the future implications of the Supreme Court's decision in *Tsilhqot'in* in terms of self-determination. As noted above, the judicial recognition of aboriginal title indicates that there must be a body of law to regulate the use and interests held under the title. The decolonization model indicates that this law has to be aboriginal law. Aboriginal title thus provides space for the development of aboriginal law-making institutions.

Legal counsel for the Tsilhqot'in did not rely on international human rights law, let alone the Declaration and the self-determination framework. However, interveners in the litigation did. Amnesty International argued

[143] McNeil, *supra* note 130 at 293 ("Unlike fee simple lands, Aboriginal title lands are vested in communities that have laws pre-dating Crown sovereignty. Such communities have the legal personality necessary for them to have real property rights that are defined and protected externally by the common law, but that are governed internally by continuing Aboriginal law.").

[144] For argument based on this alternative basis to aboriginal title, *see* Mark D. Walters, *The 'Golden Thread' of Continuity: Aboriginal Customs at Common Law and under the Constitution Act, 1982*, 44:3 McGill L. J. 711 (1999).

that the court's reasoning on aboriginal title had to be consistent with international human rights law, particularly the Declaration. The Amnesty submission cited the right to self-determination in the Declaration, although it clearly applied a human rights model. Referring to the work of James Anaya, the Declaration is said to be "grounded in fundamental human rights principles such as non-discrimination, self-determination and cultural integrity."[145] The only other reference by interveners to self-determination in the Declaration was offered by the Assembly of First Nations. This alone called for consideration of aboriginal title in the context of the decolonization model:[146]

> The promise of the law of Aboriginal title is the recognition of First Nations, both at the time of the assertion of sovereignty and in the present, as legal, political and cultural nations with a right to self-determination. These indigenous legal orders occupied, used and treated the land as their own. The modern conception of Aboriginal title must not be diluted by concerns about the impact today of recognizing the historical realities of First Nations and their interactions with the Crown. There are many and varied ways that reconciliation can be accomplished. But it must start with recognition and respect for the rights of First Nations as distinct and sovereign peoples who occupied their land and territories, in accordance with their own laws.

4.2 Claims to Freshwater in New Zealand

As noted above, treaty settlements are a prominent aspect of the indigenous rights architecture of New Zealand and many include rights to natural resources. Some relate to resources within the iwi (tribe) or hapū (sub-tribe) lands, and others are pan-tribal and national in scope, for example, the treaty settlements related to commercial fisheries.[147] This case study focuses on

[145] Tsilhqot'in Nation v. British Columbia, (2014) S.C.C. 44, Factum of the Intervener Amnesty International at para. 12, http://www.scc-csc.ca/WebDocuments-DocumentsWeb/34986/FM085_Interveners_Amnesty-International-et-al.pdf.

[146] Tsilhqot'in Nation v. British Columbia, (2014) S.C.C. 44, Factum of the Intervener Assembly of First Nations at para. 3, <http://www.scc-csc.ca/WebDocuments-DocumentsWeb/34986/FM130_Intervener_Assembly-of-First-Nations.pdf>.

[147] Treaty of Waitangi (Fisheries Claims) Settlement Act 1992 (NZ), 1992/121.

Māori claims to bodies of freshwater in rivers, lakes, and streams. Māori claims to ownership of water have increased in the face of their concern about the poor quality and pollution of water and recent government proposals to privatize interests in water. Historically, Māori have always sought recognition of their rights to waterbodies within their traditional territories. Many have a close cultural, economic, and spiritual connection with waterbodies. However, the Crown (and its successor in practice, the New Zealand government) has assumed the right to regulate its use. In the face of these claims, government has insisted that the water resource is not owned by anyone, including government, though it reserves the right to control and manage the resource on behalf of the New Zealand public.[148] The rejection of ownership rights by the government rests on the grounds that at common law water is incapable of ownership until it is captured or that water is a national resource vested in all citizens for the common good.[149] For this reason, the government says it is not possible for the Crown to offer iwi legal ownership of an entire river or lake body in a treaty settlement.[150]

So far, the strategy by Māori is to use the Waitangi Tribunal to assert a right to water. A judicial aboriginal title claim to water would face many evidential hurdles, particularly the test of continuity of use after more than a century of intensive European settlement.[151] Alternatively, a claim to the tribunal could lead to recommendations to government and negotiation of a political settlement. To date, iwi have been successful in negotiating a right of "ownership" to commercial and customary fisheries,[152] lakebeds,[153] forests,[154] Crown lands,[155] and aquaculture[156] and minerals in the coastal marine area.[157]

148 Office of Treaty Settlements, *Ka Tika ā Muri, Ka Tika ā Mua: Healing the Past and Building a Future* (March 2015), at 103.

149 *Id.* at 103 and 111.

150 *Id.*

151 Paul G. McHugh, Aboriginal Title: The Modern Jurisprudence of Tribal Land Rights (2011).

152 Treaty of Waitangi (Fisheries Claims) Settlement Act 1992; Fisheries (Kaimoana Customary Fishing) Regulations 1998.

153 Te Arawa Lakes Settlement Act 2006, s 23(1): "The fee simple estate in each Te Arawa lakebed is vested in trust in the Trustees of the Te Arawa Lakes Trust."

154 Central North Island Forests Land Collective Settlement Act 2008. The proposed sale of forests land resulted in objection by Māori who claimed an interest in the forests, and a Treaty settlement that led to the Crown keeping ownership and creation of the Crown Forestry Rental Trust (to manage rental gained from selling of cutting rights and leasing of forest lands).

155 State-Owned Enterprises Act 1986.

156 Māori Commercial Aquaculture Claims Settlement Act 2004.

157 *See* Attorney-General v. Ngati Apa, [2003] N.Z.C.A. 117, 3 N.Z.L.R. 643; and Marine and Coastal Area (Takutai Moana) Act 2011.

Ownership is not the typical means by which Māori describe their right to waterbodies, or any other natural resource. Māori prefer to use concepts like *mana* (control or authority) or *tino rangatiratanga* (political authority). Claims to ownership of resources are prompted by proposals to privatize water[158] and the fact that ownership confers the right to control access to and the use of water.[159] So far, the Waitangi Tribunal, in its Freshwater inquiry, has not had any difficulty in finding that the customary interests held by Māori in rivers are akin to proprietary rights.[160] Moreover, the tribunal has recognized that Māori interests in water extend beyond ownership like-rights to encompass governmental powers—or *tino rangatiratanga*.[161] However, government will not recognize property rights in water, let alone governmental rights. Instead, to address the impasse, the government has improved the environmental regulatory process while also encouraging the use of co-management models. Compared with many other countries, New Zealand has a robust process for environmental regulation of natural resources—including water bodies . The principal legislation for regulating natural resources is the Resource Management Act 1991 (RMA), which allows "consent authorities," usually local municipal councils, to grant a "resource consent" to take and use water up to a limit of thirty-five years. The RMA does not recognize any Māori rights to water or provide for a Māori water allocation or license. However, there are a set of protections in the Act to acknowledge Māori interests in water and other resources.[162] All decision-makers under

[158] As Richard Boast observes, "It is no accident that those natural resources which have been privatised by statute (fisheries, the radio spectrum) have attracted the greatest amount of litigation from Māori groups. If a resource is unowned, or is nationalised, there is at least some hope of securing interests in it; but it is quite otherwise once privatised." *See* Richard Boast, *Maori Fisheries 1986–1998: A Reflection*, 30 VUWLR 111, 134 (1999). Boast was speaking in the context of fisheries and efforts to privatize that industry, but the parallels to water are very close.

[159] Generally, property includes the following rights: the right to use or enjoy the property, the right to exclude others, and the right to sell or give away. *See* Milirrpum v. Nabalco, (1971) 17 F.L.R. 141 (NTSC) at 171 per Blackburn J. *See also* Kevin Gray, *Property in Thin Air*, 50 CLJ 252 (1991).

[160] *See* NZ, "Waitangi Tribunal: The Interim Report on the National Freshwater and Geothermal Resources *Claim* (Wai 2358)" 2012; at [2.8.3(3)]. [hereinafter Freshwater Report]. "Waitangi Tribunal: Te Ika Whenua Rivers Report (Wai 212)" 1998; "Waitangi Tribunal: The Whanganui River Report (Wai 167)" 1999; "Waitangi Tribunal: The Ngawha Geothermal Resource Report (Wai 304)" 1993; "Waitangi Tribunal: He Maunga Rongo: Report on Central North Island Claims (Wai 1200)" 2008. The Waitangi Tribunal has also, in other reports, found a treaty breach in relation to Māori rights to water; *see* "Waitangi Tribunal: Report of the Waitangi Tribunal on the Kaituna River Claim (Wai 4)" 1984; "Waitangi Tribunal: Report of the Waitangi Tribunal on the Manukau Claim (Wai 8)" 1985.

[161] Freshwater Report, *supra* note 160, at [2.8.3(1)], agreeing with the Whanganui River Waitangi Tribunal that "*tino rangatiratanga* was more than ownership: it encompassed the autonomy of hapū to arrange and manage their own affairs in partnership with the Crown."

[162] Resource Management Act 1991 (NZ), 1991/69, ss 6, 7, and 8.

the RMA must "take into account the principles of the Treaty of Waitangi"[163] and have "particular regard" to "kaitiakitanga" (Māori guardianship),[164] and "recognise and provide for . . . the relationship of Māori and their culture and traditions with their ancestral lands, water, sites, waahi tapu [sacred sites], and other taonga [treasures]."[165] As a result of these provisions, when a local council draws up development plans or grants resource consents to carry out some activity, it must first consider the implications of the plan and resource consent on the local tribe's customary law as it relates to *kaitiakitanga*, for example.

However, these interests do not appear to be advancing the interests of Māori. As the Waitangi Tribunal has said many times, iwi and hapū have little influence on the outcome of RMA consent applications.[166] Part of the challenge lies with the weak statutory directions to "take into account" the principles of the Treaty and the fact that the Māori interests are one of several other competing interests, including the overall commitment to sustainable development. There is also provision under the Act for "joint management agreements" between local authorities and Māori on natural resources, and devolution of resource management powers to Māori.[167] However, these functions have been rarely used.[168] There are also provisions designed to facilitate agreements between local Māori and local governments.[169] Despite these reforms, the broad view is that the protections for Māori interests in the RMA have failed. Although the RMA contains many tools to empower iwi, these have not been used due to lack of any national monitoring and oversight, resources, and mandatory language.

163 *Id.*, s 8.
164 *Id.*, s 7.
165 *Id.*, s 6.
166 *See* "Waitangi Tribunal: *Ko Aotearoa Tēnei*: A Report into Claims Concerning New Zealand Law and Policy Affecting Māori Culture and Identity" (Wai 262) 2011. *See also* Jacinta Ruru, *Indigenous Restitution in Settling Water Claims: The Developing Cultural and Commercial Redress Opportunities in Aotearoa*, 22 New Zealand Pacific Rim L. & Policy J. 311, 325 (2013), noting that "Since the enactment of the RMA in 1991, there have been about twenty instances where Māori, as objectors, have appealed council decisions that approved resource consents to take water, discharge wastewater into water, or dam water."

167 *See* Resource Management Act 1991, s 2(1), definition of "joint management agreement," and ss 36B–36E. *See, e.g.*, the agreement between Taupo District Council and Ngāti Tūwharetoa: Taupo District Council "Joint Management Agreement" (2008), <www.taupodc.govt.nz>. *See also* Gisborne District Council "Joint Management Agreement between Gisborne District Council and Te Runanganui o Ngāti Porou Trustee Limited" (Oct. 8, 2015), <www.gdc.govt.nz>.

168 Resource Management Act 1991, s 33.

169 *Id.*, s 58R (Mana Whakahono a Rohe).

Outside of the RMA, despite the government's rejection of Māori ownership of freshwater bodies, it has negotiated, through treaty settlements, alternatives to ownership in the form of co-governance agreements. Most of the agreements have been negotiated as iwi-specific treaty settlements, but also as iwi-specific joint committee agreements under the RMA. In relation to the largest river in the North Island, the Waikato River, for example, Waikato-Tainui iwi negotiated an agreement given effect in the Waikato-Tainui Raupatu Claims (Waikato River) Settlement Act 2010. This statute establishes the Waikato River Authority, which is made up of roughly equal numbers of iwi and government representatives.[170] The Authority is responsible for establishing the "vision and strategy to achieve the restoration and protection of the health and wellbeing of the Waikato River for future generations."[171] Following the confiscation of Waikato-Tainui tribal lands in the late 1800s, the Crown assumed control of the river and the river suffered from pollution due to farm run-off, coal mining, and sewage.[172] This "clean up" is to be assisted by a series of agreements with the local council that seek better integration of Waikato-Tainui tribes into the RMA planning processes, including the preparation of an "integrated river management plan" and an "environmental plan" that local councils must consider when preparing planning documents.

A more novel co-management agreement has been reached between iwi and the government over the Whanganui River—known by local iwi as Te Awa Tupua. Instead of granting the local iwi with property in the river, or political authority over it, the Te Awa Tupua (Whanganui River Claims Settlement) Act 2017 vests the river "with all the rights, powers, duties, and liabilities of a legal person."[173] The Act also establishes a trust, Te Pou Tupua, constituted of one tribal and one government member to act and speak for the river. Te Pou Tupua is required to act in the interests of the river and, in particular, the Tupua te Kawa values. These comprise "the intrinsic values that represent the essence of Te Awa Tupua" including matters like the responsibility that local iwi and hapū have for Te Awa Tupua's health and well-being.

[170] Waikato-Tainui Raupatu Claims (Waikato River) Settlement Act 2010, s 22 and sch 6.

[171] *Id.*, s 22.

[172] Linda Te Aho, *Indigenous Challenges to Enhance Freshwater Governance and Management in Aotearoa New Zealand: The Waikato River Settlement*, 20 J. WATER L. 285 (2010).

[173] Te Awa Tupua (Whanganui River Claims Settlement) Act 2017, s 14 (Te Awa Tupua declared to be a legal person). The Act gives effect to the Whanganui River Deed of Settlement signed on August 5, 2014, which settles the historical claims of Whanganui Iwi as they relate to the Whanganui River.

Recognition of the independent autonomy of the river roughly accords with the customary view that rivers possess their own *mauri* (life force). Like the Waikato agreement, the focus is on the future health and well-being of the river and its people. Measures are provided to facilitate Te Pou Tupua's engagement in the RMA planning and consent-making processes associated with the river.[174] Similar to the RMA, there are a set of directives in the Act to decision-makers to ensure the interests of Te Awa Tupua are recognized. However, Te Pou Tupua does not have a right to veto resource consents authorizing the use of the river. And like the RMA, the directives are not determinative and may be outweighed by other considerations. By vesting the river with legal personality, the government has effectively side-stepped the issue of ownership.[175]

These agreements promote iwi engagement in RMA regulatory processes, yet they remain directed at the effective participation of iwi in decision-making and the overall objective of restoring and protecting the health and well-being of the rivers for future generations.[176] The Whanganui River and Waikato River tribes cannot prevent the grant of resources consents over the river to extract or divert water or build dams, including large hydro-electric projects. Nor do they gain any benefit from use of the resource by third parties. The issue of water ownership over the river remains unresolved.

This outcome is a far cry from the recommendation made by the Waitangi Tribunal that the Whanganui River, in its entirety, be vested in the tribes, which would mean that any resource consent application would require the tribe's approval.[177] Relying on the decolonization model, Māori should be entitled to governance in its full form as well as ownership of the resource. Treaty settlements and the RMA provide Māori with more than the general right to participate in decisions relating to natural resources and extend to co-management and shared decision-making. However, they do not guarantee to Māori sufficient autonomy or the right to prevent proposals that may be counter to their values and aims, or the right to benefit from the resource's

[174] Te Awa Tupua (Whanganui River Claims Settlement) Act 2017, ss 38 and 63.

[175] *See also* the Tūhoe deal where the Crown rejected ownership of conservation land and offered, instead, to vest the park with legal personality, to be co-chaired by Māori and the Crown: Te Urewera Act 2014. *See also* s 11(2) of the Marine and Coastal Area (Takutai Moana) Act 2011, which simply declares that no one owns the foreshore and seabed.

[176] Linda Te Aho, *The 'False Generosity' of Treaty Settlements: Innovation and Contortion*, *in* International Indigenous Rights in Aotearoa New Zealand (Andrew Erueti ed., 2017). Te Aho also notes that the issue of ownership is expressly deferred by the Treaty settlement, *see* Waikato-Tainui Raupatu Claims (Waikato River) Settlement Act 2010, ss 64 and 90.

[177] NZ "Waitangi Tribunal: The Whanganui River Report (Wai 167)" 1999.

use.[178] The government has introduced proposals for reform that seek to promote co-management of the resources and respect for Māori values. In the meantime, iwi have claimed an aboriginal right to water in the courts.[179]

4.3 FPIC and the Decolonization Model

Of all the rights in the Declaration, FPIC has received the largest share of attention, particularly in the context of extractive industry and agricultural and hydro-electric projects, all of which have the capacity to negatively impact indigenous peoples and their territories. FPIC has been so prominent because the other elements of the self-determination framework are much more difficult to implement, especially self-determination and self-government and historical redress. Discourse on FPIC, on the other hand, fits with long-standing issues relating to the meaning and effect of obligations of consultation with indigenous peoples. A further reason is the growth of commercial activities on indigenous peoples' lands, especially in remote areas. Thus, there is a vast amount of literature on the right to FPIC explaining how it ought to apply in practice, and a body of jurisprudence generated by regional human rights bodies.

FPIC is referred to six times in the Declaration. Mostly, FPIC is required for proposed projects on land, or when governments seek to remove indigenous peoples from lands. If lands are taken without FPIC, there is an obligation to give redress. This includes lands traditionally occupied in the past and can include restitution or, when this is not possible, just, fair, and equitable compensation. In addition, states must consult with indigenous peoples in order to obtain their FPIC before adopting and implementing legislative or administrative measures that may affect them. These later measures are particularly controversial because they indicate that state legislatures and governments are constrained by FPIC.

[178] There are exceptions, for example, the Fisheries (Kaimoana Customary Fishing) Regulations 1998, which provide tangata whenua with power to make bylaws about customary fishing, including imposing *rahui* (prohibitions) on customary gathering. *See also* the permission and conservation rights in the Marine and Coastal Area (Takutai Moana) Act 2011 granted to holders of a marine customary title, although iwi will struggle to obtain these rights given the high evidential standards that iwi need to prove to obtain a title.

[179] Audrey Young, "South Island Iwi Ngai Tahu Takes Government to Court over Rights of Lakes and Rivers" (New Zealand Herald, 2020), https://www.nzherald.co.nz/nz/south-island-iwi-ngai-tahu-takes-govt-to-court-over-rights-of-lakes-and-rivers/LN3QMKDPR6FKYJWCMCQE5BU4ZQ/

Despite the abundant commentary on FPIC, there is little comment on its underlying normative structure and how the conceptualization of the right might affect its implementation. Human rights treaty body decisions have simply applied a human rights construction to the right to FPIC. An exception is an article by James Anaya and Sergio Puig called, "Mitigating State Sovereignty: The Duty to Consult with Indigenous Peoples."[180] Anaya and Puig intervene in the debate over the meaning and effect of FPIC and, in particular, whether it gives indigenous peoples a "right of veto" over the activities of governments and businesses or whether the right simply allows for consultation with indigenous peoples with the government reserving the right to proceed with a proposal even when consent has been withheld. This question goes to the heart of the matter of indigenous peoples' self-determination and the sovereign power of the state.

To address the conflict, Anaya and Puig offer a human rights model. In the "consent or veto approach," FPIC is characterized as a freestanding or independent right, closely associated with historical sovereignty arguments, and directed at the choice of giving and withholding consent.[181] "Although in many ways defensible," Anaya and Puig note, "this approach is in strong tension with how international law recognizes sovereignty among states as well as contrary to existing domestic constitutional arrangements."[182] By focusing on consent as the object of the process, indigenous peoples and companies/governments lose sight of the fundamental underlying rights that the right to consent is meant to preserve—including property rights. Instead, Anaya and Puig argue for a re-conceptualization of FPIC as a process for promoting the specific human rights impacted by a specific commercial project or legislative proposal. In the context of an extractive project, for example, the rights affected will likely include the rights to traditional lands and culture and even the right to self-determination. FPIC is thus part of an integrated whole instead of an independent right in its own right.

Anaya and Puig do not rule out the possibility of a right of veto. They accept that consent is required "whenever indigenous peoples' substantive rights will be materially and substantially affected by the measure promoted by the state."[183] This notion, of limiting consent to those cases where

180 James Anaya & Sergio Puig, *Mitigating State Sovereignty: The Duty to Consult with Indigenous Peoples*, 67:4 Univ. Tor. L. J. 435 (2017) [hereinafter Anaya & Puig, Mitigating State Sovereignty].

181 *Id.* at 449.

182 *Id.*

183 Anaya & Puig, Mitigating State Sovereignty, *supra* note 180, at 461.

substantive rights will be materially affected, is broadly accepted by human rights treaty bodies and organizations. But even if this is proven, Anaya and Puig argue that there may still be circumstances when it may be reasonable for a state to override the right to FPIC. The reason for this is that States may impose limitations on the exercise of certain human rights, such as the rights to property and to freedom of religion and expression.[184] Reference is made to the Declaration and to the Inter-American decisions on indigenous rights that apply this concept of reasonable limitations to indigenous rights.[185] Article 46(2) of the Declaration, for example, notes:

> In the exercise of the rights enunciated in the present Declaration, human rights and fundamental freedoms of all shall be respected. The exercise of the rights set forth in this Declaration shall be subject only to such limitations as are determined by law and in accordance with international human rights obligations. Any such limitations shall be non-discriminatory and strictly necessary solely for the purpose of securing due recognition and respect for the rights and freedoms of others and for meeting the just and most compelling requirements of a democratic society.

As we saw in Chapter 2, Article 46 of the Declaration was inserted in the compromise text prepared by the Chair of the second working group. As Anaya and Puig note, these "reasonable limitation clauses" can be found in most domestic and many international human rights instruments. However, they argue that, in order to be valid, the limitations must comply with certain standards of necessity and proportionality with regard to a valid public purpose, defined within an overall framework of respect for human rights. When applying these conditions in the context of indigenous rights, Anaya and Puig note that "no valid public objective is found in mere commercial purposes, private gains, or revenue-raising objectives."[186] In addition, "[a]ny decision to limit indigenous peoples' rights must ensure that other applicable safeguards are also implemented, in particular, steps to minimize or offset the limitation on the rights through impact assessments, measures of mitigation, compensation, and benefit sharing."[187] Finally, any decision to

[184] *Id.*
[185] *Id.* See also *Report of the Special Rapporteur on the Rights of Indigenous Peoples on Extractive Industries and Indigenous Peoples*, U.N. Doc. A/HRC/24/41, para 31–36 (July 2013).
[186] *Id.*
[187] *Id.*

limit indigenous peoples' rights should be "subject to review by an impartial authority—for instance, an independent judicial body."[188] Given these safeguards, their view is that "it will be difficult, if not impossible, to justify under the foregoing analysis any such major project that is squarely within an indigenous territory . . . without the consent of the affected indigenous people."[189]

This all presents a compelling case for a human rights approach to FPIC. Anaya and Puig offer a means to mediate the tensions between state rights and the right of indigenous peoples to veto actions affecting them. But it is not necessarily the best interpretative model in the North. The decolonization model would demonstrate three key matters. First, when determining the nature and extent of the effect of a proposal or development on indigenous peoples, that is, whether substantive rights will be materially and substantially affected, the decolonization model would emphasize that it is not only a matter of the impact on land rights and culture of the people but also their right to self-determination. Second, Anaya and Puig assume that the right to FPIC is a human right and the Declaration a human rights instrument. As noted, most human rights instruments permit the reasonable limitation of human rights subject to specific conditions and indeed Article 46(2) is an example of such a limitation clause. Article 46's inclusion in the Declaration was really the culmination of the wide acceptance of a human rights model. If the Declaration was indeed founded on human rights, it would be difficult to justify Article 46's exclusion given that human rights codes normally contain such limitation clauses.

However, the Declaration contains not only human rights but also distinctive collective historical rights—like self-determination, self-government, and FPIC—that are grounded in the decolonization model. The human rights themselves can be given a decolonization reading. This has implications for how the limitation clause should be interpreted and applied. The decolonization model means the Article 46(2) limitations must be read down when the Declaration is applied in the North. The reason is that there are strong objections to human rights limiting indigenous rights in the North due to the prominence of prior sovereignty understandings of the relationship between the settler state and indigenous peoples. There are examples in the United States, New Zealand, and Canada of inherent indigenous rights being

[188] *Id.* at 462.
[189] *Id.*

protected from abrogation by human rights. For example, section 25 of the Canadian Charter of Rights and Freedoms provides that rights in the Charter "shall not be construed so as to abrogate or derogate from any aboriginal, treaty or other rights or freedoms that pertain to the aboriginal peoples of Canada."[190] Indigenous rights are inherent and sit above human rights because they go directly to the question of the state's right to govern. Thus, the inclusion of a limitation clause in a code on indigenous rights is controversial. As noted above, Anaya and Puig reject the veto approach partly because it conflicts with state sovereignty in international and domestic law. However, this underscores what is at stake for indigenous peoples of the North. A limitation clause may be appropriate when it comes to the application of human rights. However, the decolonization model puts the Declaration in a category of its own.

The third related concern is the notion of casting FPIC as lacking any independent content—as being only dependent on other related rights such as the right to property or even the right to self-determination. This undermines the right's independent normative status and its association with the decolonization model. Nathan Yaffe has observed a widespread minimalist approach to conceptualizing FPIC applied by companies and governments in Australia and North America.[191] Businesses have been taking the lead in developing FPIC guidelines but have not adopted a self-determination approach. Instead "[c]orporate articulations of FPIC suggest companies employ a thin, liberal notion of consent, inconsistent with understanding FPIC as part of a self-determined governance process."[192] He suggests that we are "witnessing 'FPIC's normative drift': a process whereby FPIC is adopted by companies, but denuded of its normative import."[193] The answer to this dilemma, at least in the North, is to recognize the connection between FPIC and the decolonization model.

A recent proposal in New Zealand to review the constituent legislation of a national Māori organization demonstrates the importance of this connection for conceptualizing the content and effect of FPIC. In 2005, the New Zealand government proposed to amend legislation that established the New Zealand Māori Council, a pan-tribal national organization mandated

[190] The Canadian Charter of Rights and Freedoms.

[191] Nathan Yaffe, *Indigenous Consent: A Self-Determination Perspective*, 19:2 MELB. J. INTL. L. 703 (2018).

[192] *Id.*

[193] *Id.*

to engage with government on Māori matters. The council brought a claim to the Waitangi Tribunal objecting to the review process.[194] Before the tribunal, the council argued that as the legislation concerned powers of Māori self-government (or *tino rangatiratanga* under Article 2 of the Treaty of Waitangi), the council itself should lead any proposal to amend the legislation, including consultation with various Māori groups in order to produce draft legislative changes. The council would then meet with government and together agree on the draft legislation to be adopted by the legislature. Thus, the proposed changes would largely be completed by Māori and led by the council. To support its position, the council relied on the Treaty of Waitangi but it also placed great emphasis on the Declaration, especially the rights to FPIC and self-determination.

The government, in response, argued that there is no basis in the Declaration for "a sequence whereby indigenous peoples decide first on reforms to their autonomous institutions and then negotiate legislative change with the state."[195] FPIC (Article 19), it argued, envisages a process to collaborate as partners on policy and legislation with the process led by the government.[196] According to the government, the council failed to differentiate between collaboration under FPIC (Article 19) and the specific stronger rights of self-government of internal and local affairs outlined in Article 4. The government thus refused to recognize that FPIC is connected to a broader project aimed at enhancing indigenous peoples' rights to self-determination. FPIC has its roots in the decolonization model, a point the NZ government would appreciate given its long-standing participation in the Declaration negotiations. The Waitangi Tribunal ultimately agreed with the council basing its views on the many rights in the Declaration endorsing indigenous peoples' political autonomy (including the right to self-government in Article 4). These rights and the subject matter—indigenous peoples determining their own governance—indicated that indigenous peoples would take the lead in deciding what changes may be needed. This would be followed by consultation and cooperation with the state to secure legislation that gives effect to these governmental rights.[197]

[194] NZ "Waitangi Tribunal: *Whaia te Mana Motuhake*: In Pursuit of Mana Motuhake Report on the Māori Community Development Act Claim (Wai 2417)" 2015 [hereinafter *Whaia te Mana Motuhake*].

[195] *Id.* at 271.

[196] *Id.*

[197] *Whaia te Mana Motuhake*, *supra* note 194, at 272.

Conclusion

In a sort of stock taking at the local level, a collection of essays published in the *American Journal of International Law* highlights the limitations of the Declaration for the development of domestic law and policy on indigenous rights. While the Declaration has received much attention and while international, universalized propositions on the rights of indigenous peoples may present important ideals, the symposium's editor, Dwight Newman, notes:[1]

> . . . the reality remains that the implementation of Indigenous rights must take place in particular circumstances in particular states . . . the pragmatic futures of Indigenous communities and individuals may well depend on more detailed, particularistic determinations within domestic legal systems, wrestling with different interests, working through economic consequences of different positions for all the communities within the state, and trying to find ways of implementing Indigenous rights successfully rather than just theoretically.

Dealing, respectively, with themes of aboriginal land rights,[2] impact benefit agreements between indigenous peoples and extractive industry,[3] and relocation of aboriginal communities in rural Australia,[4] the contributors discuss the importance of domestic agreement-making between indigenous peoples and the state. The Declaration may provide "important ideals" to guide agreement-making but little more.

In this book, I champion the potential of the international movement for fundamental domestic reforms, and, accordingly, it is important to respond

[1] Dwight Newman, *Introduction to Symposium on International Indigenous Rights, Financial Decisions, and Local Policy*, 109 AJIL Unbound 207 (2015).

[2] Dwight Newman, *Indigenous Title and Its Contextual Economic Implications: Lessons for International Law from Canada's Tsilhqot'in Decision*, 109 AJIL Unbound 215 (2015).

[3] Ibironke T. Odumosu-Ayanu, *Indigenous Peoples, International Law, and Extractive Industry*, 109 AJIL Unbound 220 (2015).

[4] Asta Hill, *Western Australia's Remote Indigenous Communities: A Case Against Closures and a Call for New Governance*, 109 AJIL Unbound 209 (2015).

The UN Declaration on the Rights of Indigenous Peoples. Andrew Erueti, Oxford University Press. © Oxford University Press 2022. DOI: 10.1093/oso/9780190068301.003.0006

to this analytical turn to the local. I make two points in response. First, the essays in the symposium downplay the distinctive role that international law has had in all of these thematic areas. Second, and more fundamentally for the purpose of my argument, the essays overlook the implications of the mixed model for implementing indigenous rights—further evidence that the mixed model and the decolonization model, in particular, have been lost from view.

On the first point, Newman, who writes about aboriginal rights in Canada, is correct to say that the Declaration has not played a large role in the development of aboriginal rights jurisprudence. The common law courts have instead focused on traditional property concepts[5] and inquiries into whether indigenous rights have been legally extinguished by "inconsistent rights" or become defunct.[6] And while all of the common law nations have developed aboriginal rights law, they vary in approach reflecting differences of local histories and constitutional arrangements. But that is not to say that international law has not been used in aboriginal rights jurisprudence within CANZUS states. In *Mabo v. Queensland (No. 2)*,[7] the leading judgment of Brennan J. expressly relies on the International Court of Justice's decision in *Advisory Opinion on Western Sahara*[8] to justify the reversal of the 200-year-old legal rule that Australia was *terra nullius* when annexed by Great Britain.[9] In his words, "the common law does not necessarily conform with international law, but international law is a legitimate and important influence on the development of the common law."[10] International law thus affirmed the prior occupation rights of the Aboriginal peoples of Australia.

Furthermore, indigenous land rights are consistently raised and discussed at the international level: in international meetings of United Nations and regional human rights treaty bodies, and the UN indigenous-specific

[5] *See, e.g.*, Delgamuukw v. British Columbia, [1997] 3 S.C.R. 1010 (In Canada, aboriginal title is based on "exclusive occupation.").

[6] Members of the Yorta Yorta Aboriginal Community v. Victoria, [2002] H.C.A. 58.

[7] *See* Mabo v. Queensland (No. 2), [1992] 175 C.L.R. 1.

[8] Western Sahara, Advisory Opinion, [1975] 1 I.C.J. Rep. 12.

[9] Mabo v. Queensland (No. 2), *supra* note 7 ("If the international law notion that inhabited land may be classified as terra nullius no longer commands general support, the doctrines of the common law which depend on the notion that native peoples may be 'so low in the scale of social organization' that it is 'idle to impute to such people some shadow of the rights known to our law' . . . can hardly be retained. If it were permissible in past centuries to keep the common law in step with international law, it is imperative in today's world that the common law should neither be nor be seen to be frozen in an age of racial discrimination" at para. 41); *see also id. See also* the judgment of Toohey J.

[10] Mabo v. Queensland (No. 2), *supra* note 7, at para 42.

mechanisms.[11] In virtually all of their reports, successive UN Special Rapporteurs on the Rights of Indigenous Peoples speak at length about the need for states to recognize indigenous peoples' land rights. UN and regional treaty bodies elaborate on the content of indigenous rights.[12] All of this sits alongside the development of specific local laws. While Newman is right to say that particularization has to occur locally, the broader picture reveals an ongoing interactive process of argument about indigenous property—although much of the international advocacy is directed at government rather than the courts. The same point could be made about the other essays in the symposium. The Australian homelands movement has received much attention in international indigenous rights contexts,[13] as has agreement-making between indigenous peoples and extractive industry.[14]

The second broader limitation is that all of the essays focus on the North and assume international indigenous rights are universalized rights. In contrast, I argue that the Declaration contains both universal (human rights) and particular (self-determination framework) rights. Understanding the Declaration as a mixed model cannot, of course, offer specific answers to the minutiae of policy and law raised by, say, Canada aboriginal rights law. However, it does improve on the Declaration as provider of the ultimate benchmark for evaluating domestic indigenous rights reforms in the North. And this is one of the main points made in this book—both the North and the South negotiated the Declaration so as to ensure there was a meta-standard by which to judge local reforms, given their frustration with the absence of meta-standards in their home states. For the South, this was human rights and equality, and for the North, political sovereignty.

To start with this point about the South, African and Asian indigenous peoples participated in the international movement because they had few

[11] *See, e.g.*, *Petition to the Inter-American Commission on Human Rights Submitted by the Hul'qumi'num Treaty Group Against Canada*, May 10 2007, <https://lrwc.org/lrwc-on-the-merits-of-the-hulquminum-treaty> (Frustration with aboriginal title litigation led the Hul'qumi'num Treaty Group of British Columbia to bring a petition to the Inter-American Human Rights Commission claiming violation of their human right to property.).

[12] *See, e.g.*, Saramaka People v. Suriname (2007), Inter-Am. Ct. H.R. (ser. C) No. 172 (elaborating on the content of the right to FPIC).

[13] *See, e.g.*, Amnesty International – Australia, "'The Land Holds Us:' Aboriginal Peoples' Right to Traditional Homelands in the Northern Territory" (2011), <http://www.amnesty.org.au/wp-content/uploads/2016/09/AI-homelands-report-pdf>.

[14] *See, e.g.*, *Report of the Special Rapporteur on the Rights of Indigenous Peoples, James Anaya, Extractive Industries and Indigenous Peoples*, UN Human Rights Council, 24th Sess., Supp. No. 41, U.N. Doc. A/HRC/24/41 (2013).

domestic opportunities to seek recognition of basic human rights.[15] Instead, these movements sought to join the international movement centered in the UN Declaration negotiations.[16] This marks a departure from the typical "boomerang pattern" of transnational advocacy whereby activists faced with a state's opposition to reforms may activate a transnational network that lobbies other states and international organizations to exert pressure on the original state at the global level.[17] Rather than establish a transnational movement, African and Asian indigenous advocates directly engaged with international organizations, principally the UN via the Declaration negotiations.[18] Latin American indigenous advocates reached out to other movements throughout the Americas, but the UN Declaration negotiations provided a safe and high-profile setting to criticize local governments. In the South, most indigenous peoples remain on the margins of social life and there remain few means to assert human rights. The Southern indigenous movements need the UN and the human rights model in the Declaration. They need access to international institutions, including the UN indigenous-specific mechanisms.

As for the North, the struggle was directed not only at basic human rights but also *political* rights and international oversight. They were the founders of the movement forged by their sovereignty-based activism in their home states. They approached the UN during a time of local reform. Compared with the South, CANZUS states are old liberal democracies that provide the opportunity to address indigenous rights through the judicial, political, and legislative arms of the state. However, these reforms did not address their claims of greater political autonomy and territory. This lacuna remains in the indigenous rights architecture of the CANZUS states. As Cree scholar Douglas Sanderson notes, the Canadian government focuses on land rights

[15] *See generally*, Jens Dahl, The Indigenous Space and Marginalized Peoples in the United Nations (2012).

[16] *Id.* (In Africa's case, the African Commission on Human and Peoples Rights was also a site of advocacy. But this regional-based strategy was adopted after the movement first engaged with the UN.)

[17] *See* Margaret E. Keck & Kathryn Sikkink, Activists beyond Borders: Advocacy Networks in International Politics 107 (2014) (This pattern may describe the strategies of human rights movements in the Americas in the 1970s and 1980s. Keck and Sikkink see the human rights movement in Argentina as a classic example of the boomerang pattern, which underlines the fact that "international pressures [do] not work independently, but rather in coordination with national actors.").

[18] There are strong regional organizations in Asia and Africa. However, I would argue that these movements would have had little local traction without their participation in the international meetings. They gained strength and support *after* the effective participation of local advocates in the international meetings.

and not the rejuvenation of political institutions.[19] New Zealand treaty settlements deliver commercial and cultural redress, not political autonomy. The Northern indigenous movement thus needs access to the self-determination framework in the Declaration.

In his contribution to the recent symposium,[20] Newman raises the limitation of international law in development of land rights in Canadian law by focusing on the Canadian Supreme Court aboriginal title decision of *Tsilhqot'in Nation v. British Columbia*:[21]

> Working out the practical effects of particular forms of property rights within a particular legal system may well be a particularistic exercise, somewhat removed from universalized statements concerning Indigenous property rights across the world. Indeed, circumstances may even differ internally across different parts of a state.

In contrast, in the context of *Tsilhqot'in*, the mixed-model interpretation of the Declaration proposed in this book makes available a decolonization model that would draw attention to how aboriginal title provides potential space for the development of aboriginal law-making institutions. Aboriginal title is about aboriginal sovereignty not land rights.

These two grand narratives of human rights and decolonization provide the context for the application of the Declaration in domestic states. They are grounded in the fullness of the political history of the Declaration negotiations and are legally and politically justified by the uniquely equal manner in which the Declaration was negotiated. And they offer the hope of providing indigenous peoples with the elusive reforms they have always sought.

[19] Douglas Sanderson, *Redressing the Right Wrong: The Argument from Corrective Justice*, 62:1 UTLJ 93, 119 (2012).

[20] Newman, *supra* note 2.

[21] Tsilhqot'in Nation v. British Columbia, [2014] S.C.R. 257.

Index

For the benefit of digital users, indexed terms that span two pages (e.g., 52–53) may, on occasion, appear on only one of those pages.